SPORTS AND SCANDALS

How Leagues Protect the Integrity of Their Games

Edward J. Lordan

 PRAEGER

AN IMPRINT OF ABC-CLIO, LLC

Santa Barbara, California • Denver, Colorado • Oxford, England

Library of Congress Cataloging-in-Publication Data

Lordan, Edward J.
  Sports and scandals : how leagues protect the integrity of their games / Edward J. Lordan.
    pages cm
  ISBN 978-1-4408-2992-5 (hardback : alk. paper) — ISBN 978-1-4408-2993-2
(ebook) 1. Professional sports—Corrupt practices—United States—History.
2. Scandals—United States—History. I. Title.
  GV718.2.U6L67   2014
  175—dc23   2013047537

ISBN: 978-1-4408-2992-5
EISBN: 978-1-4408-2993-2

18 17 16 15 14   1 2 3 4 5

This book is also available on the World Wide Web as an eBook.
Visit www.abc-clio.com for details.

Praeger
An Imprint of ABC-CLIO, LLC

ABC-CLIO, LLC
130 Cremona Drive, P.O. Box 1911
Santa Barbara, California 93116-1911

This book is printed on acid-free paper ∞
Manufactured in the United States of America

Contents

Introduction

Like most groups of people, professional athletes run the gamut, from Ivy Leaguers and teetotalers to dullards and sociopaths. Whether people who play professional sports get in trouble more often than other members of society is debatable, but there is no question that when they do, their mistakes get a disproportionate amount of media attention. When you mess up, a few people who are close to you may hear about it. When an NFL quarterback does something scandalous, it can be the lead story in the news.

Open the sports section, turn on ESPN, or access a sports app and you are likely to find, along with the latest scores and trades, a story about a scandal. The list of possible transgressions is long—steroids, financial irregularities, spousal abuse, DUIs—but there is a good chance that, at any given time, some athlete somewhere is doing something wrong. If his mistake becomes public, the player won't be the only one forced to address the problem; his team and his league will be forced to deal with it too.

This book examines how organizations respond to scandals by reviewing some of the biggest crises in the history of American sports. Some involve individuals and some involve entire teams. Most deal with professional organizations, although two occurred at the collegiate level. Each story begins with an analysis of the transgressions made by the athletes at the center of the scandal and then looks at how the administrators at the top echelon of the sport reacted—what they did and, more specifically, how they communicated their decisions to the various publics. This book is not designed to disparage the fallen athletes, but to evaluate how effective the men in charge of the sport were in addressing the immediate problems and developing long-term solutions to reduce the possibility that the problems would occur again. When appropriate, the analysis includes discussion of ethical considerations—the degree to which the administrators acted in the best interests of all parties involved: the athlete, the team, the league, the media, the fan base, and various other publics. It is not always easy to act ethically in the midst of crises, when dealing with conflicting information, competing agendas, and the pressure of addressing embarrassing topics in a public forum. Some organizations do it well, some do it poorly, but all must live with the consequences of their decisions.

I have many people to thank for assisting me with this book. My family comes first, my wife, Mary, and sons, Daniel and Brendan, who have encouraged me throughout the research and writing process. There is a limit to how often you can deliberate the 1920s decisions of Kennesaw Mountain Landis at the dinner table, but they always stayed interested, or did a great job of acting that way. My thanks also go out to Ms. Paige Kowal, the undergraduate communication studies major at West Chester University who assisted me with my research. She was, at all times, professional and meticulous, and she brought passion to this project. Our conversations about sports scandals ranged from ethics to law to organizational policy. They not only strengthened the chapters but also provided me with the perspective of another generation, which is always helpful when the subject is history.

I must also thank various friends who stimulated my interest in sports scandals. Dr. Michael Boyle, my longtime officemate, not only has been extremely supportive about the project but is always prepared to debate the ethics of a sports topic. Little did he know how much he was adding to this book. On racquetball courts and golf courses, at poker tables and on annual trips to the Poconos, friends have argued passionately about the stories that are covered here. Their positions tell me more than how they feel about the games—they reveal their values and tell me how they view important concepts such as justice and forgiveness. Some of our debates are old, unresolved, and, seemingly, irresolvable: Does it matter if a sports league has an overwhelming percentage of black players and an overwhelming percentage of white fans? Did Shoeless Joe's batting average prove that he didn't throw the World Series? Is it fair to hold athletes to a higher standard? Others come right from today's news: What is Joe Paterno's legacy? How can the NFL protect its players from concussions? There is no real end to the debate, but that is not a bad thing.

And finally, this book is dedicated to Janet Lordan Iacono, who had minimal interest in the topic but a wonderful influence on our lives.

Chapter 1

Anatomy of a Scandal

University of California, Los Angeles (UCLA) basketball coach John Wooden once noted that "sports do not build character. They reveal it." The same can be said of sports scandals.

Athletes, like other members of society, make mistakes. But what happens next, when the individual and the organization that he or she represents respond to a scandal? Do they continue down the same path, making additional errors that exacerbate the problem? Or do they take the necessary and often difficult steps to address key audiences, bring closure to the scandal, and reduce the chances that the problem will happen again?

In evaluating organizational responses to sports scandals, it is important to determine which are specific to a particular event and which provide lessons that are applicable to any situation. Fortunately, the history of scandals in American sports provides plenty of examples of both. Scandals are almost as old as the sports themselves. The causes of the crises transcend sports and eras—human foibles such as drug and alcohol abuse, marital infidelity, greed, envy, and, most important within the context of sport, cheating. But other elements of sports scandals, such as the amount of money in athletics and the number of media covering them, have changed significantly over time, altering the frequency and extent of scandals and the organizational response when they occur.

The Codependence of Sports and Media

In 1900, baseball was a regional game that barely garnered coverage in the small local papers that constituted "the press." As the 20th century progressed, however, both sports and media expanded rapidly in America, each contributing to the growth of the other.

Today, hundreds of millions of fans use an immense network of local, regional, and national media to follow America's four major sports (football, baseball, basketball, and hockey), which are organized into professional leagues that generate tens of billions of dollars annually. Media coverage of sporting events created additional public interest, fueling revenues that led to higher salaries for players. The economic relationship was reciprocal: sports provided media with the perfect kind of stories: they occurred on a predictable schedule, were relatively easy to cover, and provided a compelling narrative. Media companies carrying sports programs earn billions of dollars in advertising revenue every year by delivering the eyes and ears of fans to the companies that pay enormous sums to reach them through advertising. Live sports coverage is one of the most profitable forms of media content in America today: sports fans, unlike consumers of other programming, want to see these events as they are happening, and advertisers will pay a premium to reach potential customers in real time.

Increased media attention brought more than money to athletes—it brought them fame as well. Prior to major media coverage of games, the best player on a team was, at most, a local hero, known primarily to regular supporters who attended home games. The print media expanded this exposure to a degree, but it was the broadcast media, radio and then television, that really made athletes famous. Prior to the introduction of major media, politicians and entertainers were the most recognized figures in society. Today, professional athletes are equal to or, in many cases, surpass these figures as the most closely followed icons in society. Michael Jordan, despite his retirement in 2003, and Tiger Woods, despite his off-the-course personal problems, are two of the most recognizable figures in America. All of this exposure has made it possible for many modern professional athletes to make far more money in product endorsements than they make through their league contracts.

The modern athlete's combination of wealth and fame has altered the relationship between the player and the fan. The vast majority of athletes from a century ago were workaday members of the community, living in the same areas as the people who attended the games and often working jobs in the off-season to supplement the income from their sports. The top athletes today live in gated communities and often shun interaction with the general public. The increased distance between the athlete and the fan base amplifies the media's role in defining the athlete. For many sports enthusiasts, everything they know about their heroes comes through the media. It can also have a detrimental effect on the athletes themselves, who are frequently unprepared for the attention that comes with their newly elevated, media-fueled positions. The extraordinary ego and sense of entitlement that often accompany the professional athlete can be exacerbated by media attention, increasing the possibility that his hubris will lead him into trouble.

The media's role in fostering athletic scandal is an unintended consequence: they are doing their job, and if their coverage encourages an athlete to shun fans, become even more egomaniacal, and make stupid mistakes, media defenders would argue that's the athlete's problem. But once a scandal does emerge, the same media that helped create the image of the athlete are quick to report and comment on the problem, from the initial revelation through each step in the process (team and league responses, legal proceedings, rulings by team officials, league offices and judges, impact on the player's career, etc.). This is simply good business, capitalizing on consumers' interest in scandal to sell more papers, generate higher ratings, or garner more clicks on a Web site.

Again, however, there are ramifications, intended or otherwise. The evolution of media has shortened the reaction time of organizations confronted with scandal: when media moved from a 24-hour news cycle, in which a story that happened today would be revealed to the news consumer in the next morning's paper, to 24/7 cable news coverage, in which stories break in almost real time, the amount of time organizations had to consider their actions and communications was reduced significantly. With the modern media system, the fan and the league sometimes find out about a scandal at the same time. The proliferation of new and more immediate media also lengthens the amount of time that the public spends focusing on the story—there are more opportunities to discuss it. Increased media coverage fuels public perception about the size and importance of a scandal, making it harder for the athlete and his organization to resolve the problem out of the public eye.

Ultimately, media have simultaneously promoted American sports, created conditions that foster scandals, and capitalized on and magnified the importance of scandals when they occur. As these media continue to grow, their influence on sports scandals will increase as well.

Battling an Archetype

Professional athletes are rich, young, privileged, and famous, so it comes as no surprise to the media or the general public when they are involved in scandal. This is part of their problem. The athlete-in-trouble is an archetype, matching a preconception that makes it easier for the press to report and the fan base to believe, regardless of the facts. The athletes discussed in this book not only disgraced themselves, they also added to the negative stereotype of the scandalous athlete and the long-term decline in public respect for their peers. Each scandal reinforces the archetype and makes it more difficult for sports organizations to put scandals to rest.

Professional sports leagues are aware of this problem and have been taking steps to combat it using a multipronged approach. First, they have introduced support programs for athletes to help them avoid mistakes to begin with. Second, they have organized and publicized pro-social activities of their players, coaches, and management. In the early days of community relations, Babe Ruth would deliver an autographed baseball to a sick boy in a hospital, and the event would be dutifully recorded by a photographer from his team or a New York newspaper. Today, teams and organizations employ entire public relations and marketing departments to identify the values of key constituents, create strategic alliances with high-profile community groups, and monitor audience perceptions of players. These efforts can be effective, but they are significantly undercut when a player gets in trouble. An editor will always run a story about a player getting arrested before a story about a team painting a local playground, and news consumers want it that way.

As in political reporting, there has also been a change in the standards and practices of sports journalism when it comes to protecting the privacy of the people they cover. In the early 1960s, reporters were well aware that President John Kennedy had affairs with women other than his wife while living at the White House, but they failed to include that information in their reporting. During the same era, it was painfully clear to writers on the New York sports beat that all-star Mickey Mantle was battling alcoholism during his years with the Yankees, but sports reporters conspired to hide the popular player's addiction. Today, such missteps by public figures would be front-page news. The culture of reporting has become so adversarial and the number of news outlets so numerous that it would be rare for a reporter to sit on a scandal for any length of time today.

Evolving Standards of What Constitutes Scandal

Sports administrators navigating the complexities of a scandal are also forced to deal with an evolving definition of the term: what, exactly, constitutes scandalous behavior? Age, education, religion, economic conditions, race, and gender all factor into perceptions of what is acceptable in society. A wealthy, suburban octogenarian might consider smoking marijuana a scandalous offense, while a teenager raised in a poor neighborhood might see it as an everyday occurrence. Media attitudes toward scandal have changed as well, a reflection of and a contribution to changing attitudes in society: over the past few decades, broadcast and print have relaxed their standards on the portrayal of a wide range of potentially scandalous issues, including obscenity, nudity, depictions of violence, interracial relationships, and drug use. They still report on them, but they often present them in less-scandalous terms.

Perceptions of scandal in the athletic arena have evolved as well. As recently as the late 1940s, the simple introduction of an African American player to professional baseball was considered an enormous scandal. Five decades later, African American running back O. J. Simpson not only starred in an integrated sports league, he married a white woman, with minimal societal response. In the 1960s, amphetamines were so ubiquitous in society that the fact that baseball players used them regularly was not even a story; in the modern era, such a revelation would be a major scandal. In 1973, the most significant trade to come out of the Yankees' training camp did not involve players but spouses, as two pitchers informed a stunned press corps that they had exchanged wives. The announcement was an embarrassment to baseball, but imagine the sensation such an announcement would cause in today's media-rich environment.

In some eras, American media have not only accepted antisocial behavior, they have embraced it. In the 1960s, films such as *Cool Hand Luke* (1967) and *Easy Rider* (1969) promoted social misfits as protagonists. In the early 21st century, television has offered up mobster Tony Soprano, high-school-teacher-turned-amphetamine-cooker Walter White, and vigilante Dexter, all as conflicted, morally ambiguous protagonists. Sports media have offered their own versions of the antihero. In 1970, major league pitcher Jim Bouton published *Ball Four,* an exposé that touched on the seamier side of baseball, including womanizing, alcoholism, and drug abuse. In 1979, *North Dallas Forty* explored the on- and off-field exploits of a thinly veiled version of the Dallas Cowboys, where coaches ignored the pill-popping, oversexed lives of their players. In a 1993 Nike advertisement, National Basketball Association (NBA) Hall of Famer Charles Barkley looked into the camera and said, "I'm not a role model. I'm not paid to be a role model," a direct negation of the traditional hero worship associated with American athletes. Antisocial behavior is now deliberately woven into the branding of some athletes to enhance their marketability to audiences with similar values. While the behavior may have a negative impact on the league, it also can help a player attract attention and differentiate himself. Dennis Rodman was known as much for his scandalous behavior as he was for his basketball skills, with actions ranging from the dangerous—kicking a photographer—to the absurd—dressing in a wedding gown. In many ways, his scandalous behavior enhanced his image with some audiences.

The Complex Ethos of Sport

The ongoing evolution of morality in society is one complication in defining a scandal; the sometimes contradictory ethos of sport is another.

Cheating, by definition, is an immoral act. Within sports, however, it is evaluated on a sliding ethical scale, based on motivation and degree. For some players, cheating is just another reflection of the will to win, an admirable trait simply being expressed in a more creative form. "If you ain't cheating, you ain't trying" and "it ain't cheating if you don't get caught" are not simply mild attempts at humor, they are an ethos that is accepted, and occasionally even encouraged, by some administrators, coaches, and players at all levels of sports. Cheating is relative.

In baseball, a runner who gets to second base is rewarded with a view of the catcher's hand signals, used to communicate the pitch selection. Runners are occasionally accused of stealing signals and tipping off batters, a trick of the trade for the offense. When done on an individual, ad hoc basis, the practice is, if not condoned, rarely challenged, but if sign stealing is raised to an institutional level, it is considered unethical.

In 2010, Major League Baseball (MLB) administrators quietly issued a warning to the Philadelphia Phillies after fielding reports that the team's bullpen coach was using binoculars to steal signs from the Colorado Rockies catcher and communicating the information via the bullpen phone to upcoming hitters. Sports reporter Andy Behrens described the transgression as "a time-honored practice that isn't formally forbidden by the rulebook," and concluded that "if a team gets reprimanded for stealing signs, then generally they're either doing it too brazenly or too well (or both)."[1] Most of the coverage of the story had a similar tone: it was mildly amusing that the Phillies had been caught, mostly because they had been so blatant about it. The potential for scandal was minimal, reporters argued, because everyone was doing it and it's part of the culture of the game.

The same lax ethical approach applies to the "it ain't cheating if you don't get caught" reasoning. Some sports figures are legendary despite—in fact, in some cases, because of—unethical practices that are connected to their names but never quite proven. National Football League (NFL) coach and team owner Al Davis was accused of ordering fields to be watered down the night before a game to slow opposing runners, footballs to be partially deflated before being handed to opposing kickers, and locker rooms to be bugged so that he could learn the halftime adjustments of opposing coaches. Most people would condemn such dishonesty, and some people in sports did. But many fans admired Davis for what was clearly unethical conduct because it reflected his craftiness and his intense desire to win. On the other hand, when New England Patriots coach Bill Belichick took Davis's techniques one step further and was caught filming the practices of his opponents, it was not only society that disapproved: he was roundly criticized by the media and fined $500,000, the largest penalty ever levied on a coach, by NFL commissioner Roger Goodell, who noted that "this episode represents a calculated and deliberate attempt to avoid long-standing rules designed to encourage fair play and promote honest competition on the playing field."[2] Even in sports, it is possible to go too far.

Sometimes a sport attempts to address a common cheating practice but still respect the efforts of those who have perfected it. MLB outlawed the spitball in 1919 but inserted a clause grandfathering protection to pitchers who were already using it. Hall of Famer Gaylord Perry used some variation of a spitball throughout his 22-year career; he went the first 20 of them without getting thrown out of a game for his dishonesty. The title of his autobiography is *Me and the Spitter.*

In contact sports, such as basketball and soccer, where a called foul can create scoring opportunities, players regularly "flop," reeling their heads back or collapsing in pain at imaginary contact from an opponent in an attempt to deceive the referees into calling the infraction. The practice is so common in basketball that columnists create "Top Ten Floppers" lists and so ingrained in soccer that a player will writhe on the ground as if his leg has been broken, be carted off in agony on a stretcher, and then return to the game within minutes, and the sports' fans find nothing unethical (or, oddly, unmasculine) about the practice. "Flopping" has become so common in soccer that leagues have instituted regular penalties against it, but there still remains no stigma attached to it, except for the mistake of being caught by a referee. These are all forms of cheating, but each is accepted, to some degree, by players, coaches, fans, and members of the media.

A critical ethical distinction in sports cheating is the objective: whether players are doing it to win or to lose. The former is relative—once intent is used as a legitimate rationale, the discussion becomes about how far is too far. But the ethos of sport is completely unambiguous if the cheating is done with the intent to lose. Here, sport is not only more absolutist than society, it places far greater weight on the transgression. A review of the halls of fame for major sports demonstrates that you can do, literally, anything—attack handicapped fans, threaten bodily harm to teammates, act with intent to injure, abuse drugs and alcohol, hit and rape women, even murder—and you can not only be forgiven but still be honored with the highest awards a sport can bestow. Cheat to lose, however, and you can be banished forever.

The critical, underlying assumption for all parties in every game is that the competitors are doing everything they can do at all times to win the game. If that assumption becomes suspect in any way, the bond between all participants is broken and the sport itself loses credibility. More than anything else, sports organizations fear and protect themselves against this taboo—you cannot cheat to lose the game.

Since league administrators fear this problem the most, they are proactive in protecting against other, lesser transgressions that can lead to it. This is why so many sports scandals center on gambling. If a person connected with the game—player, coach, referee—is involved in gambling, the theory goes, then eventually that gambler will owe a debt to a person connected to a bookie, who is most probably operating in the world of organized crime. And when that happens, the same theory holds, a fixer will inevitably offer the indebted individual a simple deal—coach, play, or referee in a way that will cause a team to lose or at least not beat the point spread—and your debts will be forgiven. The deal seems simple and undetectable enough, and the player may rationalize the decision in a variety of ways ("It's only one game in an entire season," "Other players are doing it," "I have no other way out of these debts," and, the most enticing rationalization of them all, "We don't even have to lose, I just have to keep it close"); but at that moment, the integrity of the game collapses and the bond among all involved has been broken. Gambling leads to debt, debt to thrown games, and thrown games to the rapid corrosion of the integrity of the game.

Athletes and Scandals? Really?

Increased coverage of sports scandals is more symptom than cause: there are more scandals on the sports pages not just because they sell newspapers but because there are simply more people connected with sports making bad decisions.

The Black Sox throwing the World Series was the biggest scandal in the history of American sports, but there was little competition for that dubious achievement in the year that it took place. Compare 1919 to 2010, when Washington Wizards teammates Gilbert Arenas and Javaris Crittenton pulled guns on each other in a locker room; the divorce proceedings of Frank and Jamie McCourt, the owners of the Los Angeles Dodgers, were so sordid that it threatened the future of the team; running back Reggie Bush returned his Heisman Trophy following revelations that he had received improper payments at the University of Southern California (USC); Pittsburgh Steeler quarterback Ben Roethlisberger apologized to his team and the city after being accused of sexual improprieties; and University of Louisville basketball coach Rick Pitino admitted to marital infidelity in an extortion case—all of which were buried on the inside sports pages when Tiger Woods temporarily abandoned golf to seek counsel for sex addiction after being accused of having sexual relations with a series of women, including a number of pornography stars. Any way you measure it, scandals in American sports are on the rise.

If a sociologist were to create a profile for an individual likely to be involved in a scandal, it would pretty closely match the description of the professional athlete.

The most important commonality is age—antisocial behavior is more prevalent in adolescents and young adults than in older people, for a number of reasons: younger people are more self-absorbed and less likely to be engaged in civic activity. When the vast majority of athletes sign their first professional contract, they are in their late teens or early 20s, placing them on the upper end of this cohort.

A second variable is education—risk taking that leads to scandal is more prevalent among less-educated people, who either care less about or don't grasp the ramifications of dangerous behavior. Twenty-seven percent of the adult general population of the United States has a college degree. At 47 percent, the NFL is an anomaly—the only one of the top four sports leagues in America whose athletes have a higher college completion rate than the general population. Twenty-one percent of NBA players have graduated from college, and while the National Hockey League (NHL) does not release education figures, about 30 percent of the players in the league have at least attended National Collegiate Athletic Association (NCAA) schools, but the percentage who obtained their degrees before or during their pro careers is far lower. The major professional sport with the lowest college graduation rate among active players, by far, is baseball, where a mere 3 percent of the athletes in the league have degrees. The wide variation among sports is largely the result of the differences in the gap between the college and pro experience for each sport and the different eligibility rules and drafting procedures for the leagues; but the bottom line is that a relatively small percentage of professional athletes have college degrees.

The third variable is gender. Males are traditionally greater risk takers than females, and the four largest professional sports leagues are made up entirely of men.

To summarize, participants in the Big Four sports are exclusively male, likely to lack a college degree, and almost always enter the professional ranks in their late teens or early 20s, all variables positively correlated with risky behavior. Beyond these demographic characteristics, however, there are also psychographic qualities shared by professional athletes and candidates for scandal. Athletes have an inordinate degree of self-confidence and a belief in their abilities to dominate a situation. They are successful alpha males who not only have been rewarded for aggression, they have, in many cases, been defined by it.

The effect of all of these variables on risk taking is compounded by the culture that nurtures the American athlete. The highest levels of sport are populated by athletes who not only were the most successful competitors in their schools, they often were the top players in their conferences as well. As a result, many top-echelon athletes received multiple messages during their formative years that they were different from the rest of society and that normal rules did not apply to them. From an early age, they usually were among the most popular students with both peers and authorities: if a romance with a girlfriend didn't work out, there was another girl ready to take her place, and if the athlete performed poorly in the classroom or got into trouble outside of it, his mistakes were more likely to be overlooked, especially on the eve of an important game. In other words, they have been receiving consistent messages from the earliest phases of their lives that they were different, entitled to things others weren't, and less likely to face consequences for mistakes—all messages that lead to scandalous behavior.

When they turned professional, the athletes were forced to deal with an entirely new, extremely powerful set of challenges. It may seem odd to call enormous, immediate wealth a challenge, but an unsophisticated athlete in his late teens or early twenties who is handed a multimillion-dollar signing bonus faces significant pressure: conflicting advice on financial strategies, requests for loans or gifts from family and friends, etc. He is simultaneously torn between earlier allegiances to the supporters who knew him before he became a professional and a new group of acquaintances, usually in a new location. Along with the new wealth comes a commensurate increase in performance pressure: In the season before he turned pro, his worst performance could harm his team's record. Now, a failure to match the value of his contract can cost him his livelihood. As the amount of money in rookie contracts increases, the pressure to justify that contract increases as well.

Conversely, the professional athlete at the end of his career faces a reversal of these challenges. The average length of a professional sports career varies by sport but is far less than a decade, and whether it ends in injury or retirement, it often comes as a shock to the athlete. The money, the travel, the adulation, the support, and sense of identity that come from being a part of a team all end simultaneously. Many professional athletes are unprepared academically, financially, and emotionally for the transition to a non-pro-sports lifestyle. Within five years after retirement, nearly 60 percent of former NBA players are broke, and within two years after retirement, 78 percent of former NFL players are under financial stress or have filed for bankruptcy.[3] Many of these men retire with physical problems that require ongoing expensive medical care. When they leave the game, the most exciting, glamorous, and profitable years of their lives are behind them, usually before they reach the age of 30.

The professional athlete, then, is an ideal candidate for scandal. He combines the most powerful risk-taking demographic and psychographic characteristics and operates in a social system that consistently rewards aggressive, risk-oriented behavior. When he enters the league, he is thrust into a high-stakes, high-pressure environment that he may be ill equipped to deal with emotionally and intellectually, and when he leaves it, he often leaves the wealth, the fame, and a significant part of his identity behind. None of these are excuses for scandalous behavior, but they help to explain why it occurs so often.

Are Leagues as Ill Prepared as Athletes?

In 1998, sports communication consultant Kathleen Hessert conducted a survey of 345 professional league teams from the NBA, NFL, MLB, NHL, and Division 1-A and 1-AA colleges to determine how well they were prepared to deal with the crises that occur regularly in their industry. She found that more than 70 percent of professional and collegiate teams had experienced some form of crisis in the prior year, but only 27 percent of college teams and 56 percent of professional teams had developed a formal crisis plan to address future crises.

While professional and collegiate sports administrators have become more proactive in dealing with scandals since Hessert conducted her survey, they face an uphill battle against trends that encourage scandal. Mike Paul, president of MGP & Associates PR, seconds Hessert's assessment, noting that professional athletes who excel at their sports are often far less prepared to deal with issues off the field, where they lack an overall strategy and the life skills needed to make effective decisions.

If professional sports are going to assist their employees in avoiding scandals, they need to be more effective in keeping them from failing once they leave the field.

League Considerations: Scandal Sources and Audiences

What kinds of scandals occur in sports, and what kind of audiences do leagues need to address when they occur?

Scandals come in a variety of forms and emerge from a single incident or a series of actions over time. They may involve decisions by individuals or groups, including players, managers, and officials, or policy development or implementation by administrators. Transgressions occur on the field (performance-enhancing drugs, cheating, racist statements or actions, etc.) or off (illegal non-performance-enhancing drugs, rape, murder, etc.) and can result in short-term or long-term media coverage and short-term and long-term effects for the player and the team.

The scope of sports scandals varies widely. There are scandals that are covered exclusively by sports media, with fans principally concerned about how the problem will affect the team's performance, and others that become major events beyond the sports world, covered by non–sports media and incorporated into a greater discussion of ethics, law, etc. in general society. Occasionally, the scandals will strike a nerve that reflects some of the hot-button issues in society: when a female reporter is mistreated in the all-male bastion of a locker room, it becomes part of a larger discussion of sexism; when a football player is accused of uttering a racial epithet, he opens up a much larger discussion of racism. The potential damage from the scandal varies as well: a mistake may threaten the career of the player, the fortunes of the team, or, in some cases, the integrity of the league or game itself.

In American sports, the audiences are interrelated and relatively well defined. These audiences may have aligned or competing agendas. The internal audiences are the members of the sports teams (players, coaches, administrators, staff, additional employees) as well as league administrators and other league employees, including referees. The first level of external audiences are financial supporters, beginning with advertisers and followed by fans who attend the events, then fans who follow the sport through the media and potential supporters of the sport. The press impacts nearly all other audiences because it provides ongoing information to other groups and serves as the conduit of communication between the organization and other publics. Additional external audiences include government officials (local, regional, and national) and representatives of competing sports and entertainment organizations.

One additional set of audiences that must be addressed is the representation of the players, in the form of agents and union representatives. In some situations, the objectives of these audiences are aligned with the objectives of the organization, but there is more likely to be conflict between these groups and the league than there is between the sports league and any other audience. Just as the first responsibility of league administrators is to the league, the fiduciary responsibility of a player's representative is, at all times, what is in the best interest of the player. For issues such as privacy, drug testing, testifying before league representatives or government officials, etc., the athlete's representatives often make decisions and communicate in ways that are designed to protect the athlete but do not assist the league in achieving its objectives.

Most of the time, the interests and values of the internal and the external audiences are aligned and reinforce each other. Sports audiences favor competition, individual contributions to team goals, maximum effort within the rules, fair play, and conforming to social norms. In some situations, the audiences differ in terms of prioritizing these values, and on rare occasions have completely different agendas, complicating the organization's approach to a scandal. When there are competing agendas, the organizations invariably put the interests of the organization first, whether or not they communicate this to other audiences.

In Defense of the Athlete

The following chapters tell the stories of men who have committed a litany of sins and suffered precipitous falls from the heights of popularity to the depths of public scorn. In almost every case, their wounds are self-inflicted, often the result of pride, greed, or self-centeredness. But there is also a redemptive element to some of these tales, when a player admits fault and accepts blame or a league administrator makes a difficult decision that balances the best interests of various audiences. These stories serve as a reminder that even after an athlete makes a tragic mistake, his next move does not have to compound the damage: he still has an opportunity to do the right thing.

Chapter 2

The Black Sox Scandal (1919)

Baseball is as honorable as any other business.
It is the most honest pastime in the world.
It has to be or it could not last a season out.
Crookedness and baseball do not mix. . . .
. . . The reason for the popularity of the sport is that
it fits in with the temperament of the American people
and because it is on the square.[1]

—White Sox owner Charles Comiskey, 1919

In 1919, the most important contest in America's professional sports—baseball's World Series—and the most damaging accusation in sports—throwing a game—came together in the biggest scandal in the nation's athletic history. The Black Sox Scandal—the participants, the payoff, and the players' performance, as well as the investigations and the legal proceedings that followed—was mired in controversy that remains open to debate. "Conflicting evidence, stories that changed from day to day, confessions that were later retracted, all muddy the waters sufficiently to keep many of the exact details shrouded in a fog of mystery,"[2] noted historian William Klingaman.

The story revolves around three organizations, all different but sharing one unfortunate trait: dysfunction. The first was the National Commission, the tripartite of executives entrusted with protecting the integrity of the game. The second was the Chicago White Sox, the American League team owned and ruled with an iron fist by Charles "Old Roman" Comiskey. And the third was a loose and fluid coalition of players within the team that barely qualified as an organization: the Black Sox, the eight players who allegedly agreed to accept money to throw the World Series. The relation-ships within and among these organizations were fueled by animosity, competing agendas, and conflicts of interest, and were instrumental in causing the scandal and attempting to resolve it.

American Ethics: Distinctions among Cheating, Gambling, and "The Fix"

Since the earliest days of baseball, the men in charge of the game have al-ways framed their sport as honest and transparent, where the players' per-formances are open for all to see. "According to the ideology that baseball promoted about itself, the game embodied the nation's pastoral heritage, self-reliant individualism, and democratic cooperation," explained cultural historian Daniel Nathan, "and thus it conveyed traditional American values to its participants and spectators."[3]

Nathan's description may be true, but it is undeniable that a significant part of baseball is based on deception. Catchers constantly try to outthink hitters when selecting a pitch, fielders feint defensive alignments, and run-ners disguise their intentions to steal bases. The game is played amid con-stant coded communication among head coaches, base coaches, and players. It is accepted that opponents are constantly attempting to "steal" signs to gain advantage, and, based on rumor and reporting, they often succeed: the lore of baseball is filled with stories of critical messages being stolen in criti-cal situations by infielders, coaches, bullpen pitchers, even employees in the stands. Deception and counterdeception are considered part of the game by participants, administrators, media members, and fans. For many, they are part of the allure of the game.

The critical distinction, of course, is that all of this espionage is con-ducted in attempts to *win* the game. Players, administrators, and fans may differ over what constitutes cheating, but all agree that cheating to deliberately lose a game, for whatever reason, is unethical and should be punished. The greatest danger to baseball, to any sport, is that fans come to suspect that the fix is in. In the ethical hierarchy of major sports, all possible sins—drug abuse, racism, alcoholism, womanizing, theft, finan-cial irregularities—pale in comparison to fans losing faith that the game is being played squarely.

While everyone involved in baseball agrees that throwing games is wrong, there is far less consensus on the ultimate motivation to fix a game: gam-bling. Wagering on baseball generates additional interest in the sport while simultaneously increasing the potential for corruption. As long as there has been baseball, there have been gamblers to bet on it, and as long as there have been bets on the game, there has been the temptation to fix them.

It is no coincidence that the rise of professionalism in baseball coincided with a rise in the professionalism of gambling. The first professional baseball league, The National Association of Professional Baseball Players, was formed in 1871, when representatives of 10 teams met in a New York saloon to forge a loose alliance and carve out a semi-regular schedule. At about the same time, gamblers began to organize the haphazard betting system that surrounded the game. Individual bets, which were often disputed when the games were complete, were replaced by a new "pool selling" system, in which a central organization set odds, "booked" bets on all sides, collected money in advance, and paid out winners when games were decided. Formalizing the baseball league codified the rules, legitimized the game, and made it more acceptable to interested parties. Centralizing the betting system had the same effects.

All 10 of the teams in the new league attempted to create policies to address gambling, none successfully. Baseball historian Lee Allen recalled that "the situation was especially bad in Brooklyn where the Atlantic club fostered so much open betting that one section of the grounds was known as the Gold Board, with activity that rivaled that of the stock exchange."[4] Literally and figuratively, gambling hovered around the game.

The Role of the Press

Gamblers weren't the only secondary business to profit from baseball: newspaper editors quickly recognized the value of covering the emerging game. It was news on a regular basis, easily covered, cheap to report, and followed by a sizable percentage of the readers. But many reporters, led by Henry Chadwick, writing for the *New York Clipper* and the *Brooklyn Eagle*, didn't just report the scores, they also reported on the close relationship between players and gamblers and warned that it threatened the credibility of the game. Chadwick's advocacy was a model for the media's role in sports scandals in the decades that followed: newspapers functioned as boosters and recorders, but also as gadflies, pushing management and players to maintain, or reclaim, the integrity of the sport. By heightening awareness of gambling, however, these reporters also reinforced the suspicions of many fans, increasing their skepticism when players performed poorly or managers made questionable decisions.

League officials attended the games, read the papers, and were not blind to the influences of gambling. On July 24, 1873, National Association president Bob Ferguson became so concerned that a game between the New York Mutuals and the Lord Baltimores was fixed that he stepped in to umpire the game himself. When the game ended, an incensed Ferguson leapt into the stands and confronted the gamblers, then returned to the field to accuse the players he thought were part of the fix. In the ensuing argument, the league president actually broke one player's arm with a bat. Ferguson's public confrontation with gamblers and players was an anomaly. The history of baseball is replete with administrators who would be nowhere near as direct as the National Association president, choosing to deal with the problem by ignoring it, concealing it, or dealing with it discretely and, as a result, ineffectively.

In the end, the efforts of the league president and the baseball writers failed and their predictions about the dire effects of gambling on the game came true: the amateur baseball association lasted only four years, partially because of lack of cooperation among the teams, but mostly because fans grew suspicious that so many of the games were fixed. The league's demise can be partially attributed to the failure to truly address the cancerous effects of gambling: even when accusations of fixes were substantiated, players simply moved to a rival club and played on—no one ever was expelled from the league for cheating. "The total extent of the corruption of the National Association will never be known," summarized baseball historian Daniel Ginsburg. "However, there is no question that corruption haunted the National Association from the beginning."[5]

Disbanding the league did not diminish the public interest in the game. A number of owners of National Association teams met to create a new league, designed to eliminate the problems that had killed the National Association. In 1876, they announced the formation of the National League, which brought a more businesslike approach to baseball by standardizing contracts, discouraging player movement, and formulating new policies to shield the game from gambling. Those policies very quickly proved ineffective: a year after the league was formed, members of the Louisville Grays were involved in an embarrassing game-fixing scandal. It was clear that gambling remained a part of the game, but, this time, administrators were ready to address it quickly and comprehensively: four players were banned for life from the National League. The game's new stewards were at least attempting to address the problem, but it would prove to be a difficult, ongoing challenge.

New Century, New League, New Management

The National League dominated baseball through the remainder of the 19th century, growing the game by expanding into America's largest cities.

By 1900, however, the league's development proved too aggressive, and a number of teams became too weak to compete on the field and at the box office. The league jettisoned four teams in a move to focus on its best-performing teams and create more parity.

When the National League stumbled, the smaller-market Western League pounced. Western League commissioner Ban Johnson added teams in Baltimore, Washington, and Cleveland—three of the four cities abandoned by the National League—as well as Philadelphia, Chicago, and Boston—three of the major markets still served by his larger competitor. Johnson's move was audacious but effective, and, suddenly, the Western League was on par with its competitor. The commissioner renamed his expanded organization the American League, and a rivalry was born.

Three years later, the two leagues entered into an agreement that created a new governing body, the National Commission, that would settle contract disputes, levy fines, etc., for both leagues. The new Commission consisted of three individuals: the president of the National League, the president of the American League, and a commission chairman. The first chair to be named was Cincinnati Reds owner August Hermann.

Hermann's conflict of interest was obvious from the outset. He ruled on all league decisions but owned one of the teams. By 1919, the year of the Black Sox scandal, other team owners were concerned enough about Hermann's competing agendas that they formed a committee to recommend a new approach to selecting the Commission's chair. Coincidentally, it would be Hermann's Reds who faced the White Sox in the Black Sox World Series.

Hermann's conflict was the most obvious problem with the arrangement of the Commission, but it was not the largest. The real problem was the disparity in power among the three members. In theory, commission rulings were decided on the basis of three equal votes, but, as is the case in many organizations, all votes were not equal. American League president Ban Johnson quickly emerged as first among equals, and, as the Commission began to exercise more authority, Johnson's dominance became even more pronounced. "Johnson had exercised uncontested authority well beyond his official portfolio as organized baseball's de facto overseer for almost two decades," Roger Abrams noted. "His use and abuse of power created enemies among the sixteen club owners, each used to absolute power in his own realm. Johnson, much taken with his own importance to the game, exercised authority in arbitrary fashion."[6]

From the birth of the National Commission until 1919, there was one team owner who had no complaints about Johnson's unchecked power: the White Sox's Charles Comiskey. Johnson and Comiskey were extremely close, having risen together through the Western League and bonded over their intense dislike of the rival National League. The relationship benefited both men for decades, until it exploded early in 1919, when Johnson ruled against the White Sox in a trade with the Yankees. When the season ended in the Black Sox controversy, the dysfunction within the Commission and the dislike between its strongest member and the owner of the team accused of fixing the games had an enormous impact on how the scandal played out. As Eliot Asinof noted, Johnson's "hatred of Comiskey would critically plague the development of the Series scandal and alter its history."[7] Given the animosity and competing agendas, it is not surprising that the game's administrators failed to put baseball's best interests ahead of their own when it came time to address the scandal.

The World Series Increases Interest . . . and Wagering

With two leagues of relatively equal stature, the next logical step for baseball was the creation of a season-ending showdown between the best teams from each side. Postseason championships had been held as early as 1884, but it wasn't until 1903 that the National and American Leagues agreed to play a best-of-nine showdown called the World Series.

In the inaugural series, Boston beat Pittsburgh five games to three. The victors were denied the chance to defend their title a year later, when the National League champions from New York declined to play. In 1905, the tradition resumed, and a season-ending championship series was played every fall for the next 90 years.

The new championship was one of a number of factors that led to an increased interest in baseball. It also helped that one of baseball's biggest rivals, horse racing, was in a sharp decline. America in the early 20th century was in the midst of a progressive movement designed to wipe out social ills, including gambling, and activists set their sites on eliminating what they saw as a true den of iniquity, the racetrack. For a time, their efforts were extremely successful: the number of horse racing tracks in the United States plummeted from a high of 314 in 1890 to a low of 25 in 1908. Government activity furthered the decline: in 1909, California banned betting on horses in response to corruption scandals in the sport, and New York soon followed. When World War I broke out, the federal government forced many of the remaining tracks to significantly shorten their schedules or shut down completely to support the war effort.

National antigambling sentiment and support for the war also cut into baseball, but to a much lesser degree: the 1918 regular season was shortened, ending on September 2, but the government still allowed for a World Series. The betting public stayed interested. Politicians could shut down most of horse racing, but they couldn't legislate human nature: regardless of the growth or decline of individual sports, gambling was going to continue, with many of the bets simply moving from the track to the ballpark.

The White Sox: Comiskey Creates Animosity

The history of baseball is closely connected to the history of gambling, but it also shares a long association with labor/management strife. The relationship between the opposing sides was so bad that at one point players even formed their own short-lived league in an attempt to wrestle control, and money, from the team owners.

The center of the conflict has always been the reserve clause, introduced in 1879, which kept players from switching employers to maximize salaries. The clause, despised by labor and beloved by the owners, ensured that ballplayers either negotiated a contract with the team they played for or found another way to make a living.

Many of the owners were hardnosed businessmen, but few were as callous and greedy as the White Sox's Comiskey. In 1894, Comiskey purchased the Sioux City Cornhuskers of the Western League and then quickly moved the team to St. Paul, Minnesota. In 1900, he moved the team again, to an even larger market, Chicago, as part of Ban Johnson's challenge to the National League. Comiskey renamed his team the White Stockings, which, not coincidentally, had been the original name of the city's other baseball team, the National League's Cubs. He later shortened the name to the White Sox, to fit better on the headlines of the Windy City's sports pages. The move made Chicago one of the few two-team towns in the nation, with the White Sox representing the upstart American League on the city's south side, and the Cubs representing the older, more traditional National League on the north side.

Comiskey's new White Sox were extremely successful, winning championships in 1901 and 1906, then moving into the new ballpark named for the owner in 1910. Despite the wins, the players were miserable, the result of the legendarily cheap and, in some cases, unscrupulous practices of the team's owner. Some of Comiskey's cost-cutting decisions were petty: he paid $3 per day for players' meals while the rest of the league paid $4 and refused to clean team uniforms regularly to reduce laundry bills. Some of his frugality was more than petty: he routinely paid his employees well below the league average despite their success on the field. And some of his actions were immoral: in 1917, the Chicago owner promised his players significant bonuses if the team won the pennant. When the team finished first, they were rewarded with a case of cheap champagne and nothing more. Two seasons later, the season of the fix, Comiskey promised pitcher Eddie Ciccote a $10,000 bonus if he won 30 games in a season. When the pitcher approached the magic number, Comiskey ordered him benched to avoid paying the bonus. As the regular season was winding down, the White Sox were steamrolling toward the pennant, fan interest across the nation was picking up, and the players' animosity toward White Sox management was at an all-time high.

Arranging the Fix

So much money was bet on the 1919 World Series—an estimated $2 million in New York City alone—that in the days prior to the opening game, there were actually multiple game-fixing schemes going on simultaneously. Different gamblers had different plans, but they all seemed to agree that if you wanted to bribe a player, the first man to target was first baseman Arnold "Chick" Gandil.

Gandil was no stranger to the gambling side of baseball. During most of his professional career, he was associated with bookmakers, and he had already been accused of bribing players from the opposing team in a doubleheader between the White Sox and the Detroit Tigers in 1917. A few weeks before the 1919 series began, Gandil offered to throw the series for $80,000 in a deal with bookie and long-term acquaintance Joseph "Sport" Sullivan. While he was negotiating the Sullivan deal, Gandil, along with pitcher Eddie Ciccote, was approached by two other unsavory figures, Billy Maharg and William Thomas "Sleepy Bill" Burns. Maharg was connected to organized crime, and Burns, a former White Sox pitcher, was the go-between with the players. If he could arrange a deal with both groups without either knowing about the other, Gandil could collect twice on the same transgression.

With the deal supposedly in hand, Gandil went looking for coconspirators. Cicotte was the logical choice because of his potential effect on the series—he was the team's best pitcher—and because he had been burned on the 30-win bonus only weeks earlier by Comiskey. With Cicotte on board, Gandil was in a stronger position to persuade other players, and he was able to recruit six other White Sox to join in the conspiracy: pitcher Lefty Williams, centerfielder Happy Felsch, shortstop Swede Risberg, third baseman Buck Weaver, utilityman Fred McMullin, and leftfielder "Shoeless" Joe Jackson.

More players necessitated more bribe money, however—Ciccotte allegedly demanded $10,000—but it would take 10 times that amount to cover all of the conspirators, so the small-time bookmakers, Maharg and Burns, as well as Sullivan, went looking for financial backers with deeper pockets. Coincidentally, both went to the same source. Maharg and Burns approached Abe Attell, a bodyguard and associate of Arnold "The Big Bankroll" Rothstein, one of the nation's most influential bookmakers. Sullivan bypassed intermediaries and took his case directly to Rothstein. The New York bookmaker recognized a potentially enormous payday, but, far more sophisticated than the other gamblers, he also saw the risks in fixing America's premier sporting event. Rothstein considered the best angle to play while minimizing his connection to the fix. He used Attell to relay his messages to the other gamblers, sending out convoluted, almost contradictory messages that would ensure his deniability if the scandal was revealed.

Before the first pitch of the series was thrown, the conspiracy had grown to more than a dozen men, each with his own perception of the deal, none with a thorough understanding of the big picture or of all the participants. From the inception, the agreement seemed to have little chance of working, and even less chance of staying secret.

The Games

In the opening game of the series, Eddie Ciccotte hit the first batter he faced, a prearranged sign to the gamblers that he would follow through on the agreement. After that, however, who was in on the fix, whether they were earning their bribes, and whether they continued to honor the arrangement through the entire series all became a matter of interpretation. The first of the White Sox to score a run was Chick Gandil, the alleged instigator of the plot, who also had the game-winning hit in Game Three. Joe Jackson's series batting average, .375, was the highest of any player in the series, and he was flawless in the field. Cicotte pitched extremely well in Game Four, but committed two errors that were the difference in the game. The star pitcher then demanded the ball in Game Seven and dominated in a 4–1 win.

Inconsistency on the field reflected ongoing chaos within the conspiracy. The gamblers who had offered the bribes did not follow through with all of the money, doling it out in small increments and behind the agreed-upon schedule. The players began to suspect a double cross, concerned that they had no leverage to collect their bribes if they lost the games but hadn't been paid. Gandil lost control of his scheme and the confidence of the players he had convinced to throw the games. As the series progressed, some of the conspirators may have played just poorly enough to lose; some may have reneged on the bribes out of guilt or fear that the plot had been exposed, or anger that they hadn't been paid; and some may have decided to keep what they could and try to win it all. No single person seemed to fully understand exactly how much money had been promised, delivered to intermediaries, or distributed to the players in on the fix.

Word of the fix was also spreading outside of the locker room. Rumors were rampant among baseball fans, particularly in the Chicago area. Conspiracy theories were so rampant that there even was suspicion that the opposing team was running a scam. The Reds built a 4–1 series lead and then dropped the next two games at home, extending the series, increasing both league revenues and the gambling action.

When Cincinnati clinched the final game, 10–5 in Chicago, both teams had committed six errors each, and, as historian Gene Carney writes, "there were sparkling defensive plays made by both teams and pitching gems on both sides, too."[8] The Black Sox players who were supposedly in on the fix actually outperformed their "Clean Sox" teammates who were not part of the fix.

A series of baseball games involves hundreds of decisions and actions, from pitch selection to fielding positions to decisions on where to hit and when to steal. There are many opportunities to second-guess coaches, batters, runners, pitchers, and fielders. In a championship series where players were suspected of throwing games, it was extremely difficult to tell whether, when, how, and which of the White Sox had played to lose.

The Press Catches On

By its nature, a conspiracy is difficult to prove because all of the participants prefer to keep the deal a secret. A conspiracy involving underworld figures is even more difficult to verify, because anyone who revealed the participants could be killed in retribution. But the Black Sox fix was no regular conspiracy. First, there were so many participants, on field and off, that a well-connected reporter could tap into a variety of sources to confirm his suspicions. Second, even if the conspirators managed to keep their deal a secret, there was a public component to the gambling that could not be hidden: the series odds. Once the fix was in, gamblers began to bet heavily on Cincinnati, reducing the White Sox from prohibitive 8/5 favorites to even money. Two naturally suspicious groups did what they naturally do: gamblers unconnected with the fix started betting Cincinnati even heavier, and newspaper reporters started rooting around to see if something was amiss.

The role of the press is to enlighten the public, and no reporter covering the series took that responsibility more seriously than syndicated sportswriter Hugh Fullerton. In the week before the series began, Fullerton predicted that the White Sox would win it all in a column that appeared in the *Chicago Herald and Examiner.* His series prediction would be the first of his three important predictions about the series that would prove to be wrong.

Fullerton was not alone in predicting the Sox would win: most of the Chicago players from the 1916 championship team were still part of the 1919 squad, and Cicotte was considered the top pitcher in either league. Most knowledgeable baseball writers thought the Sox were the better team. But the drumbeat of fix rumors combined with the plummeting odds caused Fullerton to change his position just before the opening pitch, when he advised his readers to avoid betting the series at all because of ugly rumors about the game. He also made an agreement with a friend, veteran pitcher Christy Mathewson, to watch the games together but keep separate scorecards, each circling plays they found suspicious. The reporter was so close to the team, he wanted a trustworthy, independent set of eyes to view the game with him.

Fullerton worked furiously to substantiate the fix story, but could not get a sufficiently reliable source to confirm it. A number of gamblers talked freely and foolishly about the fix, but bribery talk was part of every World Series, so their word was not enough for the columnist to report his suspicions as fact. As the series progressed, Fullerton struck a balance between what he knew and what he suspected: following Game Two, he questioned the White Sox's spirit; after Game Four, he pinned the loss entirely on Cicotte. By the conclusion of Game Five, Fullerton was still unable to confirm the fix, so he did the next best thing: confirm the rumors. He wrote:

> There is more ugly talk and more suspicion among the fans and among others in this series than there ever has been in any world's series. The rumors of crookedness of fixed games and plots are thick. It is not necessary to dignify them by telling that they are, but the sad part is that such suspicion of baseball is so widespread.[9]

Like many reporters, Fullerton tended to report favorably on Comiskey over the years—the owner courted the press and was liked far more by the beat writers than by his players. Before and during the series, newspapers hinted at a fix but gave the owner the benefit of the doubt. By the time Cincinnati was the champion, however, the press was no longer willing to give anyone a free pass. When the series concluded, an exasperated Fullerton blasted not only the Sox but the entire administration of baseball:

> There will be a great deal written and talked about this world's series. There will be a lot of inside stuff that never will be printed, but the truth will remain that the team which was the hardest working, which fought hardest and which stuck together won. The team which excelled in mechanical skill, which had the ability, individually, to win, was beaten. . . . [10]

In the same article, Fullerton went on to make two more predictions:

> Yesterday's game in all probability is the last that ever will be played in any world's series. If the club owners and those who have the interests of the game at heart have listened during this series they will call off the annual inter-league contests. . . .
> . . . Yesterday's game also means the disruption of the Chicago White Sox as a ball club. There are seven men on the team who will not be there when the gong sounds next Spring and some of them will not be in either major league. [11]

Author Daniel Nathan noted, "In retrospect, it is clear that no one wrote more prescient and influential articles about the 1919 World Series and the Black Sox scandal than Hugh Fullerton."[12] Yet Fullerton's three most important predictions about the series and its aftermath all turned out to be wrong, because they were all predicated on the same optimistic assumptions. Before the series began, he figured that all of the White Sox players were going to play the game to win—they did not. When the series was over, he assumed that Comiskey would clean out anyone he suspected of involvement in the fix—he did not. And, finally, Fullerton assumed that the league commissioners, the stewards of the game, would act only in the best interests of baseball—and they did not. It is not hard to see why the reporter's tone became increasingly strident as the scandal wore on—his writing reflected a consistent hope for the best in human nature and a consistent observation of the worst.

In the press box along with Fullerton was Ring Lardner, who had been covering the White Sox for the *Chicago Tribune* for six years. Lardner had enormous respect for the game, the team, and two of its major players, Cicotte and Jackson. Lardner, too, heard rumors of a fix as the series approached, and following Cicotte's dreadful Game One performance, the reporter confronted the pitcher and asked him if the fix was in. Cicotte denied the charge.

Like Fullerton, Lardner was in a bind as the series progressed. As a reporter, he was aware of the rumors and the changing betting line, and as a beat writer for the team, he was an astute judge of the Sox performance. Like Fullerton, however, he lacked adequate proof to print specific allegations. Following Game Two, Lardner got drunk enough to sing in public a version of the tune "I'm forever blowing bubbles," changing the words to "I'm forever blowing ballgames." He may have sung the song on the train ride back with the players from Ohio to Illinois, or he may have sung it in a Kentucky bar with fellow writers, depending on who tells the story. Regardless of where he sang it or who was in earshot, it is clear that the scandal helped sour the veteran sportswriter's enthusiasm for baseball: the season would be his last dedicated to the game, as he would branch out into covering subjects other than sport in 1920.

If Lardner's response was to walk away from the mess, Fullerton's was the opposite. He, more than any other writer, would continue to pursue the Black Sox scandal and keep pressure on baseball to investigate the allegations of a fix in the series.

Comiskey's Suspicions . . . and Suspicious Reaction

Following the White Sox's surprising loss in the series opener, Chicagoan Mont Tennes, one of the nation's leading gamblers, alerted Charles Comiskey to the possibility of a fix. What the owner did—and didn't do—next became a significant source of controversy.

According to Comiskey, his first decision was to send an employee and close confidante, Norris L. "Tip" O'Neill, to meet with Tennes to learn what he could about the fix. He then directed the team's manager, Kid Gleason, to address the team before the second game, informing them that management knew about a possible fix.

When the Sox lost Game Two, Comiskey directed the team's secretary, Harry Grabiner, to inform National League president John Heydler of his suspicions. He did not inform the two other members of the National Commission, Ban Johnson or August Hermann, because he didn't trust either man.

Prior to Game Three, Comiskey and Kid Gleason met personally with Heydler, explained their suspicions, and requested an investigation of the rumors. Comiskey's decision to communicate with the commission through only Heydler left the National League president in a delicate position. During the prior off-season, Heydler had made two decisions that led to accusations that he was soft on the gambling issue. First, citing lack of evidence, he had reinstated Hal Chase, a notorious gambler and member of the Cincinnati Reds who had been suspended for fixing games. Second, he had failed to respond sufficiently to rumors that the other Chicago team, the Cubs, had thrown the 1918 series. Comiskey's information gave Heydler an opportunity to improve his battered reputation, but the National League president decided to simply relay the information from Comiskey to Ban Johnson. Johnson adamantly dismissed any fix allegations as the reactions of a losing team, ending any chance of anyone in authority doing anything about the scandal while the series was still being played.

The communications among the team and league administrators would become important as the scandal unfolded, because they shifted the burden to take action from Comiskey to Heydler to Johnson. When neither member of the Commission addressed the allegations, Comiskey could (and did) claim that he had conveyed what he knew about the rumors to the executives most responsible for protecting the integrity of the game and left the solution in their hands. Participants would eventually differ on the details of the conversations—what was said, as well as when—but it is clear that no administrator from the team or Commission stepped in to address the fix while the series was played, nor did they divulge any information about a possible fix to the public until after the games were completed. Author Stanley Teitelbaum summarized the conduct of the top administrators:

> It appears that Comiskey, Johnson and Heydler were all enablers who participated in the cover-up by either turning a blind eye to what they really knew, or dropping the ball and waiting for someone else to pick it up. To expose the crookedness was too threatening to the precarious image of baseball as a sport with integrity.[13]

Post Series Maneuvers

The day after the series ended, Charles Comiskey went public.

Instead of accusing his players, however, he defended them, claiming that the rumors of a fix were the bitter response by gamblers who had bet on the Sox. His public stance, in effect, mirrored Johnson's reaction when he was informed of the rumors of a fix. Comiskey's accusation defied logic, since he had been made aware of reports that the fix had begun well before it was over. "Apparently the temptation to protect his investment overcame any original desire Comiskey might have had to get to the bottom of the mess,"[14] noted Harold Seymour.

The White Sox owner also announced a $10,000 reward for credible evidence of a fix. Comiskey may have been banking on the fact that no one involved in the conspiracy would be brazen enough to come forward to claim the reward, risking the wrath of mobsters who might be implicated. If so, he was wrong. Two Saint Louis gamblers, Harry Redmon, a theater owner, and Joe Gedeon, a ballplayer, came forward and named names. The risk came with no reward: Comiskey simply brushed aside their claims as hearsay and refused to pay. Even in the midst of the crisis, his approach to financial agreements was consistent: if he could find a way to avoid payment, he would usually take it.

Publicly, the owner was doubling down on his investment, maintaining the façade that baseball was untainted by gambling while privately maneuvering to identify the players in the scam. Comiskey withheld the World Series paychecks from suspected players as long as possible, hoping they would come in to his office for their money and provide him with a chance to interview them. The players waited him out, however, until Comiskey's attorney convinced him that he was legally required to send them their pay. The White Sox owner also hired a private detective, John R. Hunter, to quietly investigate the suspected players and the rumors of a fix. He went public with the fact that he had hired the detective, but kept Hunter's findings to himself. In the end, hiring a detective provided little more than another opportunity for Comiskey to claim that he had made every effort to find out what had really happened.

The owner's two-pronged strategy provided him with maximum control over the collection and, equally important, distribution of information about the fix. As Daniel Ginsburg pointed out:

> Comiskey would launch a half-hearted investigation, the stated purpose of which was to get to the bottom of the series rumors. In reality, Comiskey would have no intention of pushing for exposure. If the details of the scandal became public, Comiskey would be able to point to his investigations and claim that he was actually a crusader for the good of baseball, all the while working closely to ensure the coverup.[15]

But his strategy also put him in a bind. If Comiskey insisted that his team had played their best, he also would have to reward his players for their successful season. Once again, he doubled down, offering not only contracts, but substantially larger ones to most of the players, an extremely uncharacteristic move. He apparently drew the line at one player, however: suspected ringleader Chick Gandil. Comiskey offered the first baseman a contract for the same amount he had played for in 1919. Gandil counterof-fered offered, the team raised the original offer by $1,000, and when the first baseman turned it down, the front office had an opportunity to release him and frame the decision as a salary dispute. Gandil retired from base-ball, and, temporarily at least, the man who knew more about the fix than anyone else was no longer a player in the scandal.

While Comiskey's postseries agenda was to keep the Sox looking clean, Ban Johnson's goals were entirely different. The National Commission, still damaged by the gambling rumors and allegations from 1918, needed to contain this potentially larger scandal and restore the organization's reputation. Johnson launched his own investigation. If it revealed any malfeasance on the part of the White Sox owner, well, Johnson could certainly live with that.

Both Comiskey and Johnson would have preferred that the scandal simply fade away over time, so they kept the methods and findings of their investigations as private as possible. Many members of the press—led by Fullerton—saw things differently. In the months after the series, reporters throughout the country (but particularly in the Chicago area) doggedly pursued the story. By December, Fullerton's stories became too inflamma-tory for his *Chicago Herald and Examiner,* so he turned to another news-paper, the *New York Evening World,* to publish his strongest allegations. During this period, he was particularly tough on team owners and league administrators, blaming the men who ran the game as much as the men who played it. In Fullerton's view, players may have agreed to the fix, but it was the executives who had the authority to clean up the game.

Baseball was not without its supporters in the press. Some editorialists argued that Fullerton was overly moralistic and bordering on the quixotic. Some publishers, concerned that the ongoing scandal could hurt enthusi-asm for baseball and the sports pages that covered it, urged everyone to turn the page by focusing on the 1920 season. The chief defender of the sport was the nation's top baseball publication, the *Sporting News.* Through-out the series and in the year that followed, the publication's editors not only acted as though the idea of a fix was impossible but chastised anyone who entertained the idea. Years later, the *Sporting News* would question the statements and actions of some of the scandal's participants, but while the scandal and investigations were under way, the publication was the league's chief apologist, acting far more as a public relations representative for the league than a news organization interested in printing the truth.

The Cook County Grand Jury

As the 1920 baseball season began, game day news began to push stories about the investigations toward the back of the sports section, and it seemed that the league might simply wait out the coverage of the scandal. The White Sox played well in the first few months of the new season despite the ongoing scrutiny. By midsummer, the majority of the sports talk in Chicago was focused on the new club, and Comiskey Stadium was on pace to set new attendance records. Just as it appeared that Major League Baseball might weather the storm, new rumors about a baseball fix in Chicago began to circulate. This time, however, the subject was not the White Sox.

In early September, Bill Veck, president of the Chicago Cubs, announced an investigation of allegations that members of his team planned to fix a game against the Philadelphia Phillies. Veck's proactive, public approach was a marked contrast to that of Comiskey, a difference duly noted in the local press. On September 7, Chief Justice Charles A. McDonald convened a grand jury in Cook County to investigate the claim. But the charge to the jury went beyond the Cubs-Phillies game: they also were directed to investigate overall corruption in baseball, including the 1919 World Series. The Black Sox were not only back in the news—they were, for the first time, in court.

The grand jury convened on September 22, with the White Sox battling neck-and-neck for the pennant with the Cleveland Indians. The Cubs-Phillies game was almost an afterthought as the focus expanded to fixed games throughout the league and, in particular, the Black Sox. Ban Johnson promised Chief Justice McDonald the full cooperation of the American League and urged the judge to focus on the 1919 World Series. The head of the Commission did everything he could to help the court clean up the game while keeping the focus on the team of his enemy, Charles Comiskey.

For the next two and a half weeks, despite the fact that proceedings were supposed to take place in secret, newspapers throughout the country reported one stunning courtroom development after another. In the court and on the field, the White Sox provided headlines on a daily basis.

On September 23, Ban Johnson released a statement that managed to cast suspicion not only on the 1919 White Sox but on the 1920 team as well. Johnson made the astounding claim that gamblers were threatening to expose the 1919 World Series fix unless members of the 1920 team dropped out of the race so that the Indians could win the pennant. Baseball fans now had two

White Sox teams to question: the 1919 team in the World Series, and the 1920 team in the midst of a pennant race.

On September 24, Giants pitcher Rube Benton testified to the grand jury that a Cincinnati gambler had told him that a number of White Sox players had agreed to throw the 1919 series, naming names, including Ed Cicotte.

On September 25, the White Sox beat the Indians and ended their road swing. They headed back to Chicago, a half game out of first with five to play. In the next week, the White Sox would face the Detroit Tigers while the Black Sox would face the grand jury.

On September 27, the *Philadelphia North American* ran a story on a confession by Bill Maharg, in which the former baseball player charged that White Sox pitcher Eddie Cicotte had offered to fix the series, that eight members of the 1919 team were in on the fix, and that the players had been paid only $10,000 of a promised $100,000 bribe. The following day, newspapers throughout the country picked up the story. The conspiracy was unraveling.

Johnson's bombshell on the 23rd and Maharg's allegation on the 27th rocked the baseball world, but it was Eddie Cicotte's confession on the 28th that finally provided credible, on-the-record testimony from one of the conspirators. Cicotte first confessed his involvement in the plot to Comiskey, admitting that he had agreed to and received a $10,000 bribe to throw the series, and then made a similar confession under oath before the grand jury. Joe Jackson followed Cicotte with his own admission that he had accepted money to throw the game, in his case $5,000, although he insisted he played every play in the series to win.

On the morning of September 29, newspapers from New York to Los Angeles trumpeted the confessions with enormous headlines. Chicago area papers gave the story the biggest play, of course, reporting Cicotte's admission in type size usually reserved for the start of a war. The scandal had moved from the sports page to the front page, and the audience had grown from baseball fans to the entire nation. Coverage had morphed from a focus on the suspected White Sox players, to suspicion about the White Sox as a team, to an overall indictment of baseball. The *St. Louis Star* ran a cartoon of a gambler digging the grave for baseball's coffin. The grand jury's foreman, Henry Bigham, widened the circle even further, saying, "I hope the cleaning process of this investigation will extend to all the sore spots in the sporting world."[16]

Comiskey's public strategy of denying the fix was in shambles. He responded to the players' admissions by once again claiming the moral high ground. The White Sox owner declared to the *Chicago Tribune,* "I would rather close my ball-park than send nine men on the field with one of them holding a dishonest thought toward clean baseball."[17] He suspended all of the suspected players, sending each a telegram, which he also released to the press. The telegram read, in part:

> Your suspension is brought about by information which has just come to me, directly involving you in a baseball scandal now being investigated by the Grand Jury, resulting from the World Series of 1919. If you are innocent of any wrongdoing, you and each of you will be reinstated; If you are guilty, you will be retired from organized baseball for the rest of your lives, if I can accomplish it.[18]

This was a new tactic, admitting to the fix but distancing himself from the fiasco as much as possible and keeping the spotlight on the players. Ban Johnson's response bordered on the absurd: "I'm glad it's all cleaned up,"[19] he told the *Cincinnati Inquirer*. Clearly, the ballplayers' admissions were an escalation in, rather than the conclusion to, the scandal.

With a week to go in the regular season, the team was decimated. Reactions inside of baseball were varied, reflecting individual loyalties and agendas. Members of the "Clean Sox" rejoiced, because they were no longer under suspicion and no longer forced to play with Black Sox players they had long suspected of throwing games they had played their hardest to win. Their season was in tatters but their reputation was intact. Team owners loyal to Comiskey (and, by definition, opposed to Johnson), suggested that each remaining team contribute a player to the White Sox for the remainder of the season; Johnson denied the request. Major League Baseball was in chaos, making up new rules and changing others on the fly, a particularly dangerous situation for an institution in desperate need of credibility. The end of the 1920 season looked as tumultuous as the conclusion of the season that had preceded it.

In the final series of the regular season, the depleted Sox team faltered, finishing in second place, two games behind the Indians. Comiskey demonstrated uncharacteristic generosity to the unindicted players, paying each member who had also been a member of the prior year's team a bonus of $1,500—the difference between the winner's and loser's take in the World Series. The 1920 regular season was complete, but baseball's Black Sox scandal was moving on to another phase, as five gamblers and eight ballplayers—Cicotte and Jackson, along with Lefty Williams, Fred McMullin, Happy Felsch, Swede Risberg, Buck Weaver, and Chick Gandil—stood indicted on charges of conspiracy to defraud.

Changes at the Top in Baseball

Regardless of the legal outcome, the leaders of Major League Baseball knew that they needed to make major changes if their game was to survive and that the biggest changes had to come at the top of the organization. The club owners began planning a new office that would be more powerful than the discredited National Commission and began searching for a candidate with the gravitas they knew was essential for the job. The search committee considered war heroes such as General George Pershing, ex-treasury secretary William McAdoo, even former president William Howard Taft.

In the end, they decided on Judge Kenesaw Mountain Landis of the U.S. District Court in Chicago. Landis had a number of qualities that made him an appealing choice. Team owners were already familiar with him, and he had experience in baseball law, having presided over a 1914 antitrust case between the Federal baseball league and the National and American leagues. He looked, sounded, and judged like an authority from on high, a powerful figure who could purge the game of evil. If he was also tyrannical, reactionary, and self-promotional, and issued rulings that were frequently overturned on appeal, baseball could live with those shortcomings as long as he appeared to clean up the game. Daniel Ginsburg noted, "The hiring of Landis was a strong public relations move for baseball. And with the upcoming trials of the eight players, organized baseball would need all the good public relations it could get."[20]

In his negotiations for the position, Landis demanded five times his salary as a judge and insisted on unconditional authority over all aspects of baseball. He would not answer to, and could overrule, team owners and the Commission itself. The owners, desperate for a man who could put the Black Sox scandal to rest, agreed. Landis's demand would prove useful in convincing all audiences—internal and external, players, fans, and members of the media—that an entirely new authority would make decisions about the game independent of the powerful owners, and that whoever had acted—or failed to act—in ways that harmed the integrity of the game would be dealt with without bias. Ultimately, this proved not to be true, but at least Landis could present the impression of impartiality. On November 12, Major League Baseball announced his appointment.

The Trial

When the Black Sox were arraigned on February 14, 1921, it was immediately apparent that the prosecutor was working with a weak case. Potential witnesses had disappeared, and, most alarming, the players' original signed confessions had gone missing. The case was so bad that the court granted the new state's attorney an extension to strengthen it. Ban Johnson, still working behind the scenes, breathed life into the prosecution by tracking down a key witness, Bill Burns, in Mexico and persuading him to testify with a grant of immunity.

When the trial finally began on July 18, the prosecution called on Bill Burns and Billy Maharg to testify against the players. Their testimony was damaging, but, ultimately, had little impact on the jury. With the disappearance of the key documents in the case, Cicotte and Jackson recanted their confessions. On August 2, the jury debated less than three hours before returning a verdict of not guilty on all counts for everyone charged and then joined the players in a local restaurant to celebrate the victory.

The Black Sox had escaped the court of law, but not the court of public opinion. Newspapers throughout the country railed against the injustice, everyone certain that, while they weren't sure exactly what had happened, something immoral, and probably illegal, had occurred, and no one was going to answer for it. The nation didn't have long to wait for another brand of justice to be served.

Landis Lays down the Law

The day after the acquittal, Commissioner Landis announced that every ballplayer involved in the fix—Chick Gandil, Buck Weaver, Eddie Cicotte, Joe Jackson, Hap Felsch, Lefty Williams, Swede Risberg, and Fred McMullin of the White Sox, as well as Joe Gedeon of the Saint Louis Browns and Jean Dubuc of the New York Giants—was banned from baseball.

In his statement, Landis wrote:

> Regardless of the verdict of juries, no player that throws a ball game, no player that entertains proposals or promises to throw a game, no player that sits in a conference with a bunch of crooked players and gamblers where the ways and means of throwing games are discussed and does not promptly tell his club about it, will ever again play professional baseball.[21]

Landis's pronouncement shocked the nation because it was so comprehensive and because it came so soon after the players' victory in court. The decision and supporting rationale appeared to be definitive and wide-ranging, designed to restore integrity to all of baseball. On closer inspection, however, both were more arbitrary than they first appeared. Landis inexplicably failed to include Hal Chase, who had been a central figure in the gambling scandals of 1918, or Rube Benton, who had testified to the grand jury that he knew about the fix. More important, his decisions dealt only with players, with no mention of other individuals connected with the game. This could not have been coincidental: Landis's decision ignores the action and inaction of Charles Comiskey, who had indisputably heard rumors of a fix before the second game of the series, denied Joe Jackson's repeated requests to meet with him so that Jackson could tell him what he knew of the fix, and clearly had critical information about the fix that he had failed to provide to the National Commission.

The White Sox owner walked away from Landis's ruling with his reputation intact. His team, however, had been gutted by the scandal, and Comiskey would live the rest of his life without ever seeing them win another pennant.

Landis's decision generally was accepted favorably by the press and the public, although some reporters parsed Landis's announcement and quibbled with specifics. Buck Weaver, for example, hit .324 in the series, had no errors in the field, received no money from the scheme, and denied any connection with the fix before, during, and after the trial, yet he was given the same punishment as the other conspirators. Joe Jackson also claimed to have tried his hardest throughout the series, and his numbers support his contention, although he admitted to agreeing to and accepting a bribe to throw the games. Landis was unfazed: he appears to have erred in favor of too much punishment rather than too little, in an effort to remove any doubt that he had gone far enough to clean up the game.

In later years, Weaver would continue to appeal for reinstatement, and Landis would deny every appeal, arguing that his standard for banishment—failing to report knowledge of a proposed fix—was sufficient, at least for ballplayers. If there were a few innocent casualties along the way, he could live with his decision. Most fans and the general public agreed with the commissioner. As Roger Abrams noted, "(Landis') banishment of the Black Sox was necessary and proper, even if it was harsh. In the public's mind, Landis cleansed baseball of game fixing."[22]

Baseball Moves Forward

Baseball's top administrators attempted to bury the Black Sox scandal as quickly as possible, but they still had to address the ongoing corruption in their game. "Baseball discovered that the key to survival was constant vigilance against corruption," Daniel Ginsburg wrote. "Any suspicious action was investigated, any scandal was pursued, and any dishonest players were expelled from baseball."[23]

Landis had found his mission in life, and he poured his zealotry into cleaning up the game in the years that followed. After banishing the Black Sox, Landis uncovered and addressed a series of gambling plots. At each turn, he burnished his law-and-order image, making his campaign as public as possible in a constant effort to promote his efforts to purify the game and enhance his personal reputation.

Conclusion

"What deductions can be drawn about the Black Sox scandal?" asks Harold Seymour. "The task of judging the affair is doubly difficult . . . because of the lack of source material and because countless journalistic accounts have encrusted the event in layers of preconceived assumptions and questionable opinions."[24] Undeniably, there was an agreement between some White Sox players and some gamblers to throw the game. But whether and how much money changed hands, and whether the players held up their end of the agreement throughout the series, can never really be resolved.

The Black Sox story remains the most famous scandal in the history of American sports. It ended the careers of eight players and tarnished the reputation of baseball, but it also produced enormous, necessary changes at the highest levels of the sport's organization. Ultimately, these changes in both administrative structure and personnel led to the league's most important attempts to purge the game of the influence of gambling and regain the public trust.

Chapter 3

Baseball's Reaction to Jackie Robinson (1947–1956)

The story of Jackie Robinson is invariably told as a tale of triumph over adversity. As the first African American to play Major League Baseball, Robinson needed enormous courage to overcome the daily instances of racism he faced during his career, making him one of the great stories in the history of American sport. From an institutional perspective, however, the desegregation of baseball was an organizational crisis in which the sport's premier league was caught in the midst of enormous social change. From that perspective, the Jackie Robinson story was a sports crisis.

Contradictions in the Front Office: Judge Kenesaw Mountain Landis

When Baseball Commissioner Kenesaw Mountain Landis was brought in to clean up baseball in 1921, his first major task was the resolution of the Black Sox scandal. He went on to hold the league's highest office for the next 23 years, and until his death following the 1944 season, positioned himself as chief protector of the integrity of the game.

Landis had a number of advantages that were useful for this role. He had negotiated unlimited authority as part of the job, he was a tireless self-promoter, and he maintained his popularity for almost his entire tenure. If he was lacking in a few other areas—humility, judicial consistency, pliability, compassion—he could live comfortably with these shortcomings, and he assumed everyone else could, too.

Landis's rulings and the explanations that accompanied them were frequently at odds, none more so than when he dealt with the issue of race. The judge publicly maintained a position of neutrality on the issue while thwarting any attempts to integrate the game. When challenged by members of the press or antisegregationists, Landis clung tenaciously to two spurious positions. The first was that there was no rule in his league against hiring African American players, a statement that was factually correct but failed to address what author Jules Tygiel referred to as "the doctrine of common consent and coercion, the 'gentleman's agreement' to exclude non-white players."[1] When pressed, which he rarely was, Landis fell back on a second defense: black players were so successful in the Negro leagues, they would not want to switch to Major League Baseball. This position was absurd: the disparity in pay and working conditions between the black and white leagues was so great that many black players would have been happy to leave the spartan life of a barnstormer for the relative wealth, security, and fame of the National and American leagues.

Another common argument against integration, stated by league officials other than Landis, was that African American players lacked the talent to play in Major League Baseball. This position was as foolish as the commissioner's defenses, easily refuted by looking at games played between the races, particularly those involving Major League Baseball players in non league, mixed-race games. By the 1920s, this record so disproved the idea of white superiority that Landis was forced to address it. Instead of integrating the leagues or at least acknowledging that black players were as talented as white ones, the commissioner forbade league clubs from playing as a unit in the off-season. "Hereafter major league all-star squads could barnstorm during the post-season months, though Landis limited the number of players allowed from any individual team," noted Tygiel. "Black players believed that Landis invoked this rule to end the embarrassing defeats they handed championship clubs."[2]

The Bottom Line: The Bottom Line

What, then, explains the ongoing segregation of baseball, years after other American institutions had integrated? Lingering racism was one factor, but as long as America was comfortable with or oblivious to baseball's rejection of other races, there was limited social pressure to change. Beyond any social issues, however, there were economic ones. Team owners made almost all of their decisions, particularly large ones, based on how it would affect their organization's balance sheets. As business owners, the men who ran baseball viewed segregation as a good business decision because they could not predict the consequences of integration, and they did not want to risk anything that could threaten their revenue streams. For some team owners, their primary concern was alienating white fans, who, they feared, might not support a hometown team with black players or want to sit in a stadium with fans of another color.

If owners had bothered to examine demographic trends in the 1940s, they might have seen things differently. At the beginning of the decade, the vast majority of Major League Baseball teams were north of the Mason-Dixon Line while the vast majority of African Americans, representing only 10 percent of the population, lived predominantly in the South. At the time, the distribution of the races would have limited the effect of desegregation on the racial makeup of the fan base. As the decade progressed, however, a growing number of Southern blacks moved north in search of jobs, and most of them migrated to the large cities, where the teams played. They were, in effect, a growth market.

But would an increase in the black fan base be offset by a reduction in an alienated white fan base? Most owners appeared to believe so. As Tygiel noted:

> Apprehension about the impact of segregation at the box office constituted perhaps the owners' greatest and most understandable fear. Many baseball owners were businessmen. If the expectation of profit outweighed the fear of financial loss, some owners might gladly have overcome their prejudices.[3]

Trends against Segregation

The northern migration of African Americans meant that people of various races were forced to coexist in major American cities more than ever before, increasing interracial friction. In August of 1943, African Americans in Harlem rioted when a white police officer shot a black soldier. New York City mayor Fiorella La Guardia responded by forming a Committee on Unity to promote understanding among various racial and religious groups in the city. La Guardia urged a variety of institutions—manufacturing, retail, government, etc.—to end segregation and specifically pointed to the region's baseball teams—the Yankees, Giants, and Dodgers—as visible symbols of segregation, pressuring them to change.

La Guardia's desegregation efforts were part of a trend in government and society as a whole to move toward eliminating racial division. Part of the United States' rationale for fighting the Axis alliance in World War II was that the nation's enemies, particularly Germany and Japan, were corrupt societies founded on racist policies. Yet it was difficult to condemn enemy attitudes toward race when racial inequity was so apparent in the United States. This difference was as clear in baseball as in any other institution in the nation. Jonathan Eig noted:

> Black activists, trade unionists, integrationists, communists, pacifists and religious leaders in New York were exceedingly well-organized and highly

combative, and they had decided to make the integration of baseball one of their core goals. It seemed to them a relatively easy target. How could any game calling itself the national pastime, they asked, get away with excluding 10 percent of the population? The hypocrisy was so jolting that even the Japanese had picked up on it during the war, showering black troops with leaflets intended to sap morale. "If Americans are fighting for the freedom and equality of all people," the propaganda read, "why aren't Negro Americans allowed to play baseball?[4]

As the war wound down and soldiers began returning home, the pressure to end segregationist policies grew even stronger. In 2002, Scott Simon noted:

> It seems clearer now than it could have in 1945 that official segregation was a ruined and doomed institution. Racial segregation was immoral, corrupt, inefficient, and undermined by its own contradictions. The United States could not have won World War II, or beaten back the Great Depression of the 1930s, without black workers in its factories, fields and armed services. But just as Britain had discovered that it could not win a war for freedom and keep an empire, the United States was learning that it could not be considered the last, best hope for mankind while enchaining its own citizens with race laws.[5]

In 1946, President Harry Truman established a Committee on Civil Rights, which focused on a redefinition of civil rights and an end to desegregation. Truman was determined to ensure that segregation, long accepted or ignored, would come to an end in postwar America.

Political leaders may have been ready to confront racism, but their passion was not shared by many executives in the baseball business. Segregation was a polarizing issue, with a divided audience voicing strong opinions and no easy solutions—to placate one group was to antagonize another. Despite integration advances in government and industry, the national pastime seemed immune to progress: games continued to begin with the national anthem, followed by nine white men taking the field.

Branch Rickey, Baseball Pioneer

If Kenesaw Mountain Landis was baseball's past—rigid, hidebound, traditional—Branch "The Mahatma" Rickey was the game's future—innovative, unorthodox, risk taking. Both men were moralistic and exceptionally self-assured. Confrontation between two such strong-willed men seemed inevitable.

After graduating from Ohio Wesleyan University and earning his law degree at the University of Michigan, Rickey began his baseball career with the Saint Louis Browns in 1913, where he served in a variety of administrative positions for four years before moving across town to the Cardinals organization. He moved up quickly with the National League club, earning a reputation as one of the greatest innovators in the game's history. Rickey is credited with developing everything from the sport's modern farm system to its first full-time spring training facility. He reevaluated his team's entire approach to the statistical evaluation of players.

Rickey recognized and capitalized on trends before his competitors could see them, a trait that was central to his understanding that integration was inevitable in baseball, regardless of the attitudes of the men who ran it. His intimate understanding of the game and the people who played, controlled, and supported it convinced him that the change would be difficult because of the enormous stress it would bring to the culture of the game. As Jonathan Eig noted, "Rickey thought of everything, and then he thought of more. He was a lawyer by training and believed that baseball, like the law, required careful analysis as well as bold action, but more of the former than the latter."[6]

Following the 1942 season, Rickey moved east, taking the title of president and general manager of the Brooklyn Dodgers. In many ways, the details—time and place—of the midwestern Rickey's arrival to the East Coast produced an opportunity that might not have been possible in another city and another year. When Rickey came to Brooklyn, New York was a hotbed of liberalism and free thought, filled with restless people agitating for social change. Brooklyn was a densely populated cornucopia of races and cultures, all managing to coexist despite differences in language, food, and traditions. La Guardia's public push for integration dovetailed perfectly with Rickey's own plans, although, as in all things, Rickey planned to maintain as much control over the integration process as possible. The new leader of the Brooklyn team was happy to channel the New York mayor's push for desegregation, as long as it did not appear that the politician forced the team president's hand.

The Dodgers had the disadvantage of playing in the same market as two of the most deep-pocketed teams in baseball, the Yankees and Giants, making it difficult for them to attract the league's most talented players. Upon arrival at his new job, one of Rickey's first recommendations to senior management was to expand the team's scouting system to identify lesser-known talents who could be signed to less expensive contracts, an idea that team officials eagerly supported. This new scouting system,

Rickey suggested, would cover the Latin American leagues as well as the Negro leagues. He also suggested that his organization use this expanded system to develop a team for a new Negro league, the United States League, providing an additional source of revenue, as the team would play in the Dodgers' Ebbets Field. Whether the Dodgers ownership fully understood the implications of such expanded coverage is difficult to know—Rickey could be misleading when it came to his real plans—but regardless, they signed off on his new venture. The president's plan began to fall into place.

Jackie Robinson: Talent and Discipline

Rickey understood that the success of baseball desegregation would depend heavily on the man who would become the first black major league player. With his new scouting system in place, the Dodgers' general manager began looking for a player who combined two rare qualities: the talent to play with the best players in America and the temperament to deal with the abuse that would be part of the process. The Dodgers' president reviewed reports on dozens of Negro players, weighing information on off-field as well as on-field performances. After considering a number of better-known players, he identified the best candidate as Jackie Robinson, a player who not only offered both speed and power but who had already proven himself in a variety of venues, black, white, and mixed.

Robinson was a four-sport athlete at the University of California–Los Angeles and a multi-tooled player on the diamond—he could hit, field, and run. On the character side, he was a military veteran and student of the game of baseball, fastidious and devoted to his family. He neither drank nor smoked, and his temperament was, in Rickey's mind, the perfect balance: strong enough to withstand the inevitable abuse that would come his way but disciplined enough to deal with it without overreacting.

Robinson met Rickey in the Dodgers' offices on August 28, 1945. After some brief but polite conversation about family life and baseball techniques, the two began to hone in on the critical question: how Robinson would deal with the overt racism that was sure to come his way if he became the man who broke baseball's color barrier. During the interview, Rickey was relentless and deliberately provocative, baiting Robinson by mimicking one insult after another and asking the player how he would handle each assault. Finally, Robinson asked if Rickey wanted a man who was afraid to fight back. Rickey replied, "I want a man with the courage not to."

As Eig noted:

> It is testament to Rickey's sophistication and foresight that he chose a player who would become a symbol of strength rather than assimilation. It is a testament to Robinson's intelligence that he recognized the importance of turning the other cheek and yet found a way to do it without appearing the least bit weak. So long as he showed restraint when fans and players baited him, he could fight like hell on the ballfield. No one could fault him for playing too hard.[7]

An Eventful Year in the Minors

Convinced that he had found the right man, Rickey signed Robinson to a minor league contract and sent him to the Montreal Royals of the International League. The assignment worked on a number of levels. First, most baseball administrators, possibly including Rickey, felt that the Negro leagues were less serious than Major League Baseball, and even the most talented players required minor league seasoning before moving up to the parent club. Second, Robinson's stint in Montreal, as far north and away from major baseball markets as possible, would allow him to ease into his new role and give Rickey a chance to see integration in action, before any move toward the big leagues.

Despite the Dodger president's most careful planning, he quickly learned how big a story Robinson was, and how little control he had over the attention his new player would receive. Robinson was an enormous story from the moment his signing was announced, covered continuously in the press and cheered on by thousands of African American, and many white, fans. The first black player in the league would spend every day of the rest of his career—on the field and off—in the limelight. "From day one, every step Robinson took seemed tuned to the national imagination, to the dreams—and nightmares—of millions of people,"[8] wrote David Faulkner.

The two men faced antagonism from all directions: baseball administrators, teammates, opponents, fans, newspaper reporters, the general public, and even government officials from towns where the league's first black player would perform. They did not suffer any backlash from the commissioner's office. A year before Robinson's signing, Commissioner Kenesaw Mountain Landis had died, and his replacement, Albert Benjamin "Happy" Chandler, held much more progressive views on the integration of baseball. "The death of Landis removed the symbol of baseball's integrity," Jules Tygiel wrote. "It also eliminated one of the most implacable and influential opponents of integration."[9] A significant percentage of people associated with baseball would continue to fight against desegregating the sport, but it helped the Dodgers' general manager and the first black man in the majors to know that the most powerful administrator in the sport was, if not out in front supporting them, at least not actively working against them.

Robinson didn't have to go far to find racism in the new league—he didn't even have to leave the dugout. The Montreal Royals' manager, Clay Hopper, began the 1946 season less than happy to be part of the grand experiment. Hopper had even less reason to support his new player when Robinson got off to a poor start in preseason.

That changed on April 18, when Robinson made his minor league debut in Roosevelt Stadium in Union City, New Jersey. The Royals' new player enthralled his supporters with four hits, two stolen bases, a home run, and four runs scored. He would spend the rest of the summer destroying the argument about whether a black player could thrive in professional baseball.

Montreal fans embraced the Royals' new star, but Robinson's life on the road was a harbinger of the racism he would face in the majors. Taunting from opposing fans and players escalated through the season, despite, possibly because of, Robinson's stellar play. By season's end, Robinson's .349 batting average was the highest in the league, helping him earn the Most Valuable Player award. Usually, a minor league player with such impressive statistics could move up to the major leagues near the end of the season, particularly when the parent club was in a pennant drive, as the Dodgers were at the end of the summer of 1946. There was nothing normal about Jackie Robinson's career, however, and Rickey's plans to integrate the majors on his timetable trumped even his goal of having the Dodgers win the championship. Robinson would finish the season with Montreal, where he led the team to the Junior World Series title, and the Dodgers would fall just short of winning the pennant. Not coincidentally, the Royals would draw more than a million fans in 1946, setting a franchise record. Wherever Robinson played, the stands would swell; and, in greater numbers than ever before, many of these fans would be black. Team owners' fears of larger black audiences were quickly coming true: whether that would damage their relationship with white audiences remained the great unknown.

Institutional Racism: Baseball Fights Back

Rickey may have enjoyed Robinson's phenomenal season in the minors, but his enthusiasm was not shared by many other baseball executives.

At the minor league level, W. G. Bramham, president of the National Association of Professional Baseball Leagues, publicly blasted both Rickey and Robinson. Others echoed Bramham's condemnation, characterizing Rickey as irresponsible and sanctimonious and Robinson as unprepared for professional baseball. Segregationist administrators who preferred to fight their battles in private avoided public criticism but lobbied furiously behind the scenes to keep Robinson from moving to the next level. Team owners continued to cling to indefensible positions to support the status quo. Some argued that the players themselves would rebel against playing with or against black teammates, an absurdity on two levels. Polls taken as early as the late 1930s indicated that 80 percent of National League players did not object to the integration of baseball. More important, the reserve clause dominated player actions, ensuring that players' attitudes toward African Americans were irrelevant: you either played for the team that signed you or you didn't play in Major League Baseball. Owners gave very little consideration to player attitudes in any other baseball decisions— it was ridiculous to think that they suddenly worried about how their employees would react to a black teammate.

While Jackie Robinson was scoring more runs than any other player in the minors, the steering committee for Major League Baseball compiled a report designed to keep him from advancing to the majors. Since the committee consisted of both league presidents and a pair of representatives from each team in the league, it is reasonable to suggest that the report reflected the sentiment of most of the league's top administrators.

On August 27, the committee submitted a report addressing a variety of issues related to the state of the game. Their obsession with labor relations remained paramount: the majority of the report dealt with labor issues. But an appendix also addressed the issue of baseball integration, framing the process as a hypothetical, ignoring the fact that a black man was not only already playing in the league's lower level but flourishing there. The report's convoluted reasoning and antiquated language reflected a staunch defense of the status quo:

> Baseball will jeopardize its leadership in professional sport if it fails to give full appreciation to the fact that the Negro fan and the Negro player are part and parcel of the game. Certain groups in this country including political and social-minded drum-beaters, are conducting pressure campaigns in an attempt to force major league clubs to sign Negro players. Members of these groups are not primarily interested in Professional Baseball. They are not campaigning to provide a better opportunity for thousands of Negro boys who want to play baseball. They are not even particularly interested in

improving the lot of Negro players who are already employed. They know little about baseball—and nothing about the business end of its operation. They single out Professional Baseball for attack because it offers a good publicity medium.[10]

The report also included an amazingly candid analysis of the perceived financial impact of desegregation. The first economic concern was the most basic: attendance.

A situation might be presented, if Negroes participate in major league games, in which the preponderance of Negro attendance in parks such as the Yankee Stadium, the Polo Grounds and Comiskey Park could conceivably threaten the value of the major league franchises owned by these clubs.[11]

The second concern was rent: the committee predicted that taking the best players from the Negro leagues would cause those leagues to fold—a prediction that proved true—and that the demise of the leagues would end the arrangement by which the Negro leagues paid hefty fees to rent the major stadiums in northern cities for barnstorming games—which also proved true.

The report then argued that extensive minor league training (average of seven years, the report notes) developed the characters necessary for the majors, and that, by extension, since the Negro players didn't have this training they couldn't be ready for the majors. Of course, this logic prompts two immediate questions: why Negro players hadn't trained in the minors in the past and why they couldn't in the future.

Finally, the committee took the high road by pointing to the sanctity of contracts, arguing that major league teams do not—and cannot—sign players under contract to Negro clubs. "This is not discrimination," the committee reasoned. "It's simply respecting the contractual relationship between the Negro leagues and their players."[12]

Again, the logic begged a number of questions, since many prior arguments among owners stemmed from contract disputes, and the committee failed to address the possibility of negotiating the sale of the contract with a Negro league team owner or signing a player from the Negro leagues before he was under contract or after his contract had expired.

The report ended with a veiled warning about Rickey's plans without actually naming the Dodgers' general manager by name:

There are many factors in this problem and many difficulties which will have to be worked out. The individual action of any one Club may exert tremendous pressure upon the whole structure of professional baseball, and could conceivably result in lessening the value of several Major League franchises.[13]

Later in the year, administrators raised the integration issue again at Major League Baseball's winter meetings. In a secret vote, team representatives expressed their displeasure toward the movement. It is unclear whether the vote was against Robinson specifically or integration generically since the vast majority of the participants disavowed the discussion at all, but the tally made their positions extremely clear: 15–1 against, with Rickey the lone dissenter. League representatives then formed a committee to study the issue of integration. As the 1947 season approached, Rickey was as determined to introduce Robinson to the majors as the rest of baseball was determined to stop him. Baseball was headed for a crisis.

Spring Training Calamity

In the spring of 1947, Branch Rickey's segregation battles with the owners of other teams switched to a challenge far closer to home: as the team president drafted a major league contract for Robinson, a number of Dodgers began circulating a petition stating that they did not wish to play on a team with him. Leo Durocher held an impromptu private meeting with the players, a heated argument in which he insisted that Robinson was an extremely good player who could make them all rich. Rickey held a similar meeting with the players but relied primarily on moral suasion to make his case. Both ultimately threw their trump card, pulling rank and stating that anyone who couldn't play with Robinson would be traded. Rickey traded pitcher Kirby Higbe, one of the most adamant opponents of Robinson, and the rebellion, at least on the surface, was crushed.

The Dodgers' spring training included a second major disruption, when a week before Robinson's debut Commissioner Chandler suspended Durocher for a year for associating with disreputable acquaintances, including gamblers. The integration of baseball may have been the dominant issue of the day, but gambling was never far from the game.

On April 17, Rickey wired a terse telegram to his longtime friend Burt Shotton, a Dodgers scout who had been easing toward retirement. "Be in Brooklyn tomorrow morning. See nobody. Say nothing," the message said. When Shotton arrived, Rickey offered him the manager's job, a challenging position on three fronts: First, the Dodgers had been pennant contenders the prior season, so expectations would be high and press coverage would be substantial for the 1947 team. Second, the team was shaken by the sudden suspension of their veteran manager. And third, and most important, Shotton would be forced to deal with Robinson's major league debut, including interpersonal conflicts among the players and unparalleled media scrutiny.

The 1947 Season Begins

Robinson's performance in the earliest days of his first season in the majors was not as successful as the record-breaking year he had enjoyed in the minors. The competition was obviously tougher, but the public displays of racism were worse as well.

The Dodgers' new star slumped early, including an 0-for-20 streak. In the team's third series of the season, Robinson was heckled mercilessly by the visiting Philadelphia Phillies, led by their racist manager, Ben Chapman. The series featured some of the most vile, reprehensible language imaginable, and included players pointing bats at Robinson as if they were shooting at him. Years later, Robinson would concede that the series was one of the low points of his years battling segregation. At the time, however, he quietly withstood the Phillies' taunts, responding the best way he knew how—by outperforming them on the field. The first game of the series was a 1–0 Dodger win, with Robinson scoring the lone run. The Dodgers took the next two games and swept the series, but the racist abuse from the Phillies dugout never let up.

The Phillies' racist taunts were so offensive that Robinson's teammates finally began to rise to his defense. In the third game of the series, Robinson's teammate Eddie Stankey had had enough, and he challenged the Phillies to "pick on somebody who can answer back."[14] It was the first public player-to-player challenge to Robinson's abuse, a public crack in the wall of abuse Robinson was facing. The series was emotionally brutal for Robinson, but Rickey recognized the significance in Stankey's response: it was, he hoped, the first indication that the overt racism directed toward one player would bond the Dodgers to a man wearing the same uniform.

Stankey's challenge to Chapman and the Phillies was followed by a second, this time from the highest offices of Major League Baseball. When a number of members of the media, including the influential Walter Winchell, reported on the Phillies' repugnant behavior, the league offices were forced to react. Commissioner Happy Chandler and National League president Ford Frick publicly reprimanded the Phillies coach, and Chandler issued an edict that "he would fine, suspend or banish any player who couldn't express himself with a perfectly vivid profanity that did not invoke a man's race."[15] The commissioner's reaction was strong but late: baseball had to reach a new low before the executives in charge of the integrity of the game would step in to stop it.

Chapman claimed that the race-baiting of Robinson was no different from the heckling he gave other rookies, regardless of color. Phillies management, attempting to deflect the bad publicity, arranged a photo opportunity of their manager shaking hands with Robinson. Amazingly, Robinson agreed to participate, because the request came from Rickey, but when the time came for the picture, Chapman would agree only to hold a bat with the Dodgers' first baseman, not actually shake his hand.

If some Dodgers and league administrators were beginning to address the repulsive attacks on the newest Dodger, the rest of the league had a long way to go. The Phillies may have been baseball's most racist team, but they were by no means the only one. The Pirates refused to take the field in the Dodgers' first visit to Pittsburgh, playing only when threatened with a forfeit. The Cardinals and Cubs allegedly held secret votes not to play against the Dodgers, plans abandoned only when National League president Ford Frick allegedly threatened to ban any striker from baseball.

Anonymous letter writers were far worse: death threats against Robinson, his wife, and even his infant son meant that the Dodgers first baseman was forced to play under stress no one else in the league had ever dealt with. Robinson worked in a public place, surrounded by tens of thousands of people, many of whom wanted him to fail, some of whom wanted him to die, and a few who would be happy to have a hand in it.

Rickey knew that it would take more than abuse from opposing teams to get the Dodgers to support Robinson—he had to help them win, too. In the first half of May, the first baseman began to hit consistently, and his teammates began to rally around him. Once on base, he was a constant threat to steal a base, distracting pitchers and helping his teammates at the plate. Robinson's increased contributions gained him increasing acceptance with his teammates, but it also created even greater animosity among his opponents.

If the owners were ambivalent, at best, about Robinson's impact on the game, the earliest games of the season allayed one of their biggest fears: his impact at the box office. He was an enormous draw from the first day of the season—a business indicator that every team owner closely monitored. Initial attendance may have been influenced by the novelty—both casual and serious fans interested in witnessing the first Negro in the majors. As the season progressed and Robinson's play improved, however, the motivation for some fans began to change. By the time the Dodgers made their second pass through most visiting stadiums, Robinson's offensive numbers were far higher than they had been earlier in the season, and many fans paid to see an emerging star. By season's end, the Dodgers had drawn a record number of fans for their home games. Rickey's decision to bring up Robinson was altruistic, but it's undeniable that it proved to be a shrewd business move as well.

Robinson and the Press

Branch Rickey's media influence could extend only so far: he had courted key national and Brooklyn reporters for years, but he couldn't control a story as big as Robinson, and he barely influenced the local press in other major league cities. Instead, he focused on what he could control: the player himself. In preparing Robinson for the majors, Rickey spent more time advising him on how to conduct himself off the field than he did on how to play the game. He convinced Robinson to decline all endorsement offers for the first half of the 1947 season: a significant financial sacrifice for a new husband and father, who, as an emerging star, was sure to attract offers. The request was no small matter: Ricky was paying Robinson the league minimum of $5,000 for the season, and an endorsement deal could have easily earned the first baseman an additional $1,000. Robinson entered and exited Ebbets Field from a secret location, to shield him from the press and fans, and Rickey shielded him from as many interviews as possible, fearing that one misstatement or misquote would turn into a public relations fiasco. Rickey also convinced his emerging star to avoid any of the nightlife that often led other players into trouble. It was a complete double standard, but Robinson accepted it as a necessary part of the transition.

Robinson was covered extensively in the press, but the tenor of the coverage varied based on the agenda of the news organization. Niche press organizations reported on Robinson according to their political, social, or racial lens. For example, the radical left press often used his story as a vehicle for highlighting racial inequity. As Kelly Rusinack noted, the American Communist party's *Worker* publication "rarely mentioned Major League Baseball without commenting upon the exclusion of African-American players, also comparing African-American players with major league players."[16] The newspaper's readership was small but intense and politically active, and likely to pressure politicians, if not baseball insiders, to move toward integration.

African American newspapers, of course, devoted enormous coverage to the new star. Papers in Chicago, Pittsburgh, and Baltimore, hundreds of miles from the games in which Robinson played or his team's home city, reported at length on each of his at bats. Stories featured statistics, recaps, breathless play-by-play, and large photographs, and were frequently accompanied by worshipful editorials. Coverage appeared on the front pages as well as the sports pages of black papers. Of course, as in the case of Rickey, the altruism of the black press coincided with a significant financial benefit: Jackie Robinson stories sold newspapers.

The nation's most influential baseball publication, *Sporting News*, underwent as big an editorial conversion as any media outlet in the country during the 1947 season. For decades the magazine had served as a mouthpiece for Landis's segregationist logic, consistently arguing against integration. Even after Landis died, the publication gave little ground, all the way up to Robinson's first at bat in the majors. As the season progressed, however, *Sporting News* was reluctantly forced to evaluate the new Dodger using the same criteria it used for other players: the inarguable statistics produced by the daily grind of the games. As the summer progressed and Robinson's batting average continued to rise, the publication could no longer deny Robinson's contribution to his team.

In many ways, Branch Rickey's intuitive understanding of media behavior and public relations proved prescient. Most preseason and early-season articles about Robinson focused on race and the significance of breaking the color barrier, and each time the Dodgers passed through a city for the first time in the season, local writers weighed in on the integration issue. But there were only so many times a newspaperman could use the racial angle before moving on. As the season progressed, inevitably, the coverage morphed toward a focus on Robinson's performance. By midsummer, a great deal of the Jackie Robinson stories on the sports pages focused on hits and throws, long balls, and, above all, stolen bases. Privately, Robinson was forced to continue to deal with the letters and the institutional racism he faced every day in traveling with the team. Publicly, Rickey's plan seemed to be working.

Pennants and Honors

As the summer wore on, Robinson's statistics made his case: he belonged in the major leagues. The final weeks of the season featured a race between the Saint Louis Cardinals and the Brooklyn Dodgers, a repeat of the previous fall. In the final crucial series against the Cardinals at home in Ebbets Field, Robinson went 6 for 13 and the Dodgers took the pennant.

Robinson finished the year hitting .292, with a league-leading 29 stolen bases. Although Brooklyn lost the World Series to the crosstown Yankees, Robinson was named Rookie of the Year by *Sporting News*, the same publication that had argued for years against the integration of baseball. On September 27, Brooklyn celebrated with Jackie Robinson Day.

Robinson would continue to battle racism on the field throughout his career and in society for the rest of his life, but as the season came to a close in 1947, his performance, as an athlete and as an individual, effectively ended the debate over whether a black man could play Major League Baseball.

Rating Baseball's Role in Integration

The 1940s were a tumultuous decade in America, complicated by evolving attitudes toward race. Americans varying in race, age, income, religion, and social status were torn on the issue of desegregation: some favoring it enthusiastically, others tepidly; some adamantly opposed, others ambivalent or confused. Integration was a philosophical issue—an appeal to the cherished American value of equality—as well as an extremely personal one, since it would result in a greater level of interaction between races than Americans had ever experienced. Integration was unwieldy, emotional, and uncomfortable, so there was no reason to think it would be any easier for the process to unfold in baseball.

Major League Baseball was clearly behind the curve on the integration issue. It was not the last institution in America to desegregate, but integration came later to the professional game than it did to many other areas of society.

The pressure to integrate the game came as much from outside the institution as from inside. National and local political forces, large-scale social movements, and demographic trends all influenced the national pastime. The league's response to integration was reactive, inconsistent, and ineffective, even as it played out on the field. During Kenesaw Mountain Landis's reign as commissioner, the league offices offered hypocritical and indefensible positions, clinging to the fig leaf that there was no actual rule against blacks in baseball, while not only failing to promote integration but systematically working to maintain segregation. When Landis died and Happy Chandler was named commissioner, there was a significant change in the tenor of the league's leadership, but it would be an overstatement to say that baseball suddenly embraced integration. Chandler did not actively oppose integration but did not necessarily use the power of his office to ensure that it occurred, even as other institutions in society were accepting the change. Even if he had wholeheartedly embraced it, he would have faced an ongoing battle with other executives who continued to support segregation.

Once Robinson made his major league debut, most team owners maintained a public neutrality while working behind the scenes to keep integration from spreading. Because of these attitudes, they failed to prevent their employees, both players and managers, from covertly and, many times, overtly expressing their racism. It was only when league employees threatened not to play games or when their disgraceful conduct threatened the image of the league—when revenue was threatened—that owners and administrators really moved to limit the segregationists. With the obvious exception of Rickey, the leaders of the game did little to smooth Robinson's path or usher in the integration of their sport.

In the end, the integration of baseball was inevitable: it is inconceivable that the major leagues could have maintained their all-white policy as the rest of American society integrated around them. Yet the process would have been delayed even further, and been even more painful for everyone involved, if it weren't for the efforts of two men most responsible for making it happen: Branch Rickey, the baseball administrator whose will and vision created the framework for integrating the game, and Jackie Robinson, the player whose skill and temperament made it impossible to deny that black players deserved a place in the major leagues.

Chapter 4

Point-Shaving in College Basketball (1947–1951)

The responsibility . . . must be shared not only by the crooked fixers and the corrupt players, but also by the college administrations, coaches and alumni groups.[1]

—Judge Saul Streit, 1951

The average American drew a simple lesson from the 1919 Black Sox scandal: gambling is bad for sports. The average bookie, however, took away an entirely different message: gamblers were bribing the wrong athletes.

There were three factors, gamblers realized, that made baseball bribery impractical. First, one player, regardless of the position he played or his contribution to the team, could not guarantee the outcome of a game. To ensure that a baseball game was fixed, a gambler needed to bribe multiple players, and the more people in on the fix, the more it would cost and, more important, the more opportunities for it to be exposed. Second, in the wake of the Black Sox scandal, the men in charge of the game were going to police it better than ever before: players accused of fixing games, or even associating with known gamblers, faced stiffer and stiffer penalties. Kenesaw Mountain Landis had his flaws as baseball's commissioner, and he never completely eliminated fixes, but his draconian decisions clearly reduced the number of fixes in the game. Finally, the popularity of the game improved the economic conditions for the men on the field: as the century progressed, player salaries began to rise, in some cases significantly. Ironically, the salaries that fans complained were so excessive also made it far more expensive to fix a game. Clearly, it was time to find a new sport to exploit.

By the 1930s, gamblers turned their attention to an easier game to influence: college basketball. Eighteen-year-old athletes fresh out of high school were less worldly, more easily duped, and less expensive to bribe than professional baseball players, and, since a team only fielded five players at a time, fixers needed fewer participants to make their bribes succeed. Gamblers were also free to ply their trade under less restrictive conditions: antigambling policies and procedures in college basketball were not as effective or comprehensive as the rules for the American pastime. From a gambler's perspective, a bet was a bet, regardless of the sport: if you were going to try to fix a game, why not target one that offered less supervision and less expensive bribes to fewer players? Basketball was also a sport on the rise, and more fans meant more gambling, with potentially larger payoffs for those who could control the outcome of a game.

Growth of College Basketball in America

Athletics offered two significant benefits to higher education: a new source of revenue and an opportunity to increase a university's profile to important audiences, including potential, current, and former students and all forms of contributors. Basketball was already a part of higher education in America before the turn of the century, but it was during the 1930s that the college game became a national phenomenon. At the start of the decade, Adolph Rupp took over the program at the University of Kentucky, the first of the 41 seasons he would spend transforming the Bluegrass State into one of the country's dominant basketball regions. On the West Coast, the University of Southern California began a decade of dominance over rival UCLA, generating increasing interest in the sport throughout the region. And in New York City, newspaper reporter turned sports promoter Ned Irish organized the first postseason college basketball competition, the National Invitational Tournament (NIT), one of the many matchups he would organize at Madison Square Garden.

The Garden quickly emerged as center stage for many of the biggest games of the college season. Manhattan's 18,000-seat stadium was often billed as "The World's Most Famous Arena," and radio broadcaster Marty Glickman began his broadcasts from the court by announcing, "Welcome to Madison Square Garden, the basketball capital of the world." Madison Square Garden helped to promote the New York City region as a basketball hotbed, where teams from a variety of educational institutions, private and public, big and small, faced off in multigame events that generated revenue for the schools and enthusiasm for the local teams. Proximity promoted rivalries, and Ned Irish promoted a host of them to encourage press coverage and drive up attendance.

With increased interest came increased gambling. Within a month of Irish's first doubleheader at Madison Square Garden, New York newspapers reported rumors of significant payoffs to college players in local games. Reporters did not require in-depth investigation to write their stories, since gamblers were offering wagers and exchanging money in the stands through-out games. Irish understood the additional interest that gambling brought to his contests and made little effort to dissuade wagering on the games. Tickets and programs for Madison Square Garden games included a warning that gambling on the game was illegal, but no one was intimidated by the notice. Everyone, including the athletic programs, the coaches, and the arena man-agement, was making too much money to spoil the party.

As Irish's tournaments began developing a national reputation, the pro-moter expanded his lineup to include top teams from across the country. The sell was not difficult, with coaches and players jumping at the chance to showcase their games in the famous arena in America's biggest city and ath-letic department directors eager to get a percentage of the enormous gate.

The Point Spread and the Catskill Connection

As the college game's popularity grew, two other factors increased its poten-tial for a gambling scandal: the point spread and the Catskill connection.

Contrary to popular belief, bookmakers do not like to gamble, preferring to take an equal amount of action from both sides and then simply take a fee for the service they provide, regardless of the winner of the game. As college basketball became more popular, however, the gap between the best and worst teams grew as well, until eventually it was difficult for bookies to find money for underdogs commensurate with the amount that was placed on favorites. In the 1940s, they solved this problem by introducing the point spread—a number of points to be deducted from the favorite's final score—to increase the number of wagers on the underdog and the probability of equal betting on both sides. The point spread was so quickly embraced by the gambling community that newspapers even began publishing it as part of their sports coverage. The spread also created an important, unintended advantage to anyone trying to fix a game: it was now possible to bribe a player from a favored team, not to lose a game, but to "shave points," or win the game without going beyond the point spread. To some athletes, this was a moral tipping point, allowing them to honor their agreement with a fixer, collect their bribes, but not cost their teams a win.

The second development that increased the likelihood of a scandal emerged in upstate New York during summers in the 1930s and 1940s. Three hours north of Manhattan, entrepreneurs began expanding the dormant vacation re-sort business in the Catskill Mountains, catering to the growing upper-middle class from the city. Resort owners, eager to attract guests and keep them on the property once they had arrived, began organizing basketball games featuring well-known players from New York City–area college programs. Every summer, as many as 500 college players would work "summer jobs" at the region's 200 resorts, earning lucrative salaries, tips, and, occasionally, economic benefits for arranging games to turn out the way gambling patrons hoped they would. The environment was friendly and loose—the games were informal pickup games in which the players did not represent their schools, so participants felt little guilt in arranging the outcome to the advantage of a particular gambler. Players fell into a pattern of accepting money and became extremely familiar with bookmakers on vacation.

The Catskill connection was no secret to the universities: many of the players were placed at the hotels by their coaches. But it was a scene that should have horrified any college administrator responsible for keeping the game clean: gambling was an accepted element of the exhibition games, and well-known gamblers and basketball stars interacted openly. When the summer season shut down, the gambling culture, relationships, and arrangements formed in Catskill resorts did not close down with it—in many cases, the entire arrangement headed south to New York City, to be continued during the college basketball season.

One Manhattanite who escaped to the Catskills every summer was Salvatore Sollazzo, a small-time hood who had served five years in prison for his part in a jewelry robbery. When he got out of jail, Sollazzo opened his own jewelry business, a successful operation that generated plenty of profit, which he immediately burned through to support his gambling habit. As his losses mounted, he looked to improve his odds by fixing games with the help of Long Island University (LIU) player Eddie Gard. In a very short time, Gard developed into Sollazzo's middleman, recruiting players from other schools to throw games. The pair was industrious and the arrangement was profitable, and in the late 1940s, Gard and Sollazzo fixed an ever-increasing number of college games in and around New York City.

The Watchdogs: The Press and Government

The game's enormous growth should have alerted traditional watchdogs, such as the press and the local government, to the possibility of a scandal, but neither was effective in policing the sport. Occasionally an editorial on point-shaving would appear in a newspaper or a local politician would pontificate on the integrity of the game, but no concerted effort was made to curb gambling on college basketball.

The lack of aggressive news coverage reflected the codependent relationship between the press and the universities. Reporters covering college sports were often graduates of the schools they reported on or worked in university towns and for regional newspapers that valued pride in local institutions. University athletic directors encouraged fawning coverage and discouraged in-depth, objective reporting; and reporters knew that positive stories increased access to players and coaches. News readers were fine with the arrangement: a certain degree of "homerism" was assumed, almost demanded, from the local readership, and alumni were more likely to object to a reporter who was too hard on the local heroes than they were to a writer who glossed over potential problems with the game. With powerful coaches at one end of the process and boosters at the other, it was easy for reporters to function more as publicity agents for school programs than as representatives of the Fourth Estate. Muckrakers of the era may have been exposing government and business corruption, but the sports section was not their beat, so ethical problems in basketball festered with little attention.

If not the media, what about law enforcement? With Madison Square Garden drawing thousands of fans and millions of dollars in tax revenue, city officials were in no hurry to expose anything that might hurt the game. College basketball was great entertainment, growing more profitable by the year. It didn't seem to be in anyone's immediate interest to solve a problem that didn't seem to hurt anybody.

By the early 1940s, however, gambling in the arena had become so pervasive that it was impossible to ignore. Prior to the 1944 season, New York City police quietly circulated a secret phone number to college basketball coaches in the city, encouraging them to report any attempts by gamblers to influence their players. A special phone line may have been well intentioned, but it actually demonstrated how poorly authorities understood the mindset of the men most responsible for the game. Many coaches were not about to contribute to the disruption of the system that provided their livelihood. Long term, gambling might have threatened the integrity of the game, but short term, it generated a lot of interest. Gradually, law enforcement officials began to realize that they would need methods far more aggressive than a voluntary program to deal with the gambling epidemic that permeated college basketball.

CCNY and the Dream Season of 1950

One of the New York City area's premier teams was City College of New York (CCNY), coached by former New York University player Nat Holman.

Holman took over the program in 1919 at the age of 23 and built the Beaver team into a dynasty. The coach was not beloved by his players—he could be tyrannical and self-promotional—but Holman relentlessly recruited local talent and drilled his charges on the fundamentals of offense and defense. He was shrewd on and off the court, enough to realize that the more successful his team, the more likely his players were to be targeted by game fixers.

In 1944, Holman's Beaver roster included Lenny Hassman, who was suspected of dumping games throughout his career. Early in the season, Hassman approached the team's star player, Paul Shmones, with an offer to fix a game. Shmones immediately reported the conversation to his coach, who repeated the allegation to Frank Lloyd, the Chair of the CCNY's Department of Hygiene. The university's next moves were critical, since they established a pattern that would be repeated in the scandal that followed. Holman dismissed Hassman from the team, citing his poor grades and the probability that he soon would be placed on academic probation but making no mention of the bribe allegations. He did not inform the police or any authorities beyond the university about the attempted bribe. As historian Albert J. Figone noted, "[T]he risk of giving the game a bad name by exposing a disease that had grown virtually unchecked was outweighed by the unparalleled gate receipts the game was now generating."[2]

The Beaver's coach resolved the attempted fix without a public scandal, but he knew that releasing Hassman wouldn't end the problem of gamblers attempting to bribe his players—the team was just too high profile and too good. The same year that the Beaver coach swept the Hassman bribe under the rug, the New York state legislature passed a bill making it illegal to attempt to bribe a participant in an amateur or a professional sport. Law enforcement was catching on, providing new leverage and motivation for local authorities.

Holman and his Beavers didn't just survive the Hassman scandal, they thrived in the years that followed. The team ended the 1949–1950 season by winning the National Invitational and NCAA tournaments, the only team to ever win both in the same year. Both championship games were played in Madison Square Garden. The team's successes were compounded by the fact that they crushed the nationally ranked Kentucky Wildcats by a score of 89–50, the worst defeat in the legendary team's history. The local and national press were wild in their praise. Holman's Beavers were a mixed-race collection of local kids, and Adolph Rupp's team consisted, as it always did, of all white players. The racial contrast created a dramatic narrative, with the media portraying the CCNY team not only as extremely talented but also as an example of ethnic harmony and progressive thinking.

Following the game, the Beavers enjoyed a raucous homecoming on campus, with thousands of students turning out for the rally, professors cancelling classes, and college president Harry Wright proclaiming, "[T]his is one of the proudest days of my life."[3] CCNY basketball fever was national: seven members of the championship team were selected to represent the United States in the 1951 Pan American games. The honor was short lived, however, due to the more parochial interests of Ned Irish. The Pan Am games interfered with his Madison Square Garden schedule, and the promoter was not going to let a team with two national titles and the potential to pack the house stray far from the Garden.

1951: The Scandals Unfold

If 1950 was the magic year for New York City basketball, 1951 was when it all came apart; and the man who made the difference was New York City district attorney Frank Hogan. Hogan had heard the rumors of fixed games for years, and had been working doggedly to unearth a provable conspiracy that could lead him to charges against players, gamblers, or both. In 1951, his office got more evidence than the district attorney could have imagined.

On January 11, Hank Poppe, a former member of the Manhattan Jaspers, approached Junius Kellogg, the team's star player, and offered him $1,000 to dump the upcoming game against DePaul University. Poppe was no small-time player—he had been the Jaspers's captain the prior year and held the college's record for career points. Kellogg was stunned that a key member of a former team would be involved in throwing games, especially a game involving his alma mater. Like Shmones at CCNY, Kellogg's first move was to tell his coach about the bribe. Like Holman at CCNY, Jaspers coach Kenny Norton immediately consulted his superior, in this case Brother Bonaventure Thomas, the Manhattan College president. Unlike the CCNY administrators, however, Thomas immediately notified police. The district attorney finally had the lead he had been looking for, and the Bronx police moved quickly to spring a trap.

Two days before the DePaul game, at the direction of NYC detectives, Kellogg met with Poppe to discuss the bribe for a second time. Poppe not only offered the money again but coached Kellogg on how to throw the game without making it obvious.

On the night of the game, as Kellogg shot warm-up jumpers, Poppe came to the edge of the court and informed him that the spread on the game was 10 points. Kellogg was so nervous about the fix that he played horribly, scoring a mere 4 points before being benched. Manhattan eked out a 3-point win: DePaul covered the spread and the fixers who had wagered on them won their bets.

Following the game, Kellogg waited for Poppe to deliver his money, but the fixer never showed. Police arrested Poppe at his home, and the former star player quickly confessed, not only to bribing Kellogg, but also to accepting bribes during his college career. He also told police that John Byrnes, his cocaptain on the former Jaspers team, had also accepted bribes to dump games but did not implicate him in the Kellogg fix.

Hogan now had what any investigator wants: an insider willing to testify against other members of the conspiracy, creating pressure on everyone associated with the crime to confess and cut their own deals. In the district attorney's view, Poppe's confession showed that the Kellogg bribe was one incident in a much larger, long-term arrangement between gamblers and the Manhattan team. In the prior season, detectives found, gamblers paid Poppe and Byrnes $40 per week before the season and $3,000 to ensure that their team lost to the spread in three games. Oddly enough, the two players were also paid $2,000 to beat the spread in two games, which they did. Byrnes was brought in for questioning, refused to cooperate, and was arrested as part of the wider conspiracy. On January 17, Hogan's detectives arrested three gamblers, Cornelius Kelleher and brothers Benjamin and Irving Schwartzberg, charging them with bribery and conspiracy.

The Press and Public Respond

Fixers and players were now publicly connected: the scandal was in the open and Frank Hogan used one lead to generate others. The district attorney proved as adept at press relations as he was at detective work—as the scandal progressed, his office issued a steady stream of press releases about gambling arrests on a nearly daily basis. From the beginning, he worked closely with New York *Journal-American* sports editor Max Kase, who had been conducting his own investigation of fixes in New York City basketball. It was no coincidence that when the story finally made it into the papers it was Kase who broke it, since the district attorney and newspaperman shared a passion for cleaning up the game and a mutually beneficial relationship based on shared information. Throughout the investigation, Hogan provided Kase with tips and background information for his columns, and Kase used his sports page to promote Hogan and keep the scandal in the public eye. Kase, already one of the city's premier newsmen, would go on to win the Pulitzer Prize for his work on the scandal.

Reaction to the arrests from other media was hyperbolic but divided. Initial press coverage focused on the players, but in a few days, news stories and editorial pages expanded the discussion beyond day-to-day revelations and began assigning wider blame. Some papers focused on the Catskill leagues, an easy and obvious target, since game fixes in the resort community were so flagrant. Others pointed out how the college game's success had created enormous financial incentives that led to a win-at-all-costs ethos. Some editorial writers blamed the disparity between player performance and reward: regardless of how well they played, the young men's compensation was limited to their scholarships, while top programs reaped an enormous windfall. The *Journal-American* committed to extensive daily coverage of the story, with Kase directing crime reporters as well as sportswriters to cover every angle. *Life* the photography-based magazine, published a series of shots of Poppe and Byrnes fumbling away the basketball during the allegedly thrown games. The *New York Herald Tribune* pronounced the end of college basketball as a big-time sport.

Popular reaction also was mixed. To some (mostly Manhattan College fans), the story had an obvious hero: Junius Kellogg, who rejected the bribe and worked with the police to catch the culprits. Students, professors, and staff at the university held a rally in support of their star. But Kellogg's tale was an isolated incident—how many bribes went unreported and accepted, and who else was involved? Obviously, everyone heaped scorn on the gamblers, but the integrity of everyone in the game—players, administrators, etc.—was now in question. Newspapers even cast doubt on their own involvement—editors revisited policies about their handling of college basketball stories, some changing how they distributed out-of-town scores to avoid tipping off gamblers or dropped any mention of point spreads from their coverage.

One group that initially got a pass, however, was the coaches. The district attorney's office never presented evidence of a college coach taking a bribe or knowing about a bribe, and while the press lumped them in with administrators, there were no accusations and few insinuations about coaches' involvement. But coaches were so central to the game, it is hard to believe that every one of them was completely innocent. No one knew their players' abilities any better: it strains credulity that none of them knew, or suspected, that any of their players were dumping when so many of the games were fixed.

The Scandal Expands

Any possibility that New York City's gambling scandal would be limited to Manhattan College ended early in the morning on February 18, as the

CCNY Beavers returned to New York City after beating the Temple Owls in Philadelphia. When the team stepped off the train in Penn Station, they were met by detectives from Hogan's office, who handcuffed three of the players: Ed Warner, Ed Roman, and Al Roth. Coach Holman asked if he could accompany his players to the detectives' office, and his request was denied.

All three players were members of the 1949–1950 team that had swept the titles the year before. They were the face of college basketball across the country, but their fame was no help when it came time for questioning. Not only were the three players cut off from their coach, they were cut off from each other, confronted with recordings of their conversations discussing bribes, and told that their teammates had confessed. All three caved in quickly, admitting to accepting bribes between $1,000 and $1,500 to lose three games during the 1950–1951 season.

Hogan again turned his attention to the fixers. His detectives quickly arrested Salvatore Sallazzo, the gambler who had originated many of the bribes, and Eddie Gard, the former Long Island University player who served as Sallazzo's connection to the players. Sollazzo refused to cooperate, but Gard caved as fast as the Beaver players, confessing to conspiring with Sollazzo to fix games with players from a staggering number of universities, including Long Island University, New York University, and CCNY. Hogan now had two of the figures at the center of the conspiracy, and one of them was singing. It wasn't just gamblers who had reason to be nervous: players, coaches, and college administrators throughout the New York City area were worried about what would happen next.

The day after the arrest of the Beaver players, Coach Holman attempted to salvage what was left of his team and the season. At a regularly scheduled weekly press briefing, he announced the indefinite suspension of Roman, Roth, and Warner. At the event, Long Island University coach Clair Bee expressed his disappointment in former player Eddie Gard but claimed that the rest of his players were innocent. Both coaches sought to separate players who had been legally accused from those who had not, cut out the former and embrace the latter, and hoped that if Hogan had any more arrest announcements, they wouldn't include anyone connected with their schools. For both coaches, that hope would be in vain.

The 1950–1951 season was drawing to a close, and Holman's Beaver team had been gutted. The coach tried to right the ship by announcing that center Floyd Layne would be promoted to cocaptain, a decision that would prove disastrous only a month later. Holman also addressed the Beavers' supporters, encouraging an us-vs.-them mentality. Another game at the Garden loomed: the coach urged students to show up en masse to drown out the anticipated catcalls he knew the Beavers would get from a hostile crowd.

Hogan's arrest of the CCNY players cast doubt on the immediate past of the game, and his next move cast doubt on its immediate future. Two days after the Beavers' players confessed, the district attorney announced the indictment of three Long Island University players: Adolf Bigos, Leroy Smith, and Sherman White. At the time of his arrest, the 6'8" White was leading the nation in points per game, was approaching the NCAA scoring record, and had just been named the *Sporting News* Player of the Year. Hogan was charging the most well-known college basketball player in America with throwing games for money. The district attorney questioned White personally, threatening him with significant jail time unless he told everything he knew about the fixes. College basketball was in free fall, and newspapers around the country couldn't get enough of the story.

The pattern continued as the season progressed: arrests led to confessions that led to additional arrests. On February 27, the scandal turned back to CCNY, as center Floyd Lane, the new team captain, was arrested as he was leaving a class on campus. On March 26, three more of his teammates were booked: Irwin Dambrot, Norm Mager, and Herb Cohen. In the months that followed, Hogan cast his net even wider, reaching players who were not from the New York area but had played games in the Garden. In October, he announced the arrests of players Ralph Beard, Alex Groza, and Dale Barnstable, accusing them of dumping in Kentucky's 1949 National Invitational Tournament game against Chicago Loyola. Again, Hogan was reaching into the highest echelons of the game: Groza and Beard not only had played on two teams that had won national championships, they had represented the United States in the 1948 Olympics.

One New York–area school escaped Hogan's diligence: St. John's University. Some New York–area reporters felt that Hogan had as much evidence against Redmen players as he did against other schools, but no St. John's player was ever indicted. The district attorney did bring Redmen players in for questioning, but the process only served to show how the district attorney treated players from a Catholic program differently. Players from other institutions were kept in isolation prior to and during interrogations, standard procedure when attempting to intimidate a suspect. When Hogan's office brought in St. John's players, they not only were accompanied by a high-powered attorney, they were surrounded by priests from the university. To some in the press, it appeared that Hogan, a staunch Catholic, took a far lighter approach when it came to fixes involving religious schools.

By the time Hogan was done announcing arrests, however, it was clear that the college basketball fixing scandal was pervasive. The district attorney ultimately charged 32 players involving 68 games played in 17 states between 1947 and 1951. The arrests included players from four New York schools (Manhattan, CCNY, Long Island University, and New York University), two from the Midwest (the University of Toledo and Bradley University) and, finally, at one of the most prestigious basketball schools in the nation—the University of Kentucky.

Basketball Goes on Offense

As Hogan's arrest list grew, the media, the universities, and the public at large abandoned any hope that the gambling fixes were isolated incidents and began to treat the problem as systemic. On March 2, the NCAA, the governing body of intercollegiate athletics, announced that it would never again host a basketball championship at the Garden and recommended that no NCAA basketball team schedule any game there. The recommendation was nonbinding, but it served to focus the blame not on the sport's policy or administration but on a single sports facility in Manhattan. The presidents of Manhattan College, St. John's University, NYU, and CCNY quickly fell in line, issuing a statement that they would change the location of all of the games they had scheduled in the Garden for the 1951–1952 season. The universities were careful to avoid alienating their partners at the arena, however, noting that returning games to campus would not eliminate corruption, that the Garden was not solely responsible for gambling in the region, and that they would work with the arena's directors to develop policies to keep another gambling scandal from happening in the future. Clearly, games at Madison Square Garden were too lucrative to shut the door entirely.

In May, the Eastern Collegiate Athletic Conference, a division of the NCAA, banned college players from participating in games at the Catskills resorts. The perceived dens of iniquity at the heart of the corruption would have to find a non-basketball form of entertainment to keep their clientele on premises.

Meanwhile, individual universities or academic associations dealt with the scandal on their own terms. The first attempt was halfhearted and unsuccessful, when the president of Long Island University, Tristam Metcalfe, invited the leaders from seven New York–area universities to a meeting to address gambling in local basketball. The lone attendee was Bonaventure Thomas, the Manhattan College president who had originally informed the police of the Kellogg bribe—representatives of six other universities, including City College of New York, declined the invitation.

New York's Ivy League university, Columbia, had no players involved in the scandal but still acted to address the issue. The university's athletic director,

Ralph Furey, announced that, should his team qualify for the upcoming National Invitational Tournament, they would not participate. He refused to make the same statement about the NCAA championship, which struck some critics as an odd, since both the NIT and the NCAA postseason held their tournament championships at Madison Square Garden. Furey tried to differentiate between the two by arguing that the NIT was a commercial enterprise while the NCAA tournament was a playoff organized by universities. His description was a distinction without a difference; however, gamblers bet on games in both tournaments and could try to fix games in either one.

Columbia responded first, but Long Island University responded the most dramatically. LIU trustees announced the suspension of the three arrested players as well as not only the basketball team but the school's entire intercollegiate sports program. It was a sweeping decision that damaged the careers of all of the school's athletes; but the trustees grasped the enormity of the problem and chose to sacrifice all of athletics to immunize the university from additional scandals. The board even went beyond the campus borders, forbidding intramural players from participating in the summer programs in the Catskills, where so many of the relationships that led to fixes had been formed.

Nat Holman, the CCNY coach who was closest to the center of the scandal, denied any knowledge of or responsibility for the fixes. He penned articles for various publications, blaming everything from the Catskills resorts to a naïve faith in the innate goodness of his players to a general lapse in morality throughout society. In Holman's mind, neither he nor any particular arena was part of the problem. Following ancient coaching strategy, he assumed the best defense was a good offense and responded to criticism with belligerence: he ignored calls for his resignation, and, even in the midst of the crisis, attended NBA games at the Garden. To eliminate corruption, the coach recommended abolishing the point spread. In one of the more unorthodox reactions in the history of sports scandals, Holman's assistant, Bobby Sand, proposed a bizarre reorganization of the game into three periods, similar to sets in a tennis match, so that the total points scored in the contests would be irrelevant.

Like Holman, Long Island University coach Claire Bee also professed too much faith in his players. Unlike the Beavers' coach, however, Bee admitted that his win-at-all-costs philosophy contributed to the problem. The confession might have seemed a bit more sincere if Bee had not also described cash that he provided to players as loans that he anticipated would be repaid at a later date. It was an ethically questionable practice, admitted to at an inopportune time.

Universities weren't the only institutions trying to shield themselves from the scandal. As the list of player arrests escalated, Maurice Podoloff, president of the fledgling NBA, recognized that recent draft picks were like time bombs—no one knew when a player currently wearing an NBA uniform might be arrested for a bribe he had accepted in college. Podoloff urged Hogan to wrap up his investigation quickly, before the public relations problem for colleges became a similar scandal for the pros. He was prescient but too late—in November, Hogan announced another arrest, this one from the NBA ranks. It turned out that Podoloff's fears were off base, however: the arrest did not involve a former college player turned pro but NBA referee Sol Levy, whom the district attorney charged with shaving points through selective officiating. Podoloff quickly banned Levy from the league for life, although the disgraced referee's jail sentence was eventually overturned when his lawyers successfully argued that laws involving game fixing covered players and gamblers, but not referees.

When Hogan finally did charge NBA players with payoffs during their college careers, Podoloff acted quickly and decisively. He expelled former Beaver Norm Mager, one of the accused CCNY players who had joined the NBA's Baltimore Bullets, then banned from the league the six other former CCNY players who had pleaded guilty to conspiracy. Like Kenesaw Mountain Landis with the Black Sox, the NBA president cast a wide net and didn't take any chances: if a player was suspected of throwing games, Podoloff wanted him kept from the league if he wasn't in it and thrown out of the league if he was. His approach may have been harsh, but it helped keep the attention on the college game and away from the pros.

Convictions and Condemnation

By July of 1951, the legal process had moved from the detectives' office to the courtroom. District Attorney Hogan presented his evidence and General Sessions Judge Samuel S. Streit determined the punishment. All seven CCNY players pleaded guilty to misdemeanor conspiracy charges and then, one by one, testified against Salvatore Sollazo. Hogan's central target had always been the fixers, so he was willing to arrange suspended sentences for players who would testify against the gamblers.

In November of 1951 the judge granted part of Hogan's request, handing down suspended sentences to six of the seven Beaver players but sentencing Ed Warner to jail. Warner and four other players received sentences ranging from 6 months to 3 years. As Hogan had hoped, the judge ruled most harshly against the men who had initiated the fixes. Salvatore Sollazzo was sentenced to 8 to 16 years, of which he would serve 12. His middleman, Eddie Gard, received a sentence of up to 3 years.

Judge Streit may have been lenient in some of his sentencing, but unloaded on the players and everyone else connected with collegiate sports in his final statement. In a 63-page decision, he noted that all of the players charged in the scandal were at least 22 years old and should have understood what was wrong with what they had done. Streit then noted that "commercialism and over-emphasis in intercollegiate football and basketball are rampant throughout the country;"[4] blamed university officials, coaches, and alumni for their contributions to the problems in college sports; and suggested that the scandal represented only a small fraction of the corruption associated with college athletics. He dismissed the university employees' defense that they had no knowledge of the ethical lapses in their profession, stating that "the naiveté, the equivocation and the denials of the coaches and their assistants concerning their knowledge of gambling, recruiting and subsidizing would be comical were they not so despicable."[5] The judge found evidence of fraud, forgery, and the equivalent of payoffs to players and members of their families but saved his greatest condemnation for the unhealthy imbalance between sports and traditional academics in educational institutions. Finally, he warned universities to clean up the problem quickly or risk having Congress step in to make changes for them. The judge even went so far as to single out individual administrators at the University of Kentucky and Bradley University, even charging that Bradley president David B. Owen, a former public relations executive, "no doubt confused public relations with academic administration."[6] His derision for the state of athletics was complete, and, in the decades that followed, would be repeated by other authorities outside of sports.

Innocence and the Big City

Reaction to Streit's sweeping condemnation varied, with some individuals and organizations accepting the rebuke and others continuing to sputter with indignation. Generally, the farther away from New York City, the more likely the response included some form of a "big city corruption vs. rural innocence" theme, with defenders denying the validity of the charges, the jurisdictional reach of the judge, or the unfairness of an easterner imposing his distorted standards on upstanding boys from the South and the Midwest. It was no great leap for small-town audiences predisposed to mistrusting big cities to reject condemnation from the biggest American city of them all.

In May of 1952, H. L. Donovan, the president of the University of Kentucky, responded to Streit's accusations as vehemently as the judge had condemned his program. Donovan described Streit's statement as a "harangue . . . designed to destroy the reputation of the school"[7] and alleged that Streit used Kentucky and Bradley as "whipping boys" to force attention away from racketeers and gamblers in New York City. "The judge forgot that Madison Square Garden was in his bailiwick and that place is one of the rottenest gambling joints in the world,"[8] the university president thundered. The NCAA ignored Kentucky's bombast and dealt with the facts as presented by Streit. In November of 1951, citing the judge's findings, the association barred Donovan's Wildcats from intercollegiate NCAA play for a year. The university had little recourse but to accept the ban, but responded with a vote of confidence in Coach Rupp. The reaction reflected Rupp's iconic status in the community: he had amassed so much power in the Bluegrass State he was treated as infallible. At one point, he excused his players' corruption by stating, "The Chicago Black Sox threw ball games, but these kids only shaved points,"[9] and his reasoning was generally accepted in the university community. If college basketball was going to clean itself up, the process was not going to start at the University of Kentucky.

At CCNY, the school at the heart of the scandal, the administration launched an investigation of Coach Holman's involvement, but newly appointed school president Buell Gallagher did not wait for the conclusion of the investigation, suspending Holman for "conduct unbecoming a teacher and neglect of duty." The suspension was not based on any allegation that Holman had accepted any bribes but on the charge that he had concealed information about bribes offered to his team. Once again, a powerful sports figure was punished, not for the initial infraction but for failing to report it to the proper authorities. Offered early retirement, Holman declined, took a sabbatical, and sat out the season awaiting the university's report. In February of 1954, he was largely exonerated, as the committee found no evidence that the coach had any knowledge of the point-shaving by his players, although their report indicated that he should have been more aware of the potential for bribery on his team. The findings offered some vindication, but by then the veteran coach's reputation had been permanently tarnished. He returned to coach four more years at CCNY and then retired.

Can College Basketball Stay Scandal-Free?

In many ways, the 1951 college basketball scandal ended the fallacy that collegiate sports were somehow more pure than professional games. A press and public that had been willing to wave pom-poms and ignore transgressions were forced to recognize that gambling was a part of any major sport, professional or otherwise, and that where there was gambling, there was the possibility of a fix. A new cynicism emerged, with media more likely to investigate the negative side of collegiate sports and fans more aware of, and concerned about, possible abuses. The net effect of the scandal was not the purification of sports programs in universities but greater public awareness that the problems that threatened professional programs had an equal chance of occurring on college campuses.

Like baseball after the Black Sox scandal, college basketball after the Hogan investigations made some semisuccessful efforts at cleaning itself up, with similar results. The game would be damaged again by major gambling scandals in 1961 and 1979. The introduction of Internet betting, increased sports coverage on cable television, and a greater emphasis on the NCAA tournament, which has become the premier sports gambling event in America, all increase the likelihood that a major college basketball gambling scandal is more, not less, likely to occur sometime soon.

Approximately $50 billion is now wagered on the outcome of college basketball games each year, culminating in the annual NCAA basketball tournament promoted as "March Madness." College basketball's final tournament is now the largest gambling event in the country, attracting as much as 25 percent of all of the sport's wagers for the year. Regular-season action still comes from hard-core gamblers, but the season-ending tournament has helped legitimize the gambling aspect of the sport because it attracts such a high percentage of nongamblers (and even nonsports fans). For many Americans, whether it is in their office pool or a family wager, the NCAA basketball tournament represents their only bet of the year.

On December 9, 2009, Madison Square Garden celebrated 75 years of basketball at the arena with the announcement of its all-time top-ten moments in college basketball. The CCNY Beavers' dual championships in the NIT and NCAA tournaments were hailed as the greatest college basketball moment in the history of the Garden. Two of the three members of the CCNY team who took part in the commemoration ceremony were Floyd Lane and Irwin Dambrot, Beavers who had pled guilty to accepting bribes to throw games. Near the end of their lives, these players were recognized not for the scandal that had brought shame to their school six decades earlier but for the unparalleled sweep of the postseason that was also part of their story. The audience response was almost entirely positive: proof that the occasional bribery scandal weakens the sport only temporarily. In the modern American sports world, enthusiasm for college basketball is stronger than ever.

Chapter 5

Race and Drug Issues in the National Basketball Association (1970s and 1980s)

Crises in sports normally center on an individual or an incident that creates negative perceptions among key audiences. In the broadest sense, however, an organizational crisis is any situation in which the health of the organization is threatened. The cause of the threat can be real or perceived, fair or unfair. Regardless of the nature of the threat, if it has the potential to damage the organization, it can be a crisis.

In the 1970s and 1980s, the threat to the NBA was not a single scandal, an isolated incident, or a bad decision by an individual player, but an accumulation of real and perceived problems. The crisis was a reflection of attitudes toward race, changes in society, and the behavior of a portion of the league's players over a number of years. At its core, this crisis was an example of how a disconnect between an organization and its audiences can jeopardize a sport's image, stability, and potential for growth.

The NBA and the Influence of Television

The NBA was founded in 1949, the merger of two rival leagues. The National Basketball League, the older of the two organizations, centered on small midwestern towns, while the three-year-old Basketball Association of America played in the massive arenas in the eastern seaboard's biggest cities. The new league consisted of 17 teams, an unwieldy combination of large and small markets that quickly proved unsustainable. Differences in market size and ownership finances created disparity on the court, as the most profitable organizations generally produced the most powerful teams. Inevitably, within a few years of the merger, a number of teams in smaller markets folded.

In 1953, the NBA signed its first broadcasting contract, with the Dumont Television Network. The deal seemed like a natural fit, matching an emerging league with a pioneering technology. The timing of the agreement was also fortuitous in terms of audience development: until the early 1950s, the college game had overshadowed the pros, but a gambling scandal dampened enthusiasm for the university-related product, and basketball fans were eager to turn their attention to a new version of the game.

Television and professional basketball appeared to be poised for massive growth, but just below the surface, both the NBA and Dumont had significant weaknesses. Four years after its inception, the league had devolved into a plodding, low-scoring game, weighed down by a defensive strategy based on fouling to regain possession and an offensive strategy of getting the lead and freezing the ball. In a 1950 game between Fort Wayne and Minneapolis, the teams combined for eight field goals, and neither team scored more than 20 points. A 1953 playoff game between Boston and Syracuse featured 106 fouls and 128 free throw attempts. It was a challenge for the broadcaster to capture the energy and beauty of the game when so much of it was spent at the foul line. Meanwhile, some owners were concerned about the potential negative impact of television on attendance at the games—if fans could watch it on TV for free, they worried, why would they pay to see it in person? Team owners were also concerned about the strength of the network they were aligning themselves with. Television was so new that the major players had not been firmly established, and a company such as Dumont that made the wrong strategic move could be outmaneuvered, and even eliminated, by rival networks. The agreement lasted a single season, as the league and the television company struggled to find their way.

A year after the initial television contract was secured, the league contracted to a mere eight teams. The good news was that each of the survivors was financially secure. The NBA made two changes that year that dramatically improved the league's fortunes. The first was a new broadcasting contract, a more stable and lucrative arrangement with the National Broadcasting Company (NBC). NBC was far more powerful than the Dumont network, and the new deal immediately increased the league's revenues and exposure. The second change, even more significant, was to the product itself. To combat the defensive orientation of the game, Daniel Biasone, the owner of the Syracuse Nationals, convinced the league to institute a 24-second shot clock, which significantly reduced the number of fouls and sped up the pace of play, improving the experience for fans watching it in person or on TV. The change allowed NBC to offer a product with more speed, excitement, and entertainment value.

NBA owners' fears about television cutting into gate receipts proved unfounded, as broadcasting proved to have the same promotional value in basketball that it did in baseball. While it was good for the bottom line, however, the television contract also forced league administrators and team owners to begin thinking beyond the arena, to a new, larger audience viewing the games through their television sets. "In sports the crucial change had been caused by the coming of television," noted historian David Halberstam. "In the evolution of modern sport a league's success was no longer defined by the quality of its play (in this case often phlegmatic during the regular season and brilliant during the playoffs) or by the size of its live attendance (generally disappointing), but by how the networks—or more accurately the great national advertisers—saw it."[1] Instead of threatening the game's finances, the television contract provided a new source of revenues and a new opportunity to expand old ones.

Television coverage also changed the players themselves. Like their baseball counterparts, basketball players in the early days of the game were workaday members of society: with the exception of the biggest stars, players earned unexceptional wages and led middle-class lives, anonymous to all but the most avid fans. Television turned players into entertainment stars, on a par with Hollywood actors, revered in the towns in which they played and, in many cases, recognized in the cities they visited. Even more important, television revenues gave owners more revenue to increase salaries, which they reluctantly did to attract better players to improve their TV ratings. More fame and more money meant that the NBA players were no longer average Americans—for better and for worse, they were part of a new professional sports elite.

Black and White, Separate and Unequal

In post–World War II America, the game of basketball developed in two parallel worlds separated along racial lines. At the professional level, it was almost exclusively white: team ownership, officials, and league administrators were all Caucasian, and the vast majority of players on the floor, reporters on press row, and fans in the stands were white. Television contracts exacerbated this homogeneity, since decision makers in media and advertising were also almost exclusively white.

At the nonprofessional level, in large urban centers (New York, Philadelphia, Chicago), the game thrived in black communities, in recreation centers, and in public parks. (A separate, occasionally integrated game dominated by Jewish players also thrived in cities, but on a smaller scale.) African American leagues featured players and fans no less passionate about basketball than their white counterparts, but teams in those leagues did not play in the country's largest arenas and did not benefit from the collective power of national organizations.

The two worlds intersected at the college level, where schools matriculated many of the most talented local players regardless of race, but there was a disconnect between the college game and the pro game. The former served as a farm system for the latter, but owners of professional teams were years behind their college equivalents in integrating their game, concerned about the potential negative reaction from their traditional fan base.

Following World War II, however, the United States entered a period of self-reflection toward the race issue. If America claimed moral superiority over the morally bankrupt Nazis, who promoted racial purity, how could the country's black and white soldiers return from the war to a society so heavily segregated? Many Americans questioned the separation of the races, whether it occurred formally or informally; and the pressure to integrate different areas of society was intense. Business, government, and academics were all moving toward integration, but one of the most public elements of daily life, sports, clung stubbornly to old traditions. Professional baseball teams continued to trot out nine white players on to the diamond, professional basketball teams fielded five white players on the court. Professional sports were falling behind the times.

In 1950, a year after its inception, the NBA began integration, when four African Americans (Nathaniel Clifton, Hank DeZonie, Chuck Cooper, and Earl Lloyd) donned NBA uniforms for the first time. The introduction of black basketball players featured far less attention—positive or negative—than the integration of Major League Baseball, partially because Jackie Robinson had broken the color barrier in professional baseball three years earlier and partially because professional basketball was less important to the American public than the national pastime. Like their counterparts in Major League Baseball, however, NBA owners understood that fan support was the financial lifeblood of their sport and watched fan reaction to the new players very carefully. Regardless of how they personally felt about integration, they wanted to make sure that it didn't hurt the gate.

"Black" Basketball

NBA owners may have had more to be concerned about than owners in other sports, because the integration of basketball meant far more than the simple introduction of players with different skin color. "African American athletes have a distinctive style of play that separates them from their white counterparts," noted Gary A. Sailes. "[B]asketball was forever changed in its configuration when African American males began to dominate that sport."[2] Both races emphasized physical skill and intelligent decision making, but white teams emphasized team orientation and used more set plays, while black teams emphasized improvisation and individual artistry. The white game was generally more conservative in both play and expression, while the black game promoted a more flamboyant style. Would white audiences, traditionally the majority of fans who paid to see professional games, respond positively to a black version of the game? Historian David Halberstam thought that they would not. "As the games became more exciting, faster, blacker, it was moving ahead of the fans' capacity to accept it, to accept both the new level of play and the blackness of the players,"[3] he noted. Would white audiences accept a blacker version of the game? If they didn't, could the problem be offset by a corresponding growth in black audiences? Players, owners, and league officials watched carefully to find out.

Integration of the game—measured by the number of players and their impact on the style of play—happened in a hurry. Halberstam noted that basketball quickly evolved into "the blackest of the major sports. . . . The rapidity with which black athletes took over the league was astonishing. In the 1961–62 season, with no more than two or three blacks on most teams, seven out of the league's top ten rebounders were black: three years later, with perhaps three or at most four blacks on each roster (which as a rule consisted of eleven men), nine of the top ten rebounders and six of the seven top assist leaders (where, again, speed was crucial) were black."[4] African American players were not only gaining entry to the game, they were dominating it. The most valuable player of every season in the 1960s was African American. The next decade demonstrated the same pattern: the 1969–1970 All-NBA team included three black players, the NBA All-Star team was 64 percent black, and the league's All-Rookie team was entirely black.

This dominance created a quandary for segregationists. Prior to the ascension of African Americans in the league, many of those who argued against integration argued that blacks did not have the "qualifications" needed to participate in games dominated by whites. The description of the qualifications varied: often the reference was to innate intelligence, but the actual phrasing might be cloaked in euphemisms such as decision-making ability, analytical skills, or even leadership qualities. If that argument didn't work, segregationists simply fell back on moral grounds—that the races were separate and unequal and that blacks and whites simply shouldn't compete in the same games. Once African Americans joined the league and then excelled in it, the original segregationist reasoning was obviously unsustainable. It was replaced by a derivative of the separatist argument, in which blacks were described as more physically gifted than whites. This position was predicated on nature (a fundamental physiological differ-ence), nurture (generations of slavery promoted procreation of the most physically fit at the expense of the less physically fit, "breeding" blacks who were physically superior to whites), or both. The contorted narrative man-aged to explain completely contradictory evidence (African Americans increasing from zero percent of the players to dominating play) while sus-taining the underlying assumption that blacks and whites are, at the core, fundamentally different, and reconceptualized blacks from morally or in-tellectually inferior to "naturally" superior, with the emphasis restricted to physical, rather than intellectual, differences. As further proof of the differ-ences between the races, segregationists noted that players were "stacked" by position—that the positions that required the most intelligence (quar-terback in football, point guard in basketball, pitcher in baseball) remained predominantly white, while the positions that required the most brute strength (interior lineman, power forward) or speed (outfielder, wide re-ceiver) were predominantly black. The performance of black athletes did not end racism; it simply forced racists to become more creative in inter-preting new data.

If the "black" game was predicated on individual efforts and drives to the basket, television was happy to package and deliver that kind of product. ABC took over the league's broadcasting contract from 1962 to 1973 and began promoting the games as contests between individuals rather than teams (with games billed as one marquee player vs. another) and highlight-ing clever passes over the more mundane team-designed plays. When CBS took over the broadcasts in 1973, the new network continued to emphasize isolated moves and spectacular individual plays. John Papanek noted: "It focused attention on spectacular slam dunks, the epitome of playground ball, running replay after replay of them and eschewing explanations of the intricacies of team play. Halftimes were devoted to slamdunk or Horse contests."[5]

At the same time that television was promoting a "black version" of pro-fessional basketball, the American media were promoting a "black version" of the male in general. As Billy Hawkins noted, these media representa-tions reinforced negative stereotypes of African American men. Hawkins described "a mysterious re-creation of the sambo and brute nigger roles where comparable images (e.g., the ad pitch-man, menacing gang member, super-athlete, etc.) are developed which provides the mass media with a format for representing black men. This format seems to portray black men most conspicuously in the roles of super-athletes, super-entertainers, and super-criminals."[6] Network broadcasts of televised sports highlighted a black athlete who was not just physically gifted but dominant and menacing. It was a short leap to negative African American stereotypes that emphasized antisocial and often violent behavior.

Not all of the story lines were negative. Many basketball stories framed sport as a social ladder, helping poor youngsters with little hope of progress to move from poverty to economic prosperity. For this redemptive narrative to work, the basketball player, usually black, was associated with the ghetto and all of its associated evils, including unemployment, crime, and, frequently, drug addiction. But even these stories contributed to the growing problem of marketing basketball as a predominantly black sport.

In the politically and culturally tumultuous 1960s and 1970s, these stereotypes put the African American NBA player in a difficult situation. He could not simply be a basketball player; he was a representative of his race. If he rejected that classification too emphatically, he ran the risk of being considered "uppity," failing to show respect for a white-dominated system that had rewarded his play with fame and money. If he maintained the language, dress, and style of the black subculture, he was blamed for that. But if he failed to combat the stereotypes, to speak out against racism or inequality, he was ostracized by some in the black community for failing to use his good fortune for the improvement of his "people." The social terrain was difficult to negotiate, and because prior generations had been excluded from professional teams, there were very few veterans to serve as models for how African American athletes should handle newfound wealth and fame. Sports and society were changing, so whatever social norms had been in place were in a state of flux as well.

The League Begins to Stall

Average game attendance increased annually (with a few exceptions) in the late 1960s and early 1970s, but in the latter half of the decade, that growth rate stalled, until, by the early 1980s, the average number of fans going to an NBA game peaked and then actually began to decline. Television ratings, another indicator of the league's health, fell off even more precipitously than game attendance.

There was a variety of reasons for the sport's decline. The league was squeezed by competition: outside of the sport, from the ascendant NFL, and within the sport, from the increasingly popular rival, the American Basketball Association. The NBA was also too big on two levels: expansion had diluted the quality of the product, and the regular season was simply too long. Teams operating in small markets were perceived as inferior, and a season featuring multiple games every week for month after month turned exciting showdowns into everyday events.

The NBA also suffered from a malady that damaged many other sports: frequent player trades, including marquee names, alienated fans who viewed players as hired guns who sold their services to the top bidder, lacking loyalty to a team or city. The perception of this lack of loyalty was heightened by stories about increasingly lucrative contracts, especially when players known more for what they were making than how they were playing did not hustle all-out in every game, an inevitability with the grueling schedule. "Maybe the long-term contract, free agentry and big money have enabled the dollar-wise pro basketball player to contemplate retirement to an island villa at age 33," wrote John Papanek, "but they have also brought him a serious image problem."[7]

Along with all of these problems, the NBA also faced a significant racial mismatch between the men who played the game and the fans who watched them. By 1979, 75 percent of NBA players were black, and the same percentage of NBA fans were white. In a *Sports Illustrated* article summarizing the NBA's problems that year, John Papanek described the dilemma:

> The issue of race as a contributing factor to the league's troubles cannot be simply dismissed with whispers and off-the-record comments. . . . Some people are obviously turned off by the NBA for racial reasons, others may couch their rationale in more palatable—but essentially the same—terms. "A lot of people use the word 'undisciplined' to describe the NBA," says Al Attles, the black coach of the Golden State Warriors. "I think that word is pointed at a group more than at a sport. What do they mean by it? On the court? Off the court? What kind of clothes a guy wears? How he talks? How he plays? I think that's a cop-out." . . . A top executive from one of the league's charter teams said last week that the gravest problem might be that 'the teams are too black.' When it was suggested that black domination seemed to be a fact of life, and that the league has no choice but to turn it into something positive, to promote it, he replied, "The question is are they [the black players] promotable? People see them dissipating their money, playing without discipline. How can you sell a black sport to a white public?"[8]

Despite post–World War II improvements in race relations in America, racism remained an indisputable part of American society, and as the racial gap between the people who played the game and the people who paid to watch it increased, the league faced an organizational crisis.

The Drug Culture, in America and the NBA

The 1960s are often depicted as the most hedonistic in 20th-century America, but recreational drug use during that decade was generally limited to a small, mostly countercultural niche in society. According to the Gallup organization, "In popular imagination, the 1960s were the heyday of illegal drug use—but historical data indicate they probably weren't. In fact, surveys show that drug abuse was comparably rare, as was accurate information about the effects of illegal drugs." In a 1969 Gallup poll, only 4 percent of American adults said they had tried marijuana. Thirty-four percent said they didn't know the effects of marijuana, but 43 percent thought it was used by many or some high school kids.[9]

In the decade that followed, however, recreational drug use in America increased significantly, leading to a reduction in stigmatization. In 1970, public interest attorney R. Keith Stroup founded the National Organization for the Reform of Marijuana Laws (NORML) in Washington, D.C. The same year, Congress passed the Controlled Substance Act, consolidating drug laws and reducing penalties for marijuana possession. As the decade progressed, the Gallup organization found increased awareness and use of recreational drugs: "The ranks of those who had tried illegal drugs grew—in 1973, 12% of respondents to a Gallup poll said they had tried marijuana. That number had doubled by 1977. . . . As drug use increased, many Americans began to see it as a problem. In 1978, 66% of Americans said marijuana was a serious problem in the high schools or middle school in their area, and 35% said the same of hard drugs."[10]

As the decade progressed, Americans moved away from perceiving "drugs" as a generic, all-encompassing term and became more discerning about the individual and societal damages of different kinds of drugs. The federal government also appeared to evolve in its understanding of drugs during the decade: marijuana was so widely and openly used by soldiers in the Vietnam War that military commanders developed a multifront anti-marijuana campaign. The campaign reduced marijuana usage, but resulted in more soldiers turning to heroin. Some government decisions were contradictory: in 1973, President Richard Nixon established the Drug Enforcement Agency to bring a more systematic approach to America's drug

problem, but in the same year on the other side of the country, Oregon became the first of 16 states to pass marijuana decriminalization legislation. In
1975, the Ford administration released a white paper classifying marijuana
as a "low priority drug" in contrast to amphetamines, heroin, and mixed
barbiturates. In 1976, Democratic presidential candidate Jimmy Carter
campaigned in favor of relinquishing federal criminal penalties for possession of up to one ounce of marijuana.

American media offered the same contradictions as the government: a
"drugs are dangerous" theme was still prevalent across media, but films, television shows, and newspapers began to differentiate between the negative
effects of hard-core drugs and the more benign qualities of "recreational"
drugs. In a 1977 article, *Newsweek* went so far as to glamorize cocaine, minimizing its addictive qualities while playing up its social acceptance. The
American public, government, and media had developed a complex, somewhat incongruous relationship with drug culture.

The increase in drug usage and acceptance that was happening across the
country was reflected in the NBA. It is not unusual to find abuse problems
in professional sports, with the lifestyle of the newly wealthy players. Athletes spent half their time away from home, living out of hotel rooms between road games. The long grind of the season, the tedium of the travelling
life, medical problems, performance pressure, significant downtime, and
isolation from families are all conditions that make it easier for athletes to
turn to self-medication. And yet, Halberstam noted, when it came to drugs,
all games were not created equal:

> In the NBA drugs were a constant shadow; in other sports the shadows
> were slightly different. In baseball, white and rural in its roots, less rigorous
> in its daily physical demands, players in season having too much time
> to kill in alien cities, there was a surprising number of serious alcohol
> problems. Basketball players had little time for boozing, and tended, if a
> stimulant was required, toward drugs. With heavy schedules, the days were
> gone when everyone except a few religiously inclined souls went out and
> caroused at night, when by legend a coach might assign a benchwarmer the
> job of taking out a first-string buddy from an opposing team on the eve of
> the game to drink into the early hours. The new vice was drugs, not surpris-
> ing considering the salaries, the mod rootless lifestyle of many players and
> the easy availability in city after city of good dope. Smoking pot was fairly
> normal. Light use of cocaine on many teams was simply a part of the sea-
> son; on some teams, and with some stars who could afford it, the use was
> heavier. The athletes themselves were now less like old-fashioned jocks and
> more like musicians past and entertainers present; cocaine, being more of

the entertainment world, was bound to be part of sports entertainment. Coke, said one thoughtful league official, went with the territory; it was the Cadillac of modern drugs, great highs at (so its users believed) a limited physical cost.[11]

Halberstam also noted the disparity in drug use among different teams:

The exact incidence of cocaine use in professional basketball was impossible to determine unless, as one coach said, you were "a good eye, ear, nose and throat specialist and you checked every player out." Possibly, thought the same coach, 20 percent of the players in the league used coke to some degree. A few teams—usually the weakest ones, where discipline was breaking down and players were on the margin—had serious coke problems. There was general nervousness among coaches as they watched for what they believed to be the telltale signs of heavy coke usage—arrogance, it was said, mixed with paranoia. Whenever a player's game began to decline there was a lot of quick gossiping in the NBA backchannel among coaches, general managers and other players, comments that coke might be the reason. Suspicions were constantly in the air.[12]

Increased drug use by NBA players inevitably led to arrests for possession of illegal substances, reports of which merged two mediated images: the black NBA player, young, physically intimidating, and nouveau riche, and the traditional black male stereotype, violent, dangerous, and antisocial. An ongoing parade of NBA player arrests for crimes ranging from rape to drug possession to weapons charges confirmed the suspicions of many fans, but the media did nothing to dispel the stereotype of the criminal athlete: in their review of research on African American athletes and crime, Mastro, Blecha, and Seate noted a number of findings that reinforced these stereotypes, including the fact that criminality and athleticism are the two predominant depictions of blacks and that blacks are overrepresented as criminals relative to actual arrest records.[13] Media reinforced the NBA's growing reputation as a league populated by black players, frequently on drugs.

The First Drug Policy in Major American Sports

By the early 1980s, it was evident to the press, fan base, league administration, and majority of players that the NBA suffered from a serious drug problem both real and perceived; the question was how to address it. Officials could not implement rules unilaterally—since 1954, when Bob Cousy first began organizing fellow players, the league had been forced to work in conjunction with the National Basketball Players Association (NBPA) on all important policies. If the league was going to address the drug problem, it was going to have to do so within the conditions of the collective bargaining process.

Most of the time, the NBPA focused on traditional labor issues, predominantly financial ones, but it was also cognizant of players' rights issues in terms of privacy, work conditions, and health care, all of which came into play with the drug issue. Social pressure was on the side of management—it would be difficult at any time for the union to stand against a drug policy, but particularly in the early 1980s, when there was so much media attention on athletes and drugs. Union leadership wisely decided not to impede the development of a drug policy, but to help formulate one in the best interest of its players. The key details were which players could be tested, when they could be tested, what drugs they could be tested for, what could trigger a test, disciplinary measures in response to positive tests, and the appeals process.

During the negotiation process, David Stern served as a key negotiator for the league and Charles Grantham was one of the most important representatives of the union. The agreement would not only prove positive for the league, but helpful to the careers of the two principals: within a year of the agreement, Stern would be named commissioner of the NBA, and four years later, Grantham would be appointed executive director of the NBPA.

In September of 1983, the NBA and NBPA announced the formation of the first drug policy in the history of any professional American sport. The landmark agreement was designed to prevent drug abuse, identify and provide support to NBA players suffering from drug dependency, and improve the health and image of the league itself. The new policy included support for players, including both treatment and rehabilitation services, as well as protection for the league, including a set of increasingly punitive punishments for policy offenders. Penalties were incremental: players who came forth voluntarily would enter a rehabilitation program paid for by their team, with no loss of salary. Second-time offenders would also enter a rehab program but would be suspended without pay. Third-time offenders were banned "for life," although that phrasing was hyperbolic since they could appeal the decision after two years. A player who did not turn himself in but was caught taking drugs or refused to take a test was subject to expulsion. Players with admitted drug problems prior to the implementation of the policy were granted amnesty. The list of drugs covered by the new policy included cocaine, as well as amphetamine, LSD, opiates, and phencyclidine.

Reaction to the new policy was mixed. Management and the union trumpeted the new policy as a demonstration that the league was on the cutting edge of the drug issue, and congratulated themselves on taking such a daring and comprehensive stand. Critics noted a number of shortcomings, from the drugs covered to the testing process. The list of banned drugs may have been long, but it did not include marijuana, considered by many to be the most widely abused drug in the league. Testing was not random, a condition many experts felt was essential to make the policy work. Instead, league representatives or team officials who suspected a player of illegal drug use would submit evidence to an independent expert, who then determined whether to administer a test. Opponents of this part of the policy argued that it was arbitrary, and therefore more likely to result in appeals and that it would not have the deterrent effect that random testing would. Random test advocates reasoned that players who were never sure when they would be tested would be less likely to try any kind of drugs.

The new policy also represented a risk to the league's image: what if the policy worked too well—revealing a significant number of cases that would not have been made public if no policy had been put in place? League administrators and the players' association braced for a possible wave of violations, but the wave never came: in the year after the policy was enacted, only three players (John Lucas, John Drew, and Micheal Ray Richardson) reached the second level, which included loss of salary. The optimistic view was that the policy had worked—the threat of loss of salary had reduced drug use in the league. The pessimistic view was that the policy was ineffective—that the lack of violations indicated shortcomings in the testing methods (it wasn't really catching drug abusers), a poorly conceived counting method (treatment for first-time offenders was confidential, so it was impossible to know how many players were in rehabilitation), or a combination of the two.

Nevertheless, the policy allowed the NBA to legitimately claim a proactive approach that was beyond anything proposed or enacted by any other major American sports league. If it was imperfect, it was a start, and it would be subject to improvement—based on negotiations between the league and the union—in the years to come. In 1990, the list of banned substances was amended to include steroids, and again in 2000 to include newer forms of steroids, including androstenedione and testosterone. The pressure to add marijuana to the NBA's list of banned drugs intensified as the other major sports leagues instituted drug bans, including marijuana, and the number of news reports of marijuana use by NBA players increased.

Cultural attitudes toward the drug were complex, however: possession was illegal in most states, but a lot of Americans either smoked it or weren't opposed to those who did. A 1997 *New York Times* report on drugs in the NBA estimated that 60 to 70 percent of NBA players smoked marijuana and drank excessively and featured a devastating quote from former NBA player Richard Dumas: "If they tested for pot, there would be no league."[14] The NBA finally banned the drug in 1999, but that progress proved temporary.

Between 2000 and 2004, all personnel connected with the NBA, including not only players but also head coaches, assistant coaches, trainers, and other team personnel, were subjected to the latest regulations. Gradually, the league and union also agreed to amend the testing process, moving away from the ambiguous suspicion-leading-to-a-test policy to mandatory and, for some players, random testing. By 2000, all personnel were tested once during the four weeks leading up to the season, and first-year players were subject to testing three more times, randomly and without notification, during the season. In 2011, however, the union convinced the league to backtrack somewhat, limiting testing for performance-enhancing drugs in the off-season, and removing marijuana testing from the process.

Addressing, but Not Ending, Drug Abuse

In the years following the introduction of the drug policy in 1983, an occasional player made headlines for violating the rules or getting arrested on possession charges, but the league appeared to have gained control of both the problem and the league image. In 1986, however, one player's tragic decisions brought the connection between drugs and the NBA back to the front page of every newspaper in America.

Len Bias was a six-foot-eight all-American forward from the University of Maryland, his school's all-time leading scorer and a two-time Athletic Coast Conference player of the year. Bias was telegenic, articulate, and amazingly talented, exactly the kind of player the NBA wanted to promote. By the time he was ready to join the NBA, the league had succeeded in making Draft Day a major media event, and even casual fans watched closely to see which teams selected the top players. Bias was a major star of the draft, selected as the second overall pick by the Boston Celtics, one of the most prominent franchises in the league's history. He was projected to be a dominant force in the NBA for years to come, the new star in a city that loved professional basketball.

Two days after his selection, Bias died of a cardiac arrhythmia directly related to an overdose of cocaine. The drug-related death of one of the season's most prominent rookies at the height of media interest in his story was devastating not only to Bias's family and friends, but to the carefully reconstructed image of the NBA. His death was not relegated to agate type in the sports section but played out in giant headlines for weeks. After years spent developing the first drug policy in major league American sports, countless rounds of negotiations with the players' union, and an ongoing public relations program to rehabilitate the organization's image, the NBA took an enormous step backward, as Bias's death once again caused the public to reconnect the sport with drugs and question the league's ability to police itself. In the aftermath of his death, the most negative coverage was assigned to his college program and college coach, but the NBA was tarred with the same brush. The league announced plans to use private investigators to look into the lives of NBA players suspected of drug use, an approach denounced by the NBPA because, the union argued, teams might use detectives' findings to void contracts.

The NBA Goes International

While the league could enact policies to address the drug problem, it was in a far more delicate position when attempting to address the issue of race. Obviously, it would be unethical, immoral, and illegal to introduce some type of procedure designed to make the NBA less "black." By the late 1980s, however, the race issue began to dissipate as teams began to tap a pool of athletes who had been largely ignored for decades: international players.

Players born and raised outside of the United States have participated in professional basketball since the earliest games in America—Italian Henry Biasatti played in the first Basketball Association of America game in 1946, and basketball has been an Olympic sport since 1936. But the United States has traditionally dominated the competition in international play, failing to win the gold medal only three times, including the controversial final against the Soviet Union in 1972; and the occasional international player in the NBA was an anomaly in the first few decades of the sport. In the last few decades, however, the increased popularity of the game worldwide, partially driven by international broadcasting, has contributed to the development of a basketball infrastructure for non-American talent in Europe, Asia, and South America. Countries such as Czechoslovakia, Greece, Argentina, Italy, and China have produced players who not only are talented enough to play in the NBA but can dominate at every position. The league remains predominantly African American, but a wave of international players has, to a significant degree, reduced the perception that the league is "too black" for traditional white audiences to support.

The league deserves part of the credit for this, because it has encouraged market development around the world, but a large part of the trend is simply increased globalization—of basketball and other entertainment products—through mass media. However it came about, the internationalization of the game has helped to reduce the problems that came with being labeled a "black sport."

Conclusion

Today, the NBA is considered "the standard for racial and gender diversity," with the highest percentage of people of color of any professional league in America, according to the *2012 Racial and Gender Report Card* issued by the University of Central Florida's Institute for Diversity and Ethics in Sport.[15] Thirty-four percent of all professional employees in the league offices, 53 percent of head coaches, 46 percent of officials, and 82 percent of players are people of color. The internationalization of the sport continues, however, with 17 percent of the league's players coming from nations other than the United States.

The NBA's drug problem continues, despite a variety of changes designed to strengthen the drug policy first introduced more than three decades ago. It is impossible to develop a policy that will eliminate the problem, but management and labor have worked hard to move past the perilous period when, it appeared, perceptions might have caused the demise of the league.

In the second decade of the 21st century, a wave of states decriminalized marijuana, a trend that demonstrates the continual evolution of America's attitude toward drugs. Perceptions of the NBA's issues with race and drug usage will continue to evolve, not only as the league continues to change but also as the American public's attitudes toward these subjects change as well.

Chapter 6

Amphetamines and Steroids in Major League Baseball (1940s–Current)

If you had a pill that would guarantee a pitcher twenty wins, but might take five years off his life, he'd take it.

—Jim Bouton, *Ball Four* (1971)[1]

The majority of sports scandals involve the behavior of players and, occasionally, a crisis is caused by a decision at the level of the coaching or team ownership. On rare occasions, a sports scandal can be traced to leadership at the highest echelon of an organization.

Senior managers are charged with guiding an institution by setting policy at the broadest level. They are responsible for the long view, anticipating, recognizing, and addressing hazards earlier and more effectively than anyone else in the organization. When the leaders of an organization succeed, they can minimize or even eliminate threats before they damage the institution, and when they fail, threats escalate and cause greater harm.

Major League Baseball's response to performance-enhancing drugs is an example of an organization failing at the policy level and that failure leading to one of the great, still-unresolved scandals in American sports. The problem of performance-enhancing drugs in professional baseball is pervasive, damaging, and difficult to resolve. Individuals, from unscrupulous chemists who develop the drugs to misguided players who take them, are responsible for their contributions to the problem, but it is the leadership of the organization that is responsible for developing the policies that address the threats and protect the integrity of the game.

Baseball's performance-enhancing drug scandal differs from other sports scandals for a second reason: the federal government's role in addressing it. Other sports scandals have had a tangential relationship with government agencies (New York district attorney Frank Hogan's targeting of basketball gamblers to combat organized crime; New York City mayor

Fiorella La Guardia's push to integrate baseball), but none have involved such a direct connection between sports and the government. In some situations, government action impacts baseball indirectly. For example, if a league's drug policy is written specifically to address illegal drugs, then a change in the legal status of a drug influences the league policy. In other cases, the federal government has a more direct impact on the game: the president of the United States discussing baseball's drug problem in the State of the Union address or a U.S. representative calling on players to testify before a congressional subcommittee focuses national attention on the subject. But there is a limitation to this influence: it is an indication of the intractability of the performance-enhancing drug problem that, despite pressure from the highest levels of American government, Major League Baseball has still not resolved it.

Baseball's History of Drug Usage

"Greenies," as amphetamines are called in baseball, are the game's "longest-lasting addiction,"[2] dating back to the 1940s. They are designed to stimulate the central nervous system by increasing dopamine, producing a short-term, temporary sense of euphoria, increased confidence and endurance. Amphetamines produce an effect similar to adrenaline, which the human body generates naturally. When a baseball player ingests the drug in pill form, he will begin to experience the chemical reaction within about half an hour and the stimulation will last three to eight hours, well beyond the time it takes to complete the average baseball game. The potential short-term improvement in a player's performance is offset by a longer-term deterioration in athletic ability: amphetamine users develop a tolerance for the drug, not only requiring greater quantities to achieve the same results but eventually developing physical and psychological cravings if they go without it.

The typical work schedule for a professional baseball player explains how a culture of amphetamine abuse could take hold. First, there is the length of the season: some major league teams begin spring training at the end of February, even though the season opener won't be played until early April. Then, the real trek begins: 162 games, split evenly between home and the road. Over the course of the spring and summer and into the fall, players take the field as many as 20 days in a row. During these stretches, they fly multiple times between cities, sometimes from coast to coast, busing among airports, hotels, and ballparks, changing time zones and fighting jet lag. Games can be delayed by rain or extended into extra innings, or both, often by hours and late into the night. And even when nine innings are completed on schedule, players in the bullpen and on the bench sit for hours with little to do but watch. More than any other professional sport in America, the national pastime offers a mind-numbingly high percentage of time spent in tedium, punctuated by short, somewhat unpredictable moments that require speed and concentration. If you were going to invent an athletic environment that would encourage athletes to turn to amphetamines, it would be the baseball season.

The misuse of amphetamines in the middle of the 20th century was by no means limited to the baseball community, however—it was also a widely accepted practice in American society as a whole. The American medical community was aware of the short- and long-term downsides of the drug decades before the federal government took any action to control it: amphetamines were not classified as a controlled substance until 1970. For decades, Americans popped the pills to stay alert, and baseball players did the same.

Bowie Kuhn's Earliest Attempt at a Drug Policy

Bowie Kuhn was appointed baseball commissioner in February 1969, about the time that the drug problem, in America and in sports, began to escalate. As discussed in earlier chapters, the chemical dependency problem is this era was not limited to performance-enhancing drugs: the use of recreational drugs, including marijuana and cocaine, was also on the rise, and they were as prevalent in the baseball culture as they were in other sports.

Drugs were only one of the challenges Kuhn faced during his tenure, however. Throughout his 15-year term, he fought battles on multiple fronts, facing pressure from both management and labor. His authority was dependent on the support of strong-willed team owners who often asserted their positions to create whatever opportunities they could for their teams. Kuhn suspended Yankees owner George Steinbrenner in 1974 and Braves owner Ted Turner in 1977, and went to court—and won—against the As owner Charlie Finley, who fought him over a voided trade in 1976. He also grappled with an increasing hostile labor force and was forced to address the free agency controversy of 1969 and players' strikes in 1972 and 1981. The issue of drugs, recreational and performance-enhancing, loomed in the background while all these other issues played out, and Kuhn understood that if he was ever going to be able to address it, he would need the cooperation of both management and labor. Ongoing battles with both sides made it difficult to find a window of opportunity where he was on sufficiently good terms with both.

Kuhn's first attempt to address the drug issue came in a memo issued by his office prior to the 1971 season, reminding players that they were required to comply with federal and state drug laws. The memo talked tough, but was light on detail, including specific drugs and penalties for infractions. It did, however, launch the league on a strategy that based the league's drug policy on federal legislation: as written, it would expand or contract based solely on government decisions on drug classifications. Obviously, recreational drugs such as heroin, marijuana, and cocaine were clearly illegal, since they had been illegal for decades. But Kuhn's memo also ensured that amphetamines would be covered by the policy since Congress had passed the Controlled Substance Act in 1970, making it illegal to possess the drug without a doctor's prescription.

The memo was the basis of the league's drug policy for the remainder of the decade. Team owners were divided on how to move forward with the issue, and the players' union steadfastly maintained its position that the league's policy could not include mandatory testing. Despite evidence of increasing drug use among players, Kuhn was unable to strengthen the league policy beyond his feeble reminders that players were subject to federal law. A decade of opportunity was lost as performance-enhancing drugs took an even greater hold on Major League Baseball.

In the early 1980s, it became impossible for Kuhn's office to ignore the growing drug problem. The commissioner was forced to rule on drug cases involving a number of prominent players, including Willie Aikens, Jerry Martin, Vida Blue, Willie Wilson, Steve Howe, and Pascal Perez. Kuhn suspended each of them, but the string of cases convinced him that his sport needed a more proactive policy to dissuade players from ever using drugs and to assist players who were already hooked.

In June 1984, only months before his term expired, Kuhn finally succeeded in forging a policy acceptable to both the Players Association and the Player Relations Committee. The new program provided treatment for players who were found to use, or who admitted using, a number of different drugs. Players could be tested for drugs if they admitted to drug use or if there was "reason to believe" that they were using drugs. These standards were ambiguous, so the new regulations included a three-member panel that would rule on a case-by-case basis to determine which players warranted drug testing—a panel that would have to rule unanimously before any tests took place.

The new policy was not going to solve the problem, but it represented a compromise that moved the process forward. Baseball's policy no longer relied entirely on federal drug regulations, a significant breakthrough. At the same time, the union succeeded in keeping mandatory testing, to many the only real measure of the effectiveness of a drug program, off the table. Testing criteria were vague, failed tests did not result in automatic punishments, and amphetamines and steroids, the drugs most likely to damage the integrity of the game, were not even explicitly covered by the new policy.

As his tenure drew to a close, Kuhn often listed the new drug policy as one of his important contributions to the game. There is no question that Kuhn's victory represented progress, but all of the game's major audiences—administrators, the media, the fans, and the players themselves—knew that baseball had a long way to go to clean up its drug problem.

The Pittsburgh Pirates and the Grand Jury

As Kuhn and his administrators were negotiating the new policy, authorities in Pittsburgh were launching an undercover investigation that centered on one of baseball's most historic franchises. The Pirates had represented the city of Pittsburgh since 1887 and, along with football's Steelers, were a significant part of western Pennsylvania's sports identity. The team had won the World Series in 1971 behind legend Roberto Clemente and again in 1979, when Willie "Pops" Stargell starred on the team characterized by their theme song, "We Are Family." They were an interracial team that was the pride of the region and a feel-good symbol of Major League Baseball. In 1985, however, that image was erased when the Pirates became synonymous with drug abuse.

In the course of the investigation, a Pittsburgh grand jury called a series of Major League Baseball players, mostly Pirates, to testify under a grant of immunity. The players' stories were a public relations nightmare for the league: many testified about rampant drug abuse on the team, with few players differentiating between recreational and performance-enhancing drugs. Day after day, players provided astonishing details, all of which made for scandalous headlines. Former Pirate John Milner testified that he had received amphetamines from Willie Stargell, a member of the Hall of Fame, and Willie Mays, one of the most famous players in the history of the game. Former Pirate and son of Hall of Famer Yogi Berra, Dale Berra, corroborated Milner's story about Stargell, recalling how the face of the franchise had passed out amphetamines along with gold stars to members of the team. Players testified to carrying co-caine in their uniforms on the field and leaving the clubhouse in the mid-dle of a game to buy the drug from dealers associated with the team. New York Mets first baseman Keith Hernandez garnered national attention when he estimated that as many as 40 percent of Major League Baseball players used cocaine, a claim he later recanted. The story reached the level of absurdity when a player testified that the Pirates employee who worked as the team's mascot, Pirate Parrot, introduced players to a dealer and bought cocaine for himself.

Peter Ueberroth had succeeded Kuhn in March 1984, and he was de-termined to be as proactive as possible in convincing the public that the Pirates' story was an anomaly and that the new commissioner was tack-ling the drug issue. In May, shortly before the grand jury handed up indictments in its case, Ueberroth announced that all baseball personnel, from owners to scouts to front office personnel, as well as all 3,000 players in the minor leagues, would be tested for drugs. "We must stop drugs in baseball, and we will,"[3] Ueberroth said in announcing the tests. He used the announcement to urge Donald Fehr, executive director of the Players Association, and Lee MacPhail, head of the Player Relations Committee, to work together to develop a drug policy that would include the all-important mandatory testing for major league players. Ueberroth's office denied that the contents or timing of the message were in any way related to the Pittsburgh grand jury testimony, but the timing was too coincidental to ignore: events outside of Major League Baseball were pushing the league to address the issue.

As drug policy negotiations between the league and the union contin-ued, it became evident to Ueberroth that the Players Association might concede in some areas but had no intention of compromising on the all-important testing issue. He tried to go it alone, unilaterally imposing voluntary testing, but the Players Association successfully fought the decision. In 1986, the commissioner tried to introduce a mandatory test-ing clause in the standard player contract, but the union filed a grievance and had the courts remove the clause. The commissioner and the union had reached an impasse, and it would not be breached without pressure from outside of the game.

Seven Pittsburgh-area dealers were convicted of cocaine distribution, and Ueberroth suspended 11 MLB players. At the time of the suspensions, the commissioner recommended voluntary urine tests for the suspended players, a self-policing policy met with ridicule by many members of the press. In July 1987, one of the suspended players, Lonnie Smith, told reporters that baseball's commitment to stopping drug abuse was a joke and that he had not been tested during that season.[4]

Steroids "Juice" the Offensive Numbers

The Pirates' scandalous grand jury testimony was a wake-up call, but, with the exception of Hernandez's claim that 40 percent of the league used cocaine, drugs were largely an anecdote-based tale, occasional stories about the most extreme cases. In the late 1980s, however, that began to change, as the impact of drugs on baseball began to emerge in another, more easily measured form.

Baseball is America's most statistics-oriented game. Even casual fans are familiar with its most famous numbers, such as Joe DiMaggio's 56-game hitting streak and Roger Maris's 61 home runs in a season. More serious fans are attuned to more exacting metrics: earned run averages (ERAs), on-base percentages (OBPs), ball/strike ratios, and countless other measures. With decades of data to pore over, students of the game can evaluate a player's performance not only relative to his peers but also relative to thousands of players who have taken the field before him.

When a statistical outlier occurs, serious students of the game quickly identify it and attempt to understand its causes. In the late 1980s, the offensive performance of the entire league began to improve, a big enough difference that baseball experts recognized that the game was undergoing a fundamental change. The impact of performance-enhancing drugs was no longer anecdotal, it was statistically provable.

The increased offensive statistics were not the result of amphetamine usage—that had been part of the league for so long that it was incorporated into decades of data. The cause was steroids, which an increasing number of hitters were using to bump up their batting averages well beyond what they had traditionally hit. Players were also extending their careers: for decades, most players' productivity progressed on a fairly predictable trajectory. Occasionally there was an outlier, but in general, managers knew when a veteran's career would begin to decline based on his age. Suddenly, players not only seemed to defy the calendar, but they were actually improving at an age when thousands of their predecessors had begun to lose power.

The biggest difference came in the most dramatic and easily tracked offensive statistic—home runs. In a very short time, players in positions not normally associated with home runs, such as shortstop and second base, were hitting them as if they were designated hitters. The aggregate number for the league increased, and, most glaring, hitters who had been known for the long ball now began to hit home runs at a record pace.

Veteran baseball writers looked at the numbers and connected the dots. In 1988, Oakland Athletics slugger Jose Conseco became the first player in history to hit 40 home runs and steal 40 bases in a single season, an accomplishment that earned him the American League most valuable player award. *Washington Post* sportswriter Thomas Boswell, who had been reporting on the inexplicable increase in offensive production for a number of years, pounced on Conseco's achievement to make his case, claiming that Conseco's performance came with the aid of steroids. Conseco denied the allegation. In a few years, he not only would confirm Boswell's suspicions but would become the game's most outspoken insider to talk about the use and dangers of steroids. His admission would make him a pariah among his peers.

More Government Legislation, More Offensive Production

If Major League Baseball couldn't solve its problems, a larger, more powerful organization would get involved. A month after Conseco denied Boswell's accusation, the federal legislature passed the Anti-Drug Abuse Act, establishing criminal penalties for the distribution or possession of anabolic steroids with the intent to distribute for any use in humans other than the treatment of disease based on the order of a physician. In 1990, Congress strengthened the law through the Anabolic Steroids Control Act, grouping steroids into the same legal class as amphetamines and opiates.

MLB commissioner Francis T. Vincent had been elected commissioner in 1989, and, like his predecessors, he was determined to find a way to curb the use of performance-enhancing drugs in his sport. In June 1991, Vincent issued a seven-page memo to the players' union and to each team in the league, restating the league's long-standing ban on the possession of illegal drugs. "As in the past," Vincent noted, "the health and welfare of those who work in Baseball will continue to be our paramount concern. No less compelling, however, is the need to maintain the integrity of the game."[5] Vincent's memo specifically addressed steroids and prescription drugs, but his pronouncement echoed those of the men who held the office before him. Once again, a baseball commissioner talked tough, and once again, he failed to address the critical component of the plan, mandatory testing.

Congressional action and harsh words from baseball's commissioner failed to stop the growth in offensive statistics. In 1992, National League teams averaged 3.88 runs per game. The following season, those same teams averaged 4.49 runs per game,[6] an increase that league administrators were hard-pressed to explain. Baseball writers were far less reticent. In the *Los Angeles Times,* sportswriter Tim Marchman cited steroids, as well as a number of other changes to the game, as the key explanations for the increased offensive production. Marchman went further, however, explaining how increased offense not only threatened long-cherished baseball records, but the way the game itself was played:

> Many people—and I'm among them—find this an abomination. When scoring is high, baseball loses a lot of its charm. .210 hitters who make up for their weak bats with great baserunning and alert defense get turfed in favor of fat guys who stand around waiting for a ball they can hit out of the yard. There's no strategy involved in a manager sending a bunch of weightlifters to the plate to draw walks and on to the field to try to avoid torn hamstrings.[7]

Steroids were used in the dark, but their results were there for everyone to see. Players were bigger and stronger than they had ever been and were hitting balls farther than anyone had ever seen. Sports pages began to include long medical discussions, articles about telltale signs of steroid use, and more passionate indictments of the state of the game.

Labor Strike Damages the Fan Support

In 1994, the steroid scandal was overshadowed by a bigger problem, a strike that ground the game to a halt. Baseball has suffered more labor strife than any other major league sport in America—seven baseball seasons were interrupted by labor disputes between 1971 and 1990—but the work stoppage of 1994 did more damage than any of the earlier strikes. It began in August, led to the cancellation of the World Series, and spilled over into the following season, a total of 234 days. Month after month without the game increased the acrimony on both sides, and as millionaire players fought with billionaire owners, most fans wished a pox on both of their houses. Baseball enthusiasts didn't care about the intricacies of contracts, they just wanted to see their teams on the field.

Prior strikes had always drawn gripes from fans and a temporary drop in attendance, but these protests dissipated quickly as fans eventually succumbed to baseball fever. However, 1995 would be different. When the teams finally returned to the ballparks, the fans did not follow. Attendance in the first year back dropped by 20 million fans relative to 1993, a 28 percent decline. For some, staying home was a short-term protest, a reminder to the men who ran and played the game that fans, too, could turn their backs on the game. For others, the bitterness lasted longer, as the game's supporters sought their revenge on players and owners by going after them where it hurt the most. A small percentage had turned to other interests, permanently leaving the game behind. It was the risk faced by any organization caught up in a strike: if customers are forced to live long enough without a supplier's services, eventually they will find substitutes and a new norm will emerge. Getting the fan base back was not going to be easy.

Crushing the Home Run Record . . . and Baseball's Credibility

Baseball had been on hiatus, but steroid consumption had not. The 1996 season produced unprecedented levels of offense: 17 players hit 40 or more home runs during the regular season—the previous high was 8. Instead of being a problem, however, the offensive fireworks suddenly worked to the game's advantage, as fans returned to stadiums lured by high-scoring baseball. The scenario was similar to the response to the 1919 Black Sox scandal, when baseball needed a draw to lure disillusioned fans back into the game, and Babe Ruth and his home run swing provided the solution. Seven decades later, the long ball once again generated the excitement that helped people forget the game's seedier side.

Commissioner Bud Selig recognized the link between increased scoring and increased attendance but also understood that steroids were undermining the game. In May 1997, before a new season of record-breaking offense could begin, he issued a memo to all of the MLB teams warning about penalties for steroids, but it was little more than the toothless warning that players had received in 1991. Like Vincent, Selig sounded stern, and, like Vincent, he was unable to threaten the mandatory testing. Without it, players weighed the remote possibility of being caught with the pressing need to keep pace with their peers and kept on juicing. Fans filled the seats; baseballs kept clearing the fences; the steroid problem continued to grow.

The Season of Statistical Improbability

The 1997 season was embarrassing, but the 1998 season was surreal. Within the first few weeks of the spring, it became obvious that the cumulative effects of performance-enhancing drugs were about to impact some of the most important records in the sport. Not one but two stars, the Saint Louis Cardinals' Mark McGwire and the Chicago Cubs' Sammy Sosa, began to hit home runs at a pace that threatened Roger Maris's single-season home run record. Both athletes were charismatic and telegenic, and both played for iconic baseball teams. The race between the two stars made for tremendous drama—the question was not only whether the record would be broken but which player would break it. Fans filled the stadiums wherever either player appeared, watched them on TV at night, and read about their progress every morning in the local paper. Purists railed about the statistical improbability of two players beating a 37-year record in the same season, but, for the most part, sports fans were excited about the possibility of witnessing a historic moment.

Anyone who wanted to understand how the record could be broken—demolished, really—by multiple hitters in the same year needed only look at McGwire's locker for the answer: a jar of androstenedione sat in clear view. McGwire's success was at least partially attributable to the use of the drug, but the substance was not covered by the league drug policy, so the player had no reason to hide it. Sosa was more circumspect about his use of chemical assistance, but it was clear that he had bulked up in a suspiciously short time and that he was hitting home runs at a faster clip than he had ever hit them before.

When the season ended, both men had easily surpassed Maris—Sosa with 66 home runs and McGwire with 70. The contest had renewed America's interest in baseball, but the fact that both players had broken the record, and by such significant margins, ratcheted up the public debate about performance-enhancing drugs.

New Records, More Suspicion

If the McGwire/Sosa home run explosion in 1998 created suspicions, the next three seasons confirmed them. In the first 97 years of the century, a 60-homer season had occurred twice. Between 1998 and 2001, it happened six times. In the last of those years, San Francisco Giants outfielder Barry Bonds, who had emerged as one of the most likely steroid abusers, set a new single-season record, hitting 73 home runs. Prior to the season, he had never hit 50 in any year.

Bonds may have been the worst possible player for baseball to have at the center of the home run controversy. McGwire and Sosa had easy smiles, enthusiasm for the game, and a close connection with reporters and the fan base. They were a good story and easy to like. Both benefitted from their public personas, despite the abundance of evidence of steroid use. Bonds was the opposite. As his career progressed he became increasingly surly, antagonizing the press while alienating teammates and management. He was indifferent, at best, toward fans who supported him. During his record-breaking season, Bonds remained extremely popular in the town where he played, San Francisco, where fans embraced a kind of cognitive dissonance about their star's drug use. On the road, however, his quest for the record was a public relations disaster for the league. He was booed when he stepped into the batter's box anywhere beyond the Bay Area, and even more so when he hit a home run that brought him closer to the record. The reaction caused Bonds to withdraw even further from the press and public. The quest for the single-season record for home runs, which had been such an enormous celebration for Sosa and McGwire only three years earlier, devolved into a prolonged reminder that baseball's inability to resolve the steroid problem was tarnishing the game's record book.

Was the difference in the responses based on race? It was an easy explanation, since McGwire was white, Sosa was Dominican, and Bonds was black. But the fans' distaste for Bonds's assault on the record book was probably more attributable to the fact that he was so unpleasant while his competition had been so gracious and that the fans had finally caught up to the press and viewed the new records not as historic performances but as artificial and unwelcome rewards for unethical conduct. Either the rules were wrong, which was management's fault, or the players were cheating, which was their fault, but either way the fans viewed what they were seeing as unfair and harmful to the game.

The Move toward Mandatory Testing

The same year that Bonds set the new single-season home run record, Major League Baseball tried a new approach to the steroid problem. If the commissioner could still not convince the union to allow top-tier players to be tested, he could at least attempt to control drug use in the minors. In April 2001, baseball began random performance-enhancing drug tests for all league players not on major-league rosters. The penalty ranged from a 15-game suspension for first-time offenders to a lifetime ban for players who tested positive five times.

The steroid issue got fresh attention in a May 2002 *Sports Illustrated* profile of recently retired Ken Caminiti; the former All-Star not only admitted to using cocaine during his career, but also confessed to using steroids, including during 1996, the year he was named the National League's most valuable player. In the article, Caminiti estimated that half of the players in Major League Baseball were using steroids.

In August 2002, owners and players announced the Joint Drug Prevention and Treatment Program that finally included mandatory testing. There were a number of limitations: the testing would be anonymous and exploratory, designed only to establish how widespread the performance-enhancing drug problem was in the majors. There were no forms of punishment for players who failed drug tests. If 5 percent of the players tested in the following season were positive, players would be randomly tested for steroids for a two-year period. It was a limited policy but a great leap forward, since baseball's drug policy finally had the key component it had lacked for decades.

The 2003 season provided the first real indication of how prevalent performance-enhancing drugs were in baseball. In November, the commissioner's office announced that 5 to 7 percent of the 1,438 drug tests administered over the prior season were positive: random testing would begin in 2004. A first offense would lead to counseling; a second offense mandated a 15-day suspension.

Leaders from Government and Baseball Chime In

Just when it seemed that Major League Baseball had finally taken the steps necessary to address the problem, the league once again lost control of the debate. In September 2003, federal investigators raided the offices of the Bay Area Laboratory Co-operative, or BALCO, a drug development company that worked closely with Barry Bonds and a number of other high-profile athletes. The investigation led to the indictment of BALCO officials as well as Bonds's personal trainer on charges of organizing a steroid distribution ring. Just as the 1985 Pittsburgh Pirates investigation produced unsavory testimony that linked baseball and drugs, the BALCO investigation guaranteed that similar sordid testimony would become part of the public debate.

Meanwhile, baseball's steroid problem was about to attract attention from the highest levels of the federal government. It started when President George W. Bush took time to urge athletes, coaches, owners, and union representatives to end the steroid problem in sports as part of his 2004 State of the Union address. Pundits were stunned that the leader of the free world would use the same speech in which he was addressing the nation's military operations and financial condition to comment on steroids in sports, but Bush's words were a harbinger of government attention to come.

A month after Bush's speech, the leader of the nation was joined by one of the leaders of the sport. Hank Aaron, whose career home run record was being threatened by steroid-aided offensive production, told a reporter for the *New York Daily News*: "I'm sad for baseball about all of this. I played the game and we played it legitimately. Now something like this comes along and it ruins the game. All of these records blown out the window. Aside from the records, though, this could be as bad as the Black Sox scandal."[8]

If anyone in baseball understood the pressure that accompanied a home run record, it was Aaron, who had faced the vilest forms of racism, including death threats, as he had approached Babe Ruth's career record in the early 1970s. Aaron had withstood the abuse and set the record, and in the years that followed had earned a reputation as a quiet and dignified elder statesman for his game. He was initially reluctant to publicly address the steroid issue, but the assaults on the record book—not only his records but those of other greats in the game—made it difficult for him to remain silent. The closer Bonds got to the career home run record, the more frequently Aaron was asked about the Giants' slugger and the steroids issue. The entire scandal left him dismayed, not only because the sport's important records could end up tainted, but because the game he loved was increasingly linked to drugs. Aaron faced a dilemma: If he spoke out, he could be accused of being selfish since the record in question was his own. If he chose to say nothing, his silence would be open to interpretation, including the possibility that he was comfortable with the way things were going. In the end, he tried to do what was best for baseball, keeping as low a profile as possible, avoiding any statements that could damage the game.

In October 2004, President Bush translated his State of the Union speech into action, signing the Anabolic Steroid Control Act. The legislation classified hundreds of steroid-based drugs, as well as additional drugs such as the androstenedione McGwire had used during his record-breaking season, as Schedule III controlled substances, banning them from over-the-counter sales without prescription.

The federal action created pressure on the league. In January 2005, owners unanimously approved an agreement between MLB and the players' union which called for major league players to serve a 10-day suspension for a first positive drug test, a 30-day suspension for a second, a 60-day for a third, and a yearlong suspension for a fourth, each of the suspensions to be served without pay. Baseball was moving forward, but not fast enough to suit the federal government.

Congressional Investigation of Steroids—a New Low for Baseball

It might seem odd that Congress would get involved in baseball, but ever since the Supreme Court granted Major League Baseball an antitrust exemption in 1922, the federal legislature has felt compelled, every few decades, to exert influence over the game. In 2005, the House Government Reform Committee announced an investigation of steroids in sports. Just as President Bush's critics complained that his State of the Union speech was no place to talk about sports, congressional critics argued that the House of Representatives should have bigger things to worry about than baseball records. California representative Henry Waxman, the ranking Democrat on committee, defended the hearings, reasoning that the main motivation for calling them was the increased use of steroids among American children.

The committee ensured that the hearing would get maximum publicity by inviting not only the sport's top administrators but also high-profile players, including Sammy Sosa, Mark McGwire, Jose Canseco, Rafael Palmeiro, Frank Thomas, and Curt Schilling. The committee also invited Denise and Ray Garibaldi, whose son, a baseball player, had taken his own life after five years of injecting steroids. The Garibaldis put a human face on the influence of professionals on amateurs and on the dangers of steroids to the general population.

Every player and administrator called to testify knew that he faced a no-win situation. Their testimony would be under oath and broadcast live nationally, and the members of the committee would be primed to uncover the most lurid details of drug abuse from the players while demanding to know why the union leadership and league management had failed to police their sport. Commissioner Selig offered to send surrogates to testify, and the players almost universally offered excuses explaining why they could not participate. The committee responded with subpoenas—attendance was not optional. The process made baseball look even worse, as the sport's highest profile figures were dragged to the table by force of law.

The hearings proved worse than feared, if that was possible. Under oath, Palmeiro denied ever having used steroids. Six months later, he would be suspended 10 days for failing a steroid test. McGwire, the most anticipated witness, began his testimony by reading a prepared statement that appeared heartfelt and conciliatory, then deflected a series of specific questions about his steroid use by responding, "I'm not here to talk about the past." The phrase was so pathetic and McGwire repeated it so many times that it became a symbol of futility of the investigation. Sosa provided the most bizarre testimony, acting confused and incapable of comprehending the questions that were asked of him, as though English was suddenly indecipherable, although he did appear to understand enough of the language to deny ever having used steroids. Four years after his testimony, the *New York Times* reported that Sosa had tested positive for steroids two years before testifying.

Schilling, a long-term critic of steroids, agreed that performance-enhancing drugs should be barred from the game and volunteered to serve on an advisory group along with members of the House committee. The contrast between his testimony and that of other players was at least partially the result of his position: as a pitcher, he was throwing up the balls that his opponents were hitting out of the park, so it made sense that he would be more likely to condemn the use of steroids. But Schilling also took the time to rebuke Jose Conseco, whose testimony was most damning about the players and the league, warning committee members not to glorify the disgraced player or indirectly help him sell more books. It was an inopportune time for a major league player to upbraid anyone about ethical conduct.

Barry Bonds, the home run king who was arguably the player most associated with steroids, was not called to testify, to the bewilderment of the press and public. Behind the scenes, BALCO prosecutors had convinced the committee not to subpoena him, because he was under investigation in their case.

When administrators finally testified, they were as determined as the players to evade answering direct questions but were more sophisticated in their approach. Selig clung to the defense that the league had not only developed a strong program for dealing with steroids but also continued to improve it. Fehr, cast as the biggest obstacle to mandatory testing, insisted that the union did not support or condone the use of any illegal substance. The delivery was strong, the strategy questionable. For both executives, the most shameful part of their testimony came when they argued that a sharp reduction in the number of players who had tested positive was proof that the program was working. The statistics they clung to were impressive: nearly 100 players had failed tests in 2003 and only about a dozen had failed tests in 2004. They were also misleading: three years after Selig and Fehr testified, Congress determined that the baseball administrators had failed to disclose that the drug-testing program had been shut down for part of the 2004 season in response to the BALCO investigation, making the 2003/2004 comparison disingenuous and purposely misleading. When the obvious misrepresentation became public, representatives of the commissioner's office and the union used the same feeble defense: that the testimony had been "accurate," along with a cheery, pseudo-cooperative offer to respond to any additional inquiries on the subject. Their testimony was deliberately deceptive and their explanation when they were caught was shameful. Their testimony, which was widely panned as ineffective, was actually worse—a moral stand based on immoral reasoning. Congress may have been at fault for failing to understand the statistics, but the sport's administrators were the ones who presented them, and they knew at the time that their presentation was misleading.

The league also arranged for the testimony of Dr. Elliott J. Pellman, who defended the league's steroid policy and challenged the findings of opponents to the policy. "Unlike some other medical professionals you will hear from today, I have had extensive experience in the area of professional sports,"[9] the doctor told the committee. Within weeks of Pellman's testimony, the *New York Times* reported that Pellman had exaggerated both his educational and professional credentials. Democrat Henry Waxman of the House committee released a statement saying, "Major League Baseball told us Dr. Pellman was their foremost expert, but he was unable to answer even basic questions about the league's steroid policy at the hearing. This new information raises further questions about his credibility and the credibility of baseball's steroid policy."[10] This was Pellman's introduction to the general public, but it would not be the last time he would be involved in sports scandals: his controversial expertise and support for the guidelines of professional sports organizations would be questioned in yet another scandal in sports, the NFL's policy on concussions, a few years later.

In the end, players used a variety of strategies, some childish, some sophisticated, all disreputable, to avoid cooperating or telling the truth, and there is evidence that some lied under oath about their steroid use, the central issue in the investigation. Baseball administrators clung to barely defensible positions by continuously arguing that their drug-testing program was effective despite evidence to the contrary and presented statistics that were clearly designed to mislead the committee. The testimony of baseball representatives at the House investigation represents the low point in the history of the league's response to performance-enhancing drugs.

Congressional Pressure Produces Results

While baseball administrators were publicly testifying to the efficacy of their drug policies, they were working furiously behind the scenes to strengthen those policies to ward off further government intervention. In March 2006, Commissioner Selig announced that George Mitchell, the former Senate majority leader and a member of the Red Sox board of directors, would lead a comprehensive investigation into the use and abuse of performance-enhancing drugs in baseball. "Nothing is more important to me than the integrity of the game of baseball,"[11] Selig said in announcing the investigation. The commissioner promised that the report would be made public.

The federal pressure had worked: the Mitchell investigation demonstrated that Major League Baseball would finally make a serious, comprehensive attempt to understand and address one of the sport's drug issues. Once again, however, a bold move by the league was overshadowed by a related development, in this case a new expose by *San Francisco Chronicle* reporters Mark Fainaru-Wada and Lance Williams. Their book, *Game of Shadows,* detailed the performance-enhancing drug use of Barry Bonds and served as an indictment of the entire league, as the reporters explained how the game's most admired home run hitters used a variety of substances to stay competitive.

The authors quoted Yankee prospect Rob Garibaldi, whose parents had been featured prominently in the 2005 House committee hearings. Garibaldi, who would eventually commit suicide, had explained his drug abuse to his father: "I'm on steroids, what do you think? Who you think I am? I'm a baseball player, baseball players take steroids. How do you think Bonds hits all his home runs? How do you think all these guys do this stuff?"[12]

The book was excerpted in *Sports Illustrated,* quickly became a best seller, and dominated conversation in sports media. Bonds refused comment and became even more surly and uncommunicative as the attention mounted. Baseball administrators were finally making the moves needed to combat the steroids scourge, but their revised policies and in-depth investigation looked like too little, too late.

No Greenies, Less Fun

Baseball purists eagerly awaited the 2006 season, the first under the amphetamine-specific drug policy, but quickly found that greenie-less baseball would lead to some unanticipated side effects. Managers realized that some players were responding to the inability to access amphetamines by cutting back on their nightlife. "Clean livers," San Francisco Giants manager Felipe Alou said, ". . . that's what the commissioner was shooting for, right? And it didn't take very long."[13] Accidental or otherwise, the commissioner could not have been unhappy with these unintended consequences. The less time players spent in strip clubs and bars in the early morning hours, the fewer headaches for the administrators of baseball.

Whatever impact the new policy had on baseball players' nightlife, Selig insisted it was at least having the intended effect: "There's no question in my mind: the program has been very successful," he said. "The banning of amphetamines has been meaningful."[14]

By July, Selig was forced to address a potential downside of an amphetamine-free clubhouse. In a discussion with the Baseball Writers' Association of America, the commissioner was asked whether the new policy could have a negative effect on playoff drives at the end of the season. "I don't care," Selig told reporters. "It had become a serious health hazard."[15]

Selig insisted that the league was "doing okay" with the amphetamine issue, but players disagreed: in a poll taken the same month that the commissioner spoke to the baseball writers, 75 percent of MLB players surveyed believed that some players had used amphetamines during the season, with 3 percent of respondents estimating that more than half the players in the league had used them. "We need to stay ahead of the curve," Selig told reporters, "there's an acute awareness."[16]

It was impossible for the public to know who was closer to the truth, since first-time offenders were provided with counseling but not identified. Second-time offenders would be suspended and identified, and this would happen only twice in the three years after the policy went into effect. Policy supporters could point to these results as evidence that the program acted as a deterrent; policy opponents could point to the same data and conclude that players could use amphetamines until they were caught and then stop before failing a second positive test. Without knowing the number of first-time offenders, the two interpretations had equal value.

In the summer of 2006, however, there was no doubt that the league was taking on the performance-enhancing drug problem more directly than it ever had before, and baseball appeared to be moving past the embarrassment of the congressional hearings of the prior year. Once again, the momentum would be short-lived. The 2007 season loomed, and the pursuit of another home run record ensured that the league's major problem would be back in the headlines.

The New Career Home Run King

Barry Bonds entered the 2007 season with a career 708 home runs, 47 behind the all-time record of 755 that Hank Aaron had set in 1976. Bonds' 2001 pursuit of the single-season home run record had been a joyless slog, and that had been before the BALCO investigation and the publication of *Game of Shadows*. His pursuit of the career record would be even more controversial. At AT&T Park, Bonds' home stadium, the Giants outfielder remained a hero who was cheered during every trip to the plate. He received the opposite reaction from fans on the road, where his reception was an embarrassment to the league. The closer he got to Aaron's total, the more the story was covered, and the greater the antagonism from the general public.

When Bonds broke Aaron's record on August 7, 2007, it was fortunate for the player and the game that he set the record at home. The stadium was raucous, but the league's recognition was muted: neither Aaron nor Selig attended the game, although the former home run king had videotaped a congratulatory message that was played as part of the celebration and the commissioner called Bonds to congratulate him later in the evening. Even President Bush called Bonds the following day, despite his earlier statements about cleansing the game.

Bonds insisted that his record was untainted. His treatment by baseball and its supporters demonstrated how much they disagreed. The crowning moment of his career was extremely short-lived. A month after he broke the record, the Giants confirmed that they would not re-sign him. No other MLB team offered him a contract. The new home run king's days on the field were over, but his legal problems from the BALCO investigation were just beginning. Only four months after he became the all-time home run king, Bonds was indicted by a federal grand jury on four counts of perjury and one count of obstruction of justice.

The Mitchell Report Revealed

George Mitchell had demanded total independence from the commissioner in conducting his investigation, and Selig had agreed. Mitchell's team reviewed 115,000 pages of paper documents and 20,000 electronic documents. They also interviewed more than 700 witnesses, although only 68 were baseball players. In defending the investigation, Mitchell noted that the Major League Baseball Players Association had not only been largely uncooperative but had also discouraged cooperation from members of the association.

In December 2007, Mitchell filed his *Report to the Commissioner of Baseball of an Independent Investigation into the Illegal Use of Steroids and Other Performance Enhancing Substances by Players in Major League Baseball.* In the end, it appears that the union had some reasonable concerns about the privacy of information obtained for the report—Mitchell identified 89 players by name in the 311-page report, although he did not accuse them all of taking steroids.

The most surprising and heavily reported name in the report was Roger Clemens, the seven-time Cy Young winner and the dominant pitcher of his era. Clemens not only denied all allegations of performance-enhancing drug use, he went on the offensive, asking for a separate hearing to clear his name; filing a defamation suit against his former personal trainer, Brian McNamee (a suit that would eventually be dismissed); and agreeing to an interview on *Sixty Minutes* to make his case. This response prolonged his association with steroids for years. While he eventually would be exonerated in court, the lengthy and very public proceedings would seriously tarnish his reputation and, like all of the accused players, cause fans to question the legitimacy of his accomplishments.

Mitchell reached a number of conclusions in the report, finding that the use of performance-enhancing substances was illegal and unethical and that it threatened the integrity of the game. He also found that the league had been slow to develop a response to the problem, and when it did respond, the new policy had been ineffective. He noted that the league had continued to develop new policies and procedures but also found that players were switching substances to avoid detection. Mitchell concluded that while players were responsible for their individual use of the substances, the league shared some responsibility for the problem by failing to recognize and address it sooner.

The former senator also made a series of recommendations in the report, including the inclusion of an independent drug tester to improve testing capabilities, more effective methods for keeping clubhouses drug free, and improved education programs for athletes. He also called on labor and management to include the development of more effective processes based on the most up-to-date methodologies in their next round of negotiations, a relatively hollow recommendation, considering the decades-long impasse between the two sides. Interestingly, Mitchell recommended that the commissioner should not take action against players who had taken steroids in the past, including those he named in the report.

Back to Congress

If MLB administrators thought the Mitchell report would placate the federal government, they were wrong. It had the opposite effect. Once again Congress convened a committee, this time the House Oversight and Government Reform Committee, and once again they called on Bug Selig and Donald Fehr to testify. Mitchell was called before the committee as well. The commissioner went on the offensive, this time citing the Mitchell report and claiming that baseball had the strongest drug-testing program in professional sports. Selig also thanked the committee for its role in helping the league focus on the performance-enhancing drug issue, an interesting statement, given the deceptiveness of his testimony before the 2005 committee.

Instead of demanding testimony from the game's biggest hitters, as they had in 2005, the 2008 committee invited Roger Clemens to testify. In February, Clemens denied before the House committee that he had ever taken steroids or human growth hormone, despite the fact that his trainer, Brian McNamee, sat in the same room and testified to the exact opposite. "Both men stuck to their wildly divergent accounts of the truth," noted reporter Tom Verducci. "Five hours of testimony proved nothing for certain."[17] Clemens' unequivocal statements, under oath, were in such direct opposition to other testimony before the committee that it was clear that someone was lying under oath. The U.S. justice department decided it was Clemens, and, in August 2010, indicted the former pitcher on charges of perjury, obstruction of justice, and making false statements to Congress.

The Issue Fizzles . . . and Lingers

In April 2011, Barry Bonds was found guilty of one count of obstruction of justice for giving an evasive answer under oath to a grand jury in the 2003 BALCO case. In June 2012, Roger Clemens was found not guilty in a retrial. In both cases, both players acted as though the verdicts were vindications, but years of stories associating them with steroid use and perjury had damaged their reputations and the game they had dominated. By the conclusion of their trials, the American public was exhausted by 15 years of baseball's performance-enhancing drug stories, with countless details of syringes and creams, charges and countercharges, lawsuits and congressional committees. The lead for an ESPN article on the Bonds trial outcome summed up the feelings of many baseball fans: "Just like the whole Steroids Era: We'll never really know."[18]

The saga continued in August 2013, when Commissioner Bud Selig announced the suspension of 14 major and minor league players because of their connection to the Biogenesis Anti-Aging Clinic, a source of banned performance-enhancing drugs. In one of the most significant disciplinary days in the history of the game, a dozen players, some of them among the brightest stars in the sport, received 50-game suspensions. Alex Rodriguez, the New York Yankee with the largest contract in the history of the league, was suspended without pay not only for the remainder of the season but for the entire season that followed. Rodriguez immediately appealed the decision, which allowed him to play out the year.

In announcing his decision, Selig cited the suspensions as evidence that the league's antisteroid problem was working:

> This case resoundingly illustrates that the strength of our program is not limited only to testing. We continue to attack this issue on every front—from science and research, to education and awareness, to fact-finding and investigative skills. Major League Baseball is proud of the enormous progress we have made, and we look forward to working with the players to make the penalties for violations of the drug program even more stringent and a stronger deterrent. As a social institution with enormous social responsibilities, baseball must do everything it can to maintain integrity, fairness and a level playing field. We are committed to working together with players to reiterate that performance-enhancing drugs will not be tolerated in our game.[19]

Philadelphia sports columnist Bob Ford saw the suspensions in an entirely different light. He pointed out that "catching the cheaters isn't an exact science, and the drug-testing net that baseball is so proud of let these players swim right through. . . ."[20] Other detractors, while admitting that the penalties were unprecedented, noted that it was a disgruntled informant from the performance-enhancing drug company, not the league's proactive policing, that sparked the investigation. And still others interpreted the suspensions as further proof of the league's failure to deter performance-enhancing drug use: if players truly feared getting caught, or really felt that the rewards weren't worth the risks, why were so many players caught up in the investigation?

In January 2014, the court hearing Alex Rodriguez's appeal reduced his suspension from 211 games to the regular season (162 games) and possible postseason. Rodriguez claimed victory, but he was in an extremely small minority: the judge upheld the original ruling to suspend him, and if the ruling signifies the conclusion of his career, his reputation may be permanently tarnished by the longest nonlifetime suspension in the history of the game.

Conclusion

Major League Baseball's performance-enhancing drug problem is one of the most significant scandals in the history of American sports, based on how long it has lasted, how many players it has involved, and how significantly it has impacted the game. The scandal dates to amphetamine use in the 1940s and continues with a variety of drugs to this day. The total number of players involved can never be known, but the fact that the most common rationale for it is that "everybody is doing it" is at least one indication of the problem's pervasiveness. It has damaged the game in the short term, as fans wonder whether drugs are responsible for home runs hit today; and it has damaged the game in the long term, as it has tarnished some of the most important records in the league's history.

Despite the best efforts of a long line of commissioners, the sport's leadership has yet to solve the problem. Their ineffectiveness can be traced to a variety of sources: union leadership's ongoing prioritization of members' privacy rights over eliminating the drug problem; league attempts to publicly minimize the problem to protect the image of the sport; players' decisions to cheat regardless of the education the league provides or the penalties it imposes; and unethical biochemists who continue to develop steroids, human growth hormone, synthetic testosterone, and other performance-enhancing products designed to circumvent the policies and procedures of the league. The list of contributors to the problem is long; the list of solutions is insufficient.

The return of offensive production to historical norms indicates that, at least temporarily, the league has gained the upper hand on the problem, but the fact that no year goes by without major league players earning suspensions for failing drug tests indicates that the issue is nowhere near resolved. Baseball can never control those outside the sport who are determined to develop more powerful and easily masked substances, so performance-enhancing drugs will always be on the fringes of the game. But the other variables, from a more reasonable union position to more effective education programs, better testing methods and policies, and, most important, stronger penalties for infractions, must all be employed to minimize, if not eliminate, the damage that performance-enhancing drugs do to the sport. The tide appears to be shifting among the players, and it now appears that the majority of them condemn the use of performance-enhancing drugs, which would seem to indicate that a lower percentage of them are taking them.

Hopefully, the men who lead baseball and the men who play it will eventually eliminate performance-enhancing drugs from the game. If they do, at some point drug-free players will set new records that surpass the controversial marks achieved in the Steroid Era. When that happens, fans will cheer wildly, not only for the new records, but for the return of integrity to the game.

Chapter 7

Concussions and the National Football League (1900–Current)

Professional football is the most popular sport in America, featuring some of the world's fastest and strongest athletes, who capture the attention— and revenue—of billions of fans from preseason training camps in August to the Super Bowl in February. Fans revel in the complex strategies and feats of athleticism that the NFL has to offer, but they also enjoy the violence that is central to the game. In the NFL bone-crushing tackles are celebrated as much as winning touchdowns.

Modern media, particularly television, don't simply broadcast the violence of the sport, they accentuate it: in the 1990s, the ABC network opened its *Monday Night Football* broadcast with a montage that concluded with two helmets smashing against each other and bursting into sparks. Turner Network Television (TNT) promoted its first NFL broadcasts with a photo of a dazed football player sitting on the bench sucking on an oxygen mask, the ad's text stating, "Shortness of breath. Nausea. Disorientation. Memory loss. The fun begins at 8 p.m. Sunday night." In the mid-2000s, ESPN's highlight show featured a segment called "Jacked Up!," a compilation of the most bone-crushing hits from the weekend's games, accompanied by the network commentators gleefully yelling, in unison, "Jacked Up!" at each moment of collision. Analysts Carroll and Rosner summarized the media's emphasis on the game's carnage: "Television not only put fans right on top of the multiple collisions that punctuated every play, but also allowed them to reexperience those crunching impacts over and over from every angle and at every speed through the magic of instant replay."[1]

The NFL's glorified violence has made the owners, executives, coaches, and players far richer than their counterparts from earlier decades. In recent years, however, the men who supervise, coach, and play the game have become increasingly aware that their financial success has come at an enormous physical cost to the participants, with the greatest amount of damage coming in the form of concussions.

The Evolution of a Violent Game

Since the earliest days of organized football, the game's administrators have accepted that injuries are part of the sport while seeking a balance between player safety and the traditions of the game. The challenge has grown increasingly difficult, however, since changes in tactics, equipment, and players' physiques, all designed to improve a team's chances of winning, have also increased the potential for injury.

In the 1880s, college teams introduced the "flying wedge," a kick return formation where blockers created a V-shape in front of the return man, sometimes holding hands or locking arms to tighten their blocking scheme. Defensive players responded to the formation by throwing themselves at the legs of the blockers, a tactic that invariably led to injuries and occasionally even deaths. In 1904, 159 football players were severely injured and 18 died, mostly from skull fractures. The following year, President Theodore Roosevelt convened a rules committee with representatives from Harvard, Yale, Princeton, Penn, and Navy to find ways to reduce the physical destruction that had become a standard part of the game. The committee outlawed the wedge, gang tackling, and mass offensive formations and introduced a new neutral zone between the offense and defense. While some traditionalists argued that the new rules fundamentally altered the game, there was no disputing the effect of the changes on player health: in 1906 there were only 6 deaths in football games, 3 of them the result of fistfights rather than tackles.

In the modern era, current NFL commissioner Roger Goodell often retells the committee's story as a demonstration of a number of lessons. First, the sport has always been dangerous. Second, it is possible to change the rules of football while maintaining its basic integrity. Third, powerful leaders, whether American presidents or NFL commissioners, need to use whatever power they have for the greater good.

Revisions to tactics were one approach to improving safety; revisions to equipment were another. Football helmets were introduced to the game in the 1890s. They were originally made of moleskin or leather and were optional for decades. In 1938, the Riddell Company introduced the modern plastic helmet, which became mandatory equipment in the NFL in the 1940s. The helmet offered players increased protection but also created a false sense of security, encouraging some athletes to use their heads more for blocking and tackling because they mistakenly assumed that headgear protected them from brain injuries. In the last two decades, additions to the front of helmets, such as visors and more sophisticated facemasks, have increased protection for the players but may have inadvertently created new dangers, such as making it more difficult for sideline medical personnel to examine injured players, identify concussion symptoms, or communicate with players in the critical moments following a collision.

Innovations in the playing surface may also contribute to injuries. When NFL athletes began playing on Astroturf in 1968, league officials were excited about how the low-maintenance, weather-resistant fields saved money and looked on television. Players were less enthralled, however, since the synthetic field's improved traction meant sharper cuts, faster speeds, and, of course, harder collisions, and rigid subsurfaces could result in even more injuries when athletes landed on the turf. Two years after Astroturf was introduced, league commissioner Pete Rozelle predicted that every team in the league would eventually play on an artificial surface, a goal that proved overly optimistic: only half the teams in the league had installed artificial turf by 1996. Some form of synthetic surface appeared to be a permanent part of the NFL landscape, however, so the league encouraged manufacturers to develop safer, more durable products. Today, most NFL games that are played on artificial surfaces are played on "field turf," an improvement over the original artificial turf but a safety concern nonetheless.

Players: From Big to Massive

Changing rules, equipment, and playing surfaces all influenced player safety, but none had as great an impact as the changes in the players themselves. The men who play professional football have grown from big to massive. In 1970, only 1 NFL player weighed 300 pounds or more—in 2000 there were 301 and in 2009 there were 394.[2] From 1979 to 2011, the weight of the typical top-five-drafted offensive tackle increased from 264 pounds to 313 pounds, and the typical guard grew from 250 pounds to 317 pounds. The modern lineman bench-presses about 31 percent more weight than his counterparts from three decades earlier.[3] This enormous increase in size occurred with no reduction in speed—in fact, it is possible that players have gotten even faster. Advances in training, nutrition, and strength programs have all affected the growth of the average NFL player, but those improvements only account for some of the increased size. For many players, the growth can be traced to illegal performance-enhancing drugs, including steroids and human growth hormone (HGH).

Ironically, the men and their representatives who will incur the most damage from these substances are the group that fights hardest against their eradication. Football administrators who have pushed for policies to eliminate these drugs have been hindered by contractual negotiations with the NFL Players Association (NFLPA). In 2011, after years of negotiation, the NFLPA agreed to a testing program for HGH, but since that time it has been less than cooperative in implementing the program. Based on the history of the relationship between the union and management, there are reasons for the NFLPA to be suspicious about handing any additional power over to the league, but the union's failure to lead in the push for more comprehensive testing has allowed players to cause themselves more physical harm, placed players who do not use the substances at a competitive disadvantage, and reduced the union's moral stance in arguing the concussion case.

"It is estimated that two football players running full speed at 20 miles per hour can generate 1,800 pounds of force in a head-on collision,"[4] according to an *ABC News* report on football injuries. Increasingly larger players on artificial turf wearing equipment some mistakenly assume protects them from head injuries—these factors combine to make every NFL game a potential scene for career-ending injuries; and the potential for damage is on the rise.

Problems Disguised by the Warrior Mentality

The ethos of football is hypermasculine, placing premium value on performance under any conditions and individual contribution to team success. Teammates, coaches, and fans expect that an athlete should "play through pain" and be rewarded for doing so. Players, competitive by nature and petrified over the possibility of losing their positions, fight through and hide injuries to stay on the field. Coaches, making split-second personnel decisions in the heat of battle, focus on a player's availability for the next down. Fans, a safe distance from the mayhem, are preoccupied with the fortunes of the team, regardless of the sacrifices needed to win.

These priorities reinforce each other in delivering the same basic message: a player should stay on the field at all costs. Since a concussion can stop that from happening, it is in the short-term interests of everyone—player, coach, fan—to avoid dealing with it. As a result, those involved in the evaluation process often adhere to the narrowest possible definition of concussion when attempting to identify it. For example, some members of the football community argue that a concussion only occurs when a player is completely disoriented or knocked unconscious. Short of those conditions, they argue, the player should be allowed to stay in the game. They employ euphemisms such as "dinged" to describe concussion symptoms, an innocuous adjective that "equates to moments of dizziness, confusion, or grogginess that can follow a blow to the head."[5] The fact that the injury is not visible or may not immediately impede the athlete's performance can also contribute to the mistaken impression that a concussion is not serious. In 2006, Solomon et al. noted that for many years "a concussion was viewed primarily as a transient, routine event that occurred with regularity during athletic contests and was rarely taken very seriously. . . . In fact, athletic and sports medicine professionals have often shown greater initial concern for an ankle sprain than a brain sprain (concussion)."[6]

With a culture that downplays injuries and values playing through pain, a terminology that minimizes the extent of the damage, a type of injury that is not as visible as other types of physical damage, and a system that defaults to leaving a player on the field whenever possible, it is not surprising that many researchers find concussions underrecognized, underreported, and undertreated.

Concussion: An Evolving Definition

The word "concussion" is a derivative of a Latin word, "concutere," roughly defined as "shake violently." According to the Consensus Statement on Concussion in Sport, a concussion is defined as "a complex pathophysiological process affecting the brain, induced by traumatic biomechanical forces."[7] In its examination of the concussion issue, the NFL's original Mild Traumatic Brain Injury (MTBI) Committee used the following definition:

> A reportable MTBI was defined as a traumatically induced alteration in brain function, manifested by an alteration of awareness or consciousness, including but not limited to a loss of consciousness, "ding," sensation of being dazed or stunned, sensation of "wooziness" or "fogginess," seizure, or amnestic period, and by symptoms commonly associated with postconcussion syndrome, including persistent headaches, vertigo, light-headedness, loss of balance, unsteadiness, syncope, near-syncope, cognitive dysfunction, memory disturbance, hearing loss, tinnitus, blurred vision, diplopia, visual loss, personality change, drowsiness, lethargy, fatigue, and inability to perform usual daily activities.[8]

These definitions appear straightforward, but concussion research is really in its infancy, and well-meaning experts continue to differ when defining the term. "We do not have a complete understanding of the concepts, classification and metabolic effects of MTBI," notes Dr. Julian Bailes, who has written extensively on the subject. "This is especially true in contact sport athletes, who . . . are exposed inherently to multiple head impacts, and at least, subclinical, or not obvious, concussions."[9]

The lack of consensus on the term's definition makes it difficult to determine how often players are concussed. As a result, estimates vary wildly. Operationalizations, research methodologies, sampling, even question phrasing and order have a significant impact on determining the frequency of concussions: retired players are far more likely to admit to concussions than current players, self-reporting leads to lower estimates than other data collection methods, and athletes are far more likely to admit to dizziness or memory loss than to having been concussed.

The Medical Community Weighs In

Football may have been slow to address its concussion dilemma, but the medical community has been attempting to address the issue for decades. In the early 1970s, researchers began to expand their understanding of concussion symptoms, noting that a player didn't need to be unconscious or delirious to be concussed. Other, less obvious signs, such as short-term memory impairment, might also indicate mild brain trauma. Doctors also began to understand that concussions could occur in degrees, resulting in various kinds of damage.

By the early 1980s, experts began to recognize that concussions were far more dangerous than had been previously considered. First, they argued, players who were concussed were in greater danger of permanent cerebral dysfunction than previously assumed. Second, concussion probability and damage appeared to be cumulative: not only does a first concussion increase the likelihood of a second but the amount of trauma caused by the second is likely be greater than the amount of trauma caused by the first. This second finding was particularly ominous for football players. "A characteristic aspect of contact sport athletes is that they are the only groups of patients who . . . request to be allowed to return to play and thereby sustain other head impacts, and often, concussions,"[10] noted Julian Bailes.

In 1984, researchers Richard Saunders and Robert Harbaugh published a case study in the *Journal of the American Medical Association* describing a football player who suffered a head injury four days before a college game. The doctors looked past the initial trauma to focus on the damage from a second, minor injury. They hypothesized that the initial head injury significantly increased the possibility that a second injury could occur and that the second injury could be caused by far less trauma than the first. They also suggested that the second injury could produce severe swelling of the brain and the damage could be far worse than that caused by the original injury. They called this phenomenon "second impact syndrome," or SIS.

As other medical professionals contributed to the community's understanding of the concussion phenomena, they began suggesting ways to bring the medical findings to the sidelines. In 1986, building on the work of Saunders, Harbaugh, and other researchers, Robert Cantu published a set of guidelines in *The Physician and Sports Medicine* to help coaches and trainers identify concussed players and understand how long they should be kept off the field. The work was exploratory: Cantu had not developed the definitive statement on concussions but had converted the best information from research findings into a practical application. In 1997, Michael McCrea and his colleagues introduced a Standardized Assessment of Concussion, or SAC, which was refined through the McGill Abbreviated Concussion Evaluation. The University of Pittsburgh Medical Center's sports concussion program developed a "Concussion Card," a qualitative screening tool for sideline use. Research on identifying concussion grades was used to formulate return-to-play, or RTP, recommendations. The medical community was generating useful findings and offering them to the football community. What would the NFL do with the information?

On the Sideline: Working to Identify Concussions

"It's hard to take seriously an invisible injury with subtle symptoms that often seem to pass quickly,"[11] noted Carroll and Rosner. Yet the NFL assumed for many years that players, trainers, and coaches would do just that.

The first level of concussion diagnostics is self-reporting of symptoms—a player telling a coach that he is hurt and needs to leave the game. There are two immediate problems with this method. First, a severely concussed player may, by definition, lack the mental acuity to recognize and report his symptoms. Second, even if a player understands that he has a concussion, as noted earlier, players have strong incentives to hide those symptoms, including their competitive nature, their allegiance to their team, or their fear that they might permanently lose their position. Self-reporting is the most logical first indicator, but it has significant limitations.

The next level of concussion diagnostics is by trained medical personnel on the sidelines, where a team representative compares a player's responses to a preestablished baseline. "To be effective, neuropsychological testing must be quick to administer, reproducible and structured for the athlete. A baseline examination performed in the preseason period and specific for the athlete is preferred, administered by a qualified neuropsychologist,"[12] argued researcher Julian Bailes. Baseline information gathered prior to the season is flawed for the same reason that self-reporting is flawed: a player's desire to outsmart the diagnostics to stay in the game. Football players who want to remain on the field under any circumstances can purposely "flunk" the preseason test, setting the bar low so that any comparison to data collected following a possible concussion allows them to continue to play.

Collusion between the players and the medical staff can also hinder diagnostics. When a player is injured, Caroll and Rosner noted, "the trainer asks him, 'How many fingers am I holding up?' The player's answer is always the same: two. That's because the trainer makes it easy by always holding up the same number of fingers and then rewarding the correct answer by sending the player right back in the game."[13]

Potential conflicts of interest can also create diagnostic obstacles. In theory, the primary concern of a team doctor is player safety, but the medical professional is employed by the team, and the decision to keep a player on the field can impact the team's chances of winning the game. Gay Culverhouse explained:

> The doctor reports to the coach. . . . Clearly he is helping the coaches choose the incoming teams. . . . From the beginning the team doctor is invested in the success of their choices. This alignment is the crux of the problem for the players on the team. The doctor is not their medical advocate. He's not even conflicted. He knows who pays his salary; he plays golf with the coach and the owner, not the players. He is management; he makes decision for the management side of operations.[14]

There is some debate over who does—and should—make the call on whether an athlete should return to the field after an injury. According to a 2001 survey conducted by Ferrara, McCrea, Peterson, et al., team physicians are the decision makers 40 percent of the time, while athletic trainers make the call 34 percent of the time.[15] Solomon, Johnston, and Lovell noted that neuropsychologists are also called on to determine whether an athlete can return to the game: "The politics and, more important, the medicolegal considerations surrounding this issue are significant. A simple, straightforward answer to these questions cannot always be found. The circumstances, resources and professional expertise of the available sports medicine professionals of each team may dictate the answer."[16] Culverhouse also alleges that, ultimately, the medical decision may not be the most important one: "Coaches have been known to override doctor's orders."[17] The NFL is considering the use of medical professionals who are completely independent of the team to make the return-to-play decision—a move that would eliminate the conflict of interest but also create the possibility of new problems if a star player is sidelined by a league official in the middle of a crucial game.

The NFL Response: A Flawed Committee

Coaches are often portrayed as the villains in the concussion controversy, insisting that a player stay on the field when medical authorities advise otherwise. Ironically, it was an NFL coach who is credited with promoting a more scientific approach to handling concussions in professional football. In the early 1990s, Pittsburgh Steeler head coach Chuck Knoll was discussing his quarterback's recent concussion with the team's neurosurgeon, Dr. Joseph Maroon, who felt that the player should not be cleared to play. When Maroon supported his position by citing prevailing standards, Knoll asked for the basis of those standards. Maroon was unable to convince the coach that the standards were scientifically sound, and the Steelers became the first NFL team to introduce baseline neuropsychological testing for their players. The moment was a breakthrough: professional football was finally trying to truly understand, from a medical perspective, what was going on with concussions.

In 1994, the Steelers' original idea was expanded, from an ad-hoc, team-by-team examination of concussions to a systematic, league-wide approach, when Commissioner Paul Tagliabue announced the formation of the NFL Committee on Mild Traumatic Brain Injuries, a comprehensive clinical and biomechanical research study.

The new committee seemed like an excellent idea, centralizing the research and providing the funding needed to ensure that the concussion issue would be addressed across the league. In practice, it fell far short of its goals. Although the MTBI committee included experts from both inside and outside of the league, critics voiced concerns about the objectivity of the group from the start. The loudest complaints centered on the committee chair, Dr. Elliott Pellman, who served as the team doctor for the New York Jets and the NHL's New York Islanders. The biggest criticism was simple: Pellman had no expertise in neurology.

Pellman proved to be a double-edged sword for the NFL. Initially, he was the league's strongest and most credible defender, aggressively supporting league policies while generating research findings and recommendations that downplayed the cumulative effects of concussions and the need for additional league action. The problem was that his findings contradicted the consensus in the medical community. Charges that the chairman was underplaying the medical dangers escalated, but Pellman refused to back down from his positions, and his role evolved into a public relations disaster. His detractors labeled him an apologist for the league and his statements were used as evidence that the league refused to deal with the concussion problem. If the chairman of the committee investigating concussions minimized the problem, the argument went, who could players depend on to help solve it?

The committee began a five-year analysis of data from 900 traumatic brain injury cases sustained between 1996 and 2001 to determine the frequency and severity of concussions and reviewed game videos and reconstructed game-condition impacts in a laboratory setting to better understand the biomechanics of the injuries and to help manufacturers improve head protection equipment. Of 32 NFL teams, 30 participated in the research.

Pellman and his colleagues chose the journal *Neurosurgery* to release many of their findings, beginning with an October 2003 article on the group's methodologies and followed by an article in December of the same year on initial findings from the research. In 2005, they published three more articles on their findings. Each article was reported heavily in the media, the stories often highlighting the contradictions between the committee's findings and those from reputable, independent research organizations. In 2006, ESPN reporter Peter Keating noted, "Several of the country's preeminent neurosurgeons and neuropsychologists have grown increasingly concerned that the league is putting players at risk by following Pellman's lead."[18]

Pellman's aggressive defense of the NFL's positions may have bothered members of the press and other members of the medical community, but officials in the sports industry were extremely impressed. Major League Baseball liked the way the doctor faced down critics and tenaciously defended his employer so much that, when baseball administrators faced a congressional investigation into the steroids scandal in 2005, they called on the NFL committee chair to testify to the efficacy of their policies. Pellman did so, with enthusiasm, and his testimony was even more vociferous and, in some cases, uninformed than statements he had made in defense of the NFL. Baseball's new medical representative was so unimpressive that media organizations began to dig deeper into his background and within weeks of his congressional testimony started running stories questioning Pellman's academic and professional credentials. The doctor's professional trajectory was in trouble: he began representing a team, was promoted to representing a league, and then crossed over to representing a second league, but his ever-expanding profile drew greater media scrutiny, and he would soon pay the price.

Changes at the Top

The Pellman saga was only one issue the NFL was grappling with during this time—an even more important transition was happening at the top of the administration. Paul Tagliabue, who had been commissioner for 17 years, announced his retirement in the summer of 2006, setting off a scramble to identify his successor. Five finalists vied for his position, and on the fifth ballot, Roger Goodell won a close vote, although he was ultimately approved as Tagliabue's successor by a unanimous vote. He began his tenure in September 2006, a new football season with a dynamic young administrator at the helm, but he immediately faced the same vexing concussion problem that was left unresolved by his predecessor.

The new commissioner had spent the early part of his NFL career in public relations, and he quickly recognized that the Committee on MTBIs could not be effective in advancing the league's cause in its current form. In March 2007, less than a year after Goodell took the helm, Pellman resigned from his chairmanship of the MTBI committee, although he retained his position as a committee member. In a commentary two months later, *New York Times* reporter Selena Roberts compared Pellman's relationship with the league's administration to sycophants who reinforce poor decisions by players, writing, "Sometimes, organizational loyalists need reference checks, too."[19] (It would take a few more years, but by 2010, the NFL committee would sever all ties with Pellman and Major League Baseball would replace him with a new chief medical director.)

Goodell was reshaping the research team, but he was not waiting around for a report to take action on the field. In 2007, he introduced the league's first official set of return-to-play rules, which stated that a player could not return to a game or a practice in which he lost consciousness.

Pellman's successors, Dr. David C. Viano and Dr. Ira Casson, wasted little time in distancing themselves from some of Pellman's more controversial positions, and the committee began to gain some grudging respect from the press and other concussion researchers. Despite the progress, the two new chairs would still not acknowledge the key claim that was now being argued by a growing number of players and their union: that head injuries in football result in long-term brain damage. The cochairs continued to argue that the evidence was insufficient to make the claim conclusively. Their insistence that they would not fully accept the connection between the two was medically questionable but fit into the league's legal strategy: an increasing number of former players were beginning to file brain damage–related lawsuits against the league; and if the chairmen of the league's own committee publicly acknowledged a link between on-field brain injuries and concussions, those lawsuits would be significantly strengthened. Insisting that the lack of evidence made the connection unsupportable eventually became untenable, and by November 2009, Viano and Casson, too, resigned their chair positions.

After nearly 15 years, the league's MTBI committee had generated reams of data, more than a dozen research articles, and an enormous amount of controversy but had made little real progress on the concussion issue. In some ways, the committee's efforts had even been counterproductive: their findings would become a weapon in the players' lawsuits, more players had been injured in the interim, and the league's credibility on a critical issue that was not going away had eroded with important audiences, including fans and players. The league had spent more than a decade finding ways to avoid the problem instead of solving it.

Goodell's words and actions at the time were the first glimpse of the strategies he would use consistently during his time as the commissioner. He moved quickly, decisively, and in a number of directions simultaneously. He allocated resources to gather whatever data were necessary to help everyone understand the issue and made fundamental changes in the game to protect the players while also attempting to maintain the integrity of the game. But he worked equally hard to protect the financial interests of the league, and gave no ground on any position that would provide support for anyone who sued or might sue his league.

Congress Gets Involved

Over in the baseball world, the steroid problem had corrupted the record book to such a degree that, by 2005, Congress held hearings to find out what Major League Baseball was doing to clean itself up. Four years later, it was the NFL's representatives who were called to Washington to squirm in the spotlight. This time it wasn't the decimation of records that worried politicians, but the destruction of the players themselves. Older retired players were showing an alarming rate of dementia and other symptoms of brain injury, and current players were being carted off the field almost every Sunday afternoon. Congress wanted to know what professional football was doing about it.

The House Judiciary Committee hearings on football-related head injuries began in October 2009. There were a number of similarities between the baseball and football investigations. First, both committees justified their actions by referencing the influence that professional athletes had on children and young adults. Second, both witness lists featured players, league administrators, and families impacted by the leagues' failure to resolve their problems. Third, both processes damaged the credibility of the leagues, although the concussion committee did not attract quite as much attention as baseball's steroid inquiry. And finally, the most aggressive inquisitor in each committee was a California Democrat: for baseball in 2004, it was Henry Waxman; for football in 2009, Linda Sanchez.

A union member and a tenacious lawyer, Sanchez was eager to question Commissioner Goodell when he was called to testify. She forced him to read directly from the player's handbook and challenged him on his position on secondary concussions. Goodell parried, claiming that there was no issue he had devoted more time and attention to than player safety. When pressed, however, he refused to admit to a connection between football head injuries and cognitive erosion. His testimony was a critical moment in the history of concussions and of the NFL—as late as 2009, the most powerful administrator in the NFL refused to accept the connection between head injuries in the game and brain injuries in retirement, despite the fact that the NFL retirement board had already awarded disability payments for crippling brain injuries due to football injuries to at least three players. Goodell may have been embarrassed, but his greater priority was the financial stakes of his testimony. Any admission of a connection would strengthen the former players' lawsuits, and the commissioner was loath to give them ammunition.

Player safety advocate Gay Culverhouse noted that "it became apparent to those in the gallery that day and to the witnesses present that Roger Goodell was either poorly informed, had not read a paper in two years, or he was deliberately obfuscating."[20] Sanchez didn't stop at the league commissioner: she also skewered NFLPA head DeMaurice Smith and even threw the "tobacco card," accusing league representatives of using the same tactics that had failed the cigarette industry.

The tobacco analogy is an apt one, because the league was basing an increasing amount of its argument on a risky position. In tobacco lawsuits, claimants argued that the tobacco companies knew of the health dangers of nicotine but failed to take adequate action and shielded litigants from critical information. Eventually, a big part of the tobacco settlement was based on the "what did they know and when did they know it?" question, and the companies' liabilities increased with every damning study they had completed. Goodell was refusing to admit to the connection between football injuries and brain damage at the same time that he was announcing and funding further research on that very connection, research that would eventually produce data that undermined his position.

The three doctors who had served as chairs of the Committee on MTBIs, Elliott Pellman, Ira Casson, and David Viano, never appeared before the committee. When House Committee chair John Conyers asked Roger Goodell why Casson was not present to testify, the commissioner responded that the committee had not requested him. Conyers disputed the response and Goodell responded that he would have to get back to him to clarify his answer. The absence of the committee members was a glaring indication that the league had either lost faith in its top medical officials or did not want them to get trapped in a public discussion of the committee's methodologies and findings. Either way, the hearings were a communication disaster for the NFL.

Stronger Policies and a New Committee

Two months after the congressional hearings, the NFL announced a revised return-to-play policy for players who sustained concussions and stiffer penalties and suspensions for players who broke the revised safety rules. The new return-to-play policy mandated that a player who suffers a concussion or concussion symptoms not return to practice or play on the same day and that a player who demonstrated those symptoms must have neurological and neurophysiological testing and be cleared to return by both his team physician and an independent neurological consultant before returning to the field. In the memo to the clubs announcing the changes, Goodell sounded like an administrator who not only wanted to improve safety but also wanted to remind a variety of audiences that his league had already made progress on the concussion issue:

> The evidence demonstrates that team medical staffs have been addressing concussions in an increasingly cautious and conservative way. This new return-to-play statement reinforces our commitment to advancing player safety. Along with improved equipment, better education, and rules changes designed to reduce impacts to the head, it will make our game safer for the men who play it, and set an important example for players at all levels of play.[21]

Goodell knew that the stronger policies were an important step, but he also recognized that more would be needed to placate Congress. In March 2010, he announced the formation of the Head, Neck, and Spine Medical Committee to replace the disgraced Committee on MTBIs. This time the league got it right from the start, beginning with the appointment of two prominent neurosurgeons, Dr. H. Hunt Batjer and Dr. Richard G. Ellenbogen, as cochairs. The league also announced that Pellman would no longer be a member of the committee, that the new chairs would have complete control over the composition of the new group, and that the chairs would receive no compensation beyond expenses. The three announcements created separation between the two committees and shielded the new group from the accusations of hidden agendas that had hounded its predecessors.

In June the cochairs announced that the methodologies and data from the first committee would not be part of the work of the new committee, further reinforcing the clean break, and announced that Dr. Robert Cantu, the neurologist who had emerged as one of the most renowned specialists on concussions, would serve as the senior adviser for the group. The new committee consisted of highly respected experts with minimal prior connections to the league.

The commissioner now had a group that could provide him and the players with useful information and would demonstrate the league's commitment to addressing the concussion crisis.

It did not, however, mean a reduction in the carnage on the field. In December 2010, Steeler linebacker James Harrison, notorious for violent hits and a staunch defense of his style, knocked Cleveland quarterback Colt McCoy senseless in a tackle. Harrison was penalized for the hit, fined, and suspended for a game. The more damaging issue for the league, however, was that McCoy returned to the game only two plays after sustaining the concussion. Goodell used the incident to introduce a new league-wide policy that required an independent trainer to observe games and alert team medical and training staffs to possible head injuries. The change was significant: the league was starting to move the decision on return-to-play from a person affiliated with the team to a medical professional who reported to the league. Policy changes were no match for the video evidence of what was happening on the field, however: media reports on the new policy were overshadowed by continual replays of Harrison's brutal hit. Goodell was losing the public relations battle.

More Policy Changes, More Messages

Kickoffs have always been a particular area of concern in the concussion debate, because they produce an inordinate percentage of concussions relative to other plays. The athletes begin the play at a maximum distance apart, allowing them to achieve the highest possible speeds in a direct line toward opposing players. Returners are often in the most defenseless position possible, looking up to receive the kick split seconds before they are hit. In March 2011, team owners agreed to move kickoffs from the 30-yard line to the 35-yard line, which resulted in more touchbacks and fewer returns. The 5-yard difference was significant: a team with a kicker who consistently booted the ball beyond the end zone line could eliminate the threat of an opponent's return man. Some of the teams with the best kick returners balked, but the new rule had an immediate impact: concussions on kickoffs dropped 40 percent from the 2011 season to the 2012 season.

Traditionalists accused Goodell of implementing a rule that altered the fundamentals of the game, but the commissioner did not back down and made his priorities clear. Speaking at the 2011 Congress of Neurological Surgeons, he told a receptive audience:

> There is nothing more important to the N.F.L. than the safety of our players, and there is no issue of greater importance when it comes to player safety than the effective prevention, diagnosis and treatment of concussions. . . . The more we can learn about the brain, the better for all. And we can be the leaders.[22]

The Lawsuit That Changed the Equation

In June 2012, lawyers representing more than 2,000 NFL players filed a "master complaint" lawsuit in Philadelphia, accusing the NFL of concealing information that linked football-related injuries to brain damage. The plaintiffs also charged that the "NFL exacerbated the health risk by promoting the game's violence" and "deliberately and fraudulently" misled players about the link between concussions and long-term brain injuries."[23] The suit was a compilation of more than 80 concussion-related court cases against the NFL that had been filed in a series of states, including New York, New Jersey, Florida, California, and Georgia. On the day the suit was filed, former Bears quarterback Jim MacMahon told ESPN "We didn't know about the head trauma and they [the NFL] did. That's the whole reason for the lawsuit."[24]

As part of the suit, the players' lawyers argued that the league's Committee on MTBIs generated false findings that obscured information about the problem rather than helping the league and players to understand it. Whatever the original intent of the MTBI committee had been, at this point it had evolved into a liability for the league, a symbol of the NFL's deliberate decision to downplay the role of concussions in brain injuries.

The class action was staggering in its scope. It wasn't only the number of players involved—the biggest group to ever sue the league—but also the stature of the players—it included some of the highest-profile athletes to ever play the game. It wasn't only the biggest lawsuit in the history of football, it was the biggest in the history of American sport. An ABC News report announcing the legal action concluded that "concussions have become football's No. 1 issue."[25]

The power of the class action lawsuit to sway public opinion was magnified by the strong relationship fans had with many of the athletes as well. Fifteen months before the suit was filed, former Bear safety Dave Duerson shot himself in the chest after texting his family that he wanted his brain to be used for research into the effects of football injuries. A month before the suit, former San Diego Charger linebacker Junior Seau died from a self-inflicted gunshot wound. Their stories humanized the damage, and their voices and actions carried significant weight. To the football fans, these were not nameless, faceless men, they were their heroes and they were suffering terribly.

Players and ex-players did not speak with a single voice on the issue, however. James Harrison, the Steeler who had concussed quarterback Colt McCoy and had been fined multiple times for illegal hits, was openly contemptuous of Goodell's attempts to implement policies that improved player safety. Hall of Famer and network analyst Deion Sanders not only claimed that the game was safe and the equipment better than ever but accused half of the former players who were part of the lawsuit of being in it only for the money. They were in the minority, but their prominent positions demonstrated that the players were not united and that the problem was more complex than the lawsuit suggested.

Lawyers representing the players did not stop at the NFL when assigning blame: they also argued that equipment manufacturers play a role in the problem and blasted the media coverage, including NFL partner NFL Films, because of their glorification of the violent aspects of the game.

The NFL Plays Offense

In March 2012, the league's credibility on attempts to prevent concussions took an enormous blow when it announced that members of the New Orleans Saints coaching staff had paid bounties to players who had knocked opponents out of games. It was a sensational story that dominated the sports world for months. Fans and reporters pored over game tape, identifying which Saints had injured which players, focusing on player reactions on the field and on the sidelines. Opposing players who had been knocked out of games against the Saints were asked their opinions, and members of the media asked everyone in the New Orleans organization the "what did you know and when did you know it?" question. Goodell announced suspensions of four Saints: linebacker Jonathan Vilma for six games; general manager Mickey Loomis for eight games; head coach Sean Payton for a year; and defensive coordinator Gregg Williams indefinitely. He also fined the Saints $500,000 and took away two second-round draft choices for the following season. Around the league, fans and players debated the fairness of the penalties. The blow to the Saints' prestige and prospects was considerable—the damage to the league's position on player safety was even bigger.

In the last week of August 2012, the NFL announced a partnership with the U.S. Army designed to better understand the impact of head injuries on the two organizations' employees: football players and soldiers. The announcement linked the league with the American military and connected the league's head injury research to national defense. A week later, the league announced a $30 million contribution to the National Institutes of Health (NIH) to be used at the organization's discretion, the largest donation in the history of the league. Both actions expanded the NFL's efforts beyond addressing its own concussion problems. Goodell insisted that the Army agreement and NIH donations had "absolutely nothing" to do with the lawsuit. In between the announcements, the league filed a motion to dismiss the suit, a motion that was denied.

In September 2012, just as another season was about to begin, the National Institute for Occupational Safety and Health (NIOSH) released a study on the incidence of neurodegenerative disease among NFL players. The report found that NFL athletes who played at least five seasons had developed Alzheimer's disease or Lou Gehrig's disease at rates disproportionate to the general population. Two months later, three of the NFL's starting quarterbacks suffered concussions on the same Sunday.

Penalties for dangerous play were up and concussions were down, but football continued to account for more concussions than any other sport in America. Even the most well-funded communications campaigns would have trouble explaining those kinds of facts, but that didn't stop the commissioner from trying. He stayed on point, regardless of the studies and injuries that undercut his position. Speaking at the Harvard School of Public Health, the commissioner cited rules changes such as penalties for hits to the head, moving the kick-off line, and faster concussion diagnoses on the sideline as proof that the league was making progress on the issue of head injuries. He also suggested that the league's "warrior mentality" caused some players to deliberately hide concussions to avoid being removed from a game. A "cultural shift," he suggested, was needed to combat the mentality.

By now, Goodell had honed his message to its core principles. The *New York Times* reported in December 2012:

> Goodell said he was pleased with some steps that have been taken in regard to player safety—including the use of video monitors on the sidelines and spotters in the press box to help identify potential injuries, particularly concussions. He noted that internal video reviews show that players are adjusting their hits away from the head and neck area in response to a crackdown on such plays.[26]

A *Time* magazine profile of Goodell in the same month noted that:

> After years of downplaying the dangers of concussions, the NFL has instituted policies and rules to reduce the risk of long-term injury. But things like sanctions for dangerous hits—especially the punishment handed down to the New Orleans Saints for allegedly running a bounty system that gave cash rewards for injuring opposing players—and stricter return-to-play guidelines are just the beginning of a safety-first orientation. . . . From changing tackling techniques to altering the stance of offensive linemen so they don't launch themselves headfirst into opponents, everything is up for discussion. And Goodell sits at the center of the table.[27]

The commissioner's efforts to improve safety policies and communicate the league's priorities convinced some key audiences that the league was serious about the concussion issue, but it did little to halt the ever-growing legal case that threatened the game: by the end of the summer of 2013, more than 4,500 former players or their families were a part of the suit. Concussions were not only the game's biggest public relations problem, they were also its largest open-ended financial liability.

Settling the Suit without Solving the Problem

On August 28, 2013, a week before the opening of the new season, the NFL reached a settlement with the plaintiffs, agreeing to pay $765 million to retired players who demonstrated medical evidence of brain injuries. The agreement set limits on the payout a player could receive for each type of medical problem: $3 million for dementia, $4 million for chronic traumatic encephalopathy, and $5 million for amyotrophic lateral sclerosis.

The league agreed to pay half of the money in the first 3 years, with the remainder to be paid out over the following 17 years. The dollar figures may seem exceptional until they are considered in the context of the sport's economics: at the time of the agreement, the league's annual revenues were between \$9 and \$10 billion, a number expected to increase significantly when the NFL negotiates its next television contracts.

With the agreement, the league finally had a cap on what was previously an unknown liability. The pact made it increasingly difficult for other players to introduce new lawsuits related to concussions and ended the possibility that the plaintiffs' legal team would expose in court whatever damaging information they had about questionable league decisions. Many legal experts, economists, and public relations professionals pronounced it a positive outcome. "The league is keenly sensitive to its public image. [The Agreement] changes the conversation and really lets the air out of the publicity balloon,"[28] explained Michael LeRoy, a professor of labor law at the University of Illinois at Urbana-Champaign. Peter King, *Sports Illustrated*'s veteran analyst, summarized the outcome: "All things considered, that's a very fair deal to buy peace of mind for the next decade. . . . In essence, the league won."[29]

The league admitted no liability or wrongdoing in the agreement. Even as it was announced, the NFL continued to insist that it was a leading proponent of research on concussions and policies designed to minimize their effects on its players. NFL executive vice president Jeffrey Pash said in a statement that "this agreement lets us help those who need it most and continue our work to make the game safer for current and future players. . . . Commissioner Goodell and every owner gave the legal team the same direction: Do the right thing for the game and for the men who played it."[30]

The settlement provided economic comfort to thousands of players impacted by concussions, and many NFL retirees and their surviving families supported the decision. They had feared a drawn-out, multiyear lawsuit, with a potential for a payout, if it ever came, delivered long after it could help cover medical bills. Some retired and current players balked at the decision, but most of their complaints focused on the amount of money rather than the decision to settle.

The agreement did not resolve the NFL's concussion dilemma. The issue continues to be surrounded by claims and counterclaims, facts and anecdotes, legal issues and research studies. The fundamentals of the discussion, including what constitutes a concussion, how many players are being concussed, return-to-play rules, and who makes the final decision on the return remain largely unresolved. Researchers Mark Fainaru-Wada and Steve Fainaru conclude that "three years after Congress pressured the NFL to overhaul its concussion program, the league effort remains marked by inconsistencies in how it tracks, manages and even describes serious head injuries, making it difficult to assess the league's progress on the issue."[31]

The NFL continues to develop policies designed to reduce the probability of injuries—in 2013, the league instituted a new rule that bars ball carriers from using the crown of their helmets to initiate contact—and as part of the new agreement, the NFL committed $10 million to additional research and education and $75 million for ongoing medical exams for players. Additional funding will help the league and players better understand concussions, and more stringent contact rules will probably reduce how often they occur, but neither will come close to eliminating them, and the settlement does not cover current and future players. The agreement is a very big step in a very long journey.

Concussions and the Bigger Picture

Goodell consistently states that player safety is a top priority of the league, but his actions do not always support that assertion. For example, at the beginning of the 2012 season, the commissioner honored the hard-line position of team owners and pushed for the lockout of referees who were negotiating for better pay and benefits. The decision was a disaster—the league dug in over a relatively small amount of money while placing the on-field supervision of the game in the hands of officials who were, in some cases, unqualified for the job. Replacement refs made an inordinate number of questionable calls, including a game-changing touchdown decision on the final play of a nationally telecast game. For the players, however, the potential for blown calls wasn't the big problem. Replacement referees demonstrated that Goodell's top priority was not their safety. If the commissioner is so worried about our health, players argued, why does he have second-rate officials overseeing our games? The league eventually negotiated a settlement but not without considerable damage to the administrators' reputations.

Goodell has also occasionally floated the idea of an extended regular season, a schedule that players feel will result in more injuries, particularly if the athletes are more fatigued late in the season because of the additional games. So far the union has been able to successfully block any expansion, but the league has not abandoned the idea. Players cite any discussion of more games as further proof that safety is not the league's highest priority.

The commissioner continues to cite a variety of league investments, committees, policies, fines, and suspensions to support his message that safety comes first, but his critics counter with an equally long set of league decisions that demonstrate that professional football has other priorities as well.

Football's problems also go beyond the NFL, to areas that the commissioner has very little ability to influence. At the game's lower levels, fewer young people are playing the game, as parents see professional athletes carted off the field and decide their children will be safer in other sports. Between 2007 and 2011, the number of kids age 6 to 12 participating in tackle football dropped 35 percent. Medical specialists and representatives of the game itself have called for a ban on full-contact football until a player becomes a teenager, and if the idea gains momentum, even fewer kids will play the game. The NFL supports the Zachary Lystedt Law, which promotes concussion awareness and strict return-to-play policies for young athletes in a variety of sports but is opposed to banning play at any level.

In a caustic *New Yorker* article on the future of the league, reporter Steve Coll recently wrote:

> So far, Goodell and the owners have responded to the concussion problem in a way that is familiar from the N.F.L.'s past handling of existential threats: litigation, delay, denial, and inadequate, incremental fixes, all constructed to outlast and outflank opponents. That strategy helped the N.F.L. overcome antitrust allegations, but it won't work in the concussion litigation. If Goodell and the owners don't change the League's rules fast enough to reduce concussions to a level comparable to that present in baseball and basketball—where concussions are very rare accidents—then the League will face a devastating reckoning. The tobacco and asbestos industries' experiences show that, in the long run, if a commercial product causes widespread injuries among customers or workers, the manufacturer will pay—and government regulators may step in even before courtroom verdicts are fully calculated.[32]

Ever the shrewd communicator, Goodell attempts to frame the issue in the form of a rhetorical question: "Can I solve the problems for everybody?" he asks. "I don't think that's possible."[33] Undeniably, the commissioner has worked hard to address the toll that the game of football has taken on the men who play it. Equally undeniably, his efforts have not been enough. This football season, hundreds of NFL players will be hit so hard that they will suffer a concussion. Every time an athlete is carted off the field, it is not only the player who is damaged, it is also the game itself.

Chapter 8

The Penn State University Football Child Molestation Scandal (2009–2013)

Success without honor is an unseasoned dish; it will satisfy your hunger, but it won't taste good.

—Joe Paterno, Penn State University football coach

If the Black Sox were the biggest sports scandal of the 20th century, the sex crime debacle at Penn State University (PSU) is, to date, the biggest of the 21st. For the perpetrator, former PSU football coach Jerry Sandusky, the crime was child molestation. For the institution, the crime was turning a blind eye to, and then covering up, Sandusky's horrific behavior.

An Insular Institution

Pennsylvania State University, the state's only land-grant university, is located in State College in Centre County, a region nicknamed Happy Valley. Like many land-grant schools, Penn State dominates the town and region that surrounds it—the university is the central focus of a rural area, geographically insulating it from outside influences or authority. This insularity was a significant factor in fostering the culture that contributed to the school's biggest scandal.

Penn State is not an anomaly: on many college campuses in America, football is a religion. The ritual of the Saturday afternoon game takes on an importance far beyond any other activity at the university. Players are treated as a higher caste than other students, with unrivalled status and privileges. However, even the greatest players have a relatively limited period in the limelight, with only four years of eligibility for their sport. At football-centric universities, it is the coaches who become the ultimate symbols of their teams and, in many ways, their schools. With their enormous contracts, year-round media exposure and, in particular, decades representing the institution, college football coaches are often the highest-paid, most-recognized, and most-revered figures on campus—synonymous not only with their teams but with their universities. They take on an almost pope-like aura: Grambling's Eddie Robinson, Knute Rockne at Notre Dame, Ohio State University's Woody Hayes, and, of course, Paul "Bear" Bryant at Alabama were often perceived as infallible.

Among the most powerful was Joseph Vincent Paterno, or JoPa as he was known to the worshipful alumni of Penn State University. Born in Brooklyn and educated at Brown University, Paterno arrived as an assistant in 1950 and spent his entire coaching career with the Nittany Lions. He married his college sweetheart, Suzanne, a native of nearby Latrobe, Pennsylvania, in 1962, the year she graduated from Penn State, and they raised five children who all graduated from the university. JoPa took over as head coach of the Nittany Lions in 1966 and coached the team until shortly before his death in January of 2012. Along the way, he developed the most successful program in American college football history: JoPa's teams had five undefeated seasons and 24 bowl victories, and he won more games (409) than any coach in Division I history.

Paterno wasn't just known for winning, however; he was also celebrated for the way that he won. He espoused a "Penn State way" of doing things, and peppered his gridiron talk with musings on honesty, integrity, and responsibility. His organization was often cited as a model when media and fans discussed the right way to run a program, a reputation Paterno did nothing to dissuade. While he was deified in parts of Pennsylvania, his moralism didn't play as well in other parts of the country. "To his rivals, he was a holier-than-thou prig who intimated he was more principled than they were,"[1] one observer noted. He was a man on a tall pedestal, and his fall from grace would be all the more dramatic because of it.

Charges Lead to an Investigation

Early in 2009, a student at Central Mountain High School in Clinton County, Pennsylvania, complained to school officials that Jerry Sandusky, an assistant coach for the school's football team who had been a member of the Penn State University football team coaching staff for 30 years, had touched him inappropriately while they were alone in the gymnasium. Officials referred the case to Children and Youth Services, who then brought the case to the office of the attorney general, Tom Corbett. By summer, Corbett's office had convened a grand-jury investigation to investigate allegations against the former PSU assistant coach. In Pennsylvania, a grand jury is a powerful fact-finding group, 32 members of the public operating in secret with the ability to compel evidence and force testimony via subpoena. They do not determine whether a subject is guilty or innocent but recommend to the attorney general whether there is enough evidence to file charges.

Corbett's role in the investigation and the time line for the development of the case would become controversial in themselves because the attorney general was running for governor in the fall of 2009, and any investigation that included Coach Joe Paterno would be controversial enough to sway some votes in a Pennsylvania election. His critics contended that the attorney general dragged his feet on the investigation and the grand jury decision to keep the issue from damaging his campaign. He was elected governor on November 2, 2010, before the jury's report was made public. Coincidentally, his new role as governor made him an automatic member of the Pennsylvania State University Board of Trustees.

Grand Jury Report Shocks the Sports World

On November 5, 2011, Corbett's successor as Pennsylvania attorney general, Linda Kelly, and Pennsylvania State Police commissioner Frank Noonan announced the results of the grand-jury investigation. The authorities charged Jerry Sandusky, the former Penn State assistant football coach and founder of The Second Mile charitable foundation, with 40 counts related to sex crimes with children over a 15-year period. They also charged Penn State athletic director Tim Curley and senior PSU administrator Gary Schultz with perjury and failure to report a crime. Kelly accused Curley and Schultz of perjuring themselves by repeatedly denying, during the grand-jury investigation, that they were told in detail about a 2002 incident involving Mike McQueary, a graduate football assistant who walked in on Sandusky while the former coach was showering with a young boy and reported what he had seen to Paterno, Curley, and Shultz. Conviction on the perjury charges could lead to up to 7 years' imprisonment. Neither Coach Paterno nor the university's president, Graham Spanier, were initially charged, although both appeared to have been part of the investigation.

The grand jury report set off a chaotic, rapid-fire chain of events that produced one astonishing development after another, none of which appeared to be coordinated or adequately considered. Two of the university's top officials were publicly targeted in the legal proceedings, and the two most high-profile members of the institution, the president and the legendary football coach, were widely suspected of involvement at some level. It appeared that the decision-making process and line of command at the top levels of the university disintegrated in a single week. It also appeared that university officials and the leaders of the football program were astonishingly ill prepared to handle the communications component of the scandal.

On November 8, three days after the release of the report, Coach Paterno attempted to go about his regular practice, planning to hold his customary midday press conference. Paterno's attempt to project normalcy demonstrated that he either didn't grasp the severity of the problem or continued to cling to the idea that he could control a situation by sheer force of will. Both options were alarmingly naive. Spanier cancelled the press conference, according to Paterno, without conferring with him. The coach told local members of the press that he was open to talking about the scandal at the press conference as well as discussing the upcoming Nebraska game. PSU's assistant athletic director/communications Jeff Nelson seemed equally delusional, sending a release to the press advising that the primary focus of the press conference would be the upcoming game against the Cornhuskers.

The attempts at dictating the press angle were symptomatic of the larger problem—Penn State administrators continued to insist that they were in control, even of the media, and even as the delusion that they were calling the shots was collapsing around them. By this time, the *New York Times* was reporting that Paterno's coaching tenure would be completed within days or weeks and the *Chronicle of Higher Education* Web site claimed that Spanier and Paterno might be out of work by the end of the week.

Paterno's supporters, still convinced that he was the moral figure he had long claimed to be and unable to recognize how quickly the landscape was changing, rallied around their icon. The coach returned home at the end of the day to find hundreds of supporters on his lawn, chanting, "We are Penn State!" and "Joe-Pa-ter-no!" His son insisted that Paterno was still the coach and that there was no exit strategy. When Paterno addressed the crowd, however, there was some indication that he was beginning to come to terms with the gravity of the situation. "No matter what happens to some people," he told the students, "I'm proud of you."[2]

The following day, November 9, a defeated Paterno released a statement to the press announcing his resignation:

I am absolutely devastated by the developments in this case. I grieve for the children and their families, and I pray for their comfort and relief. I have come to work every day for the last 61 years with one clear goal in mind: To serve the best interests of this university and the young men who have been entrusted to my care. I have the same goal today. That's why I have decided to announce my retirement effective at the end of this season. At this moment the Board of Trustees should not spend a single minute discussing my status. They have far more important matters to address. I want to make this as easy for them as I possibly can. This is a tragedy. It is one of the great sorrows of my life. With the benefit of hindsight, I wish I had done more. My goals now are to keep my commitments to my players and staff and finish the season with dignity and determination. And then I will spend the rest of my life doing everything I can to help this university.[3]

To his supporters, Paterno's announcement was not only heartbreaking but a further demonstration of the coach's high moral standards. In their minds, the coach had dedicated his life to building winning football teams and mentoring young men, and the final moments of his career were being tarnished by the scandal. To many, the announcement signified more than the conclusion of the coach's career: Paterno had often railed against retirement, citing how quickly another legend, Bear Bryant, had died after ending his days as a coach. It was clear that Paterno was talking about more than his departure from the game.

The resignation was complicated by the fact that Paterno was agreeing to quit after four more games, however. "I want to make this as easy for [the board of trustees] as I possibly can," he said, but the statement was disingenuous. The employee was altering the formal decision making chain of the termination and simultaneously demanding that the employer move on to more important issues. The coach was chastising his employer while dictating the terms of his termination. Paterno had also abandoned traditional channels—meetings, phone calls, face-to-face conversations—and was communicating with his superiors through the press. His announcement to the public was his announcement to the administration.

The board of trustees now faced a number of options, none of them good and all requiring quick decisions. The university's beloved coach had announced—not offered—his resignation, but on his own time line. With Athletic Director Tim Curley gone, members of the board of trustees felt that the decision on how to address Paterno's contract was in their hands. Many felt that he had usurped their authority in announcing his decision.

That evening, 32 members of the board assembled to determine the coach's fate (the state's new governor, Tom Corbett, phoned in to the meeting). Board members felt that Paterno had lost the support of the room for three reasons: based on the grand-jury report, Paterno should have done more to address the Sandusky scandal; the coach's announcement was an unacceptable challenge to the board's authority; and Paterno's continued presence on the sideline, representing the university, would be a distraction to the team and a reminder of the university's complicity in the cover-up. At 10:00 p.m., Vice Chair John Surma surveyed the board, asking everyone if there was any objection to asking the coach to step aside and no longer serve as the coach of the team. No one spoke up, and the vote was unanimous.

The communication among the players in the drama had broken down to the point that even informing Paterno of the board's decision was a lose-lose proposition: Send a delegation to Paterno's house, and they might be in danger from pro-Paterno students who were already bordering on violent. Wait until the morning to talk with Paterno, and the story was likely to leak to the press, at which point the coach would probably learn about his dismissal from a reporter asking for a comment.

An assistant athletic director was sent to the Paterno's house, where the coach and his wife were already dressed for bed. The messenger handed Paterno a piece of paper with a phone number on it and asked that he call it, with no additional information. Paterno called the number, and John Surma told him, "In the best interests of the university, you are terminated." Paterno hung up and repeated what he had been told to his wife. She grabbed the phone, redialed, and told Surma, "After 61 years he deserved better."[4]

The moment would be frequently cited by Paterno supporters as evidence that the coach's termination process was mishandled and that, in the end, the coach was not treated with the dignity he deserved. In fairness to the board, Paterno had forced their hand, cutting off communication with them while they faced tremendous external pressures to address his status. There were better ways to handle the dismissal, but Paterno did not, as he described it, "make this as easy for them as I possibly can."

In the same meeting in which the coach was fired, the board held a second unanimous vote forcing out Spanier, the university's president, and named Rodney Erickson, the university's executive vice president and provost, as interim president of the university. If the dysfunction of the situation needed any further demonstration, it was provided when the majority of the media reports summarizing the board meeting led with the dismissal of the coach, and, further down in the reports, noted the change in the presidency of the university.

The board's fear of violence proved prescient: in the hours after Paterno's firing was announced, the campus erupted. Thousands of students gathered to protest the coach's dismissal, chant his name, and denounce Sandusky and the board of trustees. Rioters damaged light posts and a news truck, and 38 people were arrested, 35 of them students. An undergraduate student, a sister of one of Sandusky's victims, told the *Patriot-News,* "If there was any pride left at PSU, it's gone now."[5]

Terminating a Controversial Witness

Chaos reigned in the boardroom and across the campus, but there were still football games on the schedule. Interim president Erickson named Tom Bradley, Paterno's defensive coordinator, as interim head coach for the remainder of the season. Among Bradley's many immediate concerns was what to do about McQueary, the key witness in the grand-jury investigation, who remained an assistant for the team and was scheduled to be on the sidelines for the Nittany Lions' final home game of the season.

Local reaction to McQueary ran the gamut. He was labeled everything from coward ("How could he have reported the molestation but not stepped in to stop it?") to hero ("He was the only person to be truthful about what happened") to victim ("He got caught up in something he didn't cause and is now accused of lying by administrators who are trying to save themselves"). In a press conference, Bradley insisted that McQueary was still a member of the staff and would be on the sidelines at the game. By midweek, however, various news agencies reported death threats on the assistant coach, forcing Bradley to backtrack and announce that his assistant coach would not be on the sidelines for the game. On the Friday before the game, the university president announced that McQueary had been placed on administrative leave.

McQueary would never appear on the Penn State sidelines again. When the team eventually hired Bill O'Brien as their permanent head coach, O'Brien declined to interview the long-term assistant coach for a position on the new staff. McQueary, who had quarterbacked the 1997 Nittany Lions and hoped to spend his entire career as a PSU coach, was unable to find a coaching position with another team. He sued the university for $4 million in a wrongful termination lawsuit in October 2012.

Sandusky, in His Own Words

In the vast majority of court cases, defense attorneys instruct their clients to repeat the words "no comment" as often as possible and shield them from the press. Jerry Sandusky's counsel took the opposite approach, agreeing to an interview request from NBC's Bob Costas. On November 14, the network aired the interview, and a national audience watched the former assistant coach proclaim his innocence, deny the charges, and refute the claim by McQueary. But the interview raised as many questions as it answered. When Costas asked Sandusky basic questions about questionable conduct with children, the beleaguered coach struggled with his responses. "I could say that I have done some of those things. I have horsed around with kids. I have showered after workouts. I have hugged them and I have touched their legs without intent of sexual contact," Sandusky told Costas. When the interviewer asked if he would concede to any wrongdoing, Sandusky replied, "I shouldn't have showered with those kids."[6] The most stunning moment in the interview came when Costas asked Sandusky if he had a sexual attraction to underage boys. The coach paused and then replied, "I enjoy young people. I love to be around them, but no, I'm not sexually attracted to young boys." To many viewers, it seemed odd that a man facing 40 counts of child molestation would answer the question with anything other than an unequivocal denial. Legal analysts questioned the wisdom of Sandusky's legal team for exposing their client to unscripted questions in a national interview. It would not be the last time Sandusky's advisers would be second-guessed.

The Freeh Investigation

The terminations of Paterno and Spanier were critical decisions by the board of trustees, but they were by no means the end of the scandal. It was obvious, for legal and public relations purposes, that the university would have to go outside of its own personnel to conduct an investigation. The board quickly appointed a special investigation task force to coordinate the effort, and on November 21, 2011, the task force retained Louis Freeh and his law firm, Freeh Sporkin & Sullivan, LLP, to conduct the investigation, charging them with establishing the facts and circumstances of the university's conduct regarding Sandusky's child abuse.

Freeh was an excellent choice: given the emotional nature of the case, the explosive charges being investigated, and the impeccable reputations and enormous popularity of the targets of the investigation, it was inevitable that the investigation's methods and findings would be attacked by a variety of sources, regardless of the findings. Sandusky's reputation was ruined, but Tim Curley and Gary Schultz were highly regarded university administrators, university president Graham Spanier was an internationally recognized leader in higher education, and, of course, Joe Paterno was the university's most trusted and beloved icon.

Freeh had no direct connection with Penn State; he had earned his degrees at Rutgers University and New York University—academic credentials that helped establish his objectivity. He served in the U.S. Attorney's office before being appointed judge for the United States District Court, then served eight years as the director of the Federal Bureau of Investigation, establishing his credentials as a thorough investigator. If there was a weak point in the hiring process, it was the role of the people who hired him: there was clearly a potential conflict of interest if the investigation led to the people who had hired the investigator. Nevertheless, his résumé and reputation made him the right man for the job.

Freeh's investigation was complicated by the fact that it ran parallel to a series of other investigations from the Pennsylvania attorney general's office, FBI, Department of Education, and Pennsylvania State Police, as well as Sandusky's prosecution. His work would be a delicate dance based on uncooperative witnesses and conflicting testimony, all under the glare of the national media.

Freeh assembled a team of veteran investigators that included lawyers, prosecutors, former FBI agents, and state police. Over the next seven months, his investigative team interviewed more than 430 subjects and reviewed 3.5 million e-mails and documents. Three of the central figures in the investigation did not testify—Curley and Shultz declined, and Paterno, whose health deteriorated rapidly after his dismissal, died before he could be interviewed by the committee. Freeh's investigation was also encumbered by the request of the state's attorney general not to interview a number of witnesses who would appear at the Sandusky trial.

Paterno's Final Days

Paterno may have felt too ill to meet with Freeh's investigators, but he still wanted to get his side of the story out. In early January, he met at his home with *Washington Post* reporter Sally Jenkins for an interview that she reported on in the paper's January 14 edition. Since his firing, Paterno had announced that he was suffering from lung cancer, and during the interview, he sat at his kitchen table in a wheelchair, covered by a blanket and struggling for breath.

If Sandusky is guilty, "I'm sick about it,"[7] Paterno told Jenkins. In explaining his failure to address the situation, the former coach said:

> I didn't know exactly how to handle it and I was afraid to do something that might jeopardize what the university procedure was. So I backed away and

turned it over to some other people, people I thought would have a little more expertise than I did. It didn't work out that way.[8]

The ex-coach also explained his side in the story of Sandusky's retirement from the program in 1999. The former assistant coach's departure from the program had always been considered an oddity, since most of the Penn State assistants had signed on to the Nittany Lion program for their entire careers. Paterno explained that he had recommended to Sandusky that he retire because the university was offering a particularly generous buyout at the time and that he had told Sandusky that he would not recommend him as his replacement when he retired. Paterno also suggested that Sandusky had been spending so much time with his Second Mile charity, the same one that he would use to recruit his victims, that he was not fulfilling his obligations to the football team. Critics who were suspicious that Paterno had long known more about Sandusky's illegal behavior than he let on pointed to the unusual departure as evidence. In the Jenkins interview, Paterno insisted that he had no indication of Sandusky's deviant behavior until assistant coach Mike McQueary told him what he had witnessed in 2002.

McQueary's conversations with Paterno and other school officials became one of the most controversial focal points of the entire cover-up. According to Paterno,

He [McQueary] was very upset and I said why, and he was very reluctant to get into it. He told me what he saw, and I said, what? He said it, well, looked like inappropriate, or fondling, I'm not quite sure exactly how he put it. I said you did what you had to do. It's my job now to figure out what we want to do. So I sat around. It was a Saturday. Waited till Sunday because I wanted to make sure I knew what I was doing. And then I called my superiors and I said: "Hey, we got a problem, I think. Would you guys look into it?" Cause I didn't know, you know. We never had, until that point, 58 years I think, I had never had to deal with something like that. And I didn't feel adequate.[9]

In the preliminary hearing for Curley and Shultz, McQueary testified that, out of respect for the coach, he had been reluctant to go into specific detail about what he had seen, and Paterno implied that he did not fully grasp what his assistant coach was telling him. Paterno's explanation was unconvincing—if a member of his staff had described, even in the most euphemistic way, a sexual assault of a minor by a direct report, it is hard to believe that he wouldn't take stronger action or at a minimum ask follow-up questions to clarify what had happened. Instead, all parties agreed,

Paterno simply arranged for McQueary to meet with Curley and Shultz. According to the law and according to administrative policy, Paterno argued, he had done what he was required to do, although he readily admitted, "In hindsight, I wish I had done more."[10]

At the end of the interview, Paterno attempted to remain positive. "I've had a wonderful experience here at Penn State," he told Jenkins. "I don't want to walk away from this thing bitter. I want to be helpful."[11]

Eight days after the interview was published, Paterno died of lung cancer at the age of 85. His long-term fear that he would suffer the same fate as Bear Bryant proved true, but it was clear that the scandal, along with the cancer and the retirement, factored into his death. Paterno's passing only increased his supporters' bitterness and the rifts among the Penn State factions. In the hours after his death, hundreds of supporters flocked to his statue outside of Beaver Stadium, leaving candles, notes, pom-poms, and flowers.

Columnists and sportswriters throughout the nation attempted to summarize the coach's life. The *Washington Post* announcement stated:

> Mr. Paterno's ascent, followed by his sudden firing at age 84, formed one of the most tragic narratives in modern athletic history and constitutes something of a conflicted legacy. He was the most successful head coach in the history of major college football, but the circumstances of his dismissal led to a stain both on the football program and the man who ran it for so long.

The Sandusky Trial

In early June, the Penn State scandal shifted to the Centre Country courthouse, where jury selection began in Jerry Sandusky's child molestation trial. It was extremely challenging to identify jurors who had not heard about or didn't have a strong opinion about Sandusky, but the defense opposed bringing an out-of-town jury in for the case. This was one of a number of questionable moves by Sandusky's legal team, but no one in the community or press expressed any concern about inadequate representation: the vast majority of Pennsylvanians were hoping for a fast conviction on as many counts as possible. Media from around the world swarmed into the picturesque town to cover every detail of the case. Sandusky continued to protest his innocence, but testimony from the victims was overwhelming and compelling.

On June 22, Sandusky was convicted on 45 of 48 counts of child sexual abuse. Relief that a child rapist would spend the rest of his life behind bars was almost universal, but what the conviction meant to the university and football team was open to interpretation. Many PSU supporters hoped that the court decision could help begin the healing and assist the institution in moving forward—wishful thinking since Freeh had not yet concluded his investigation. Fault lines among university groups, most based on the degree of loyalty toward Paterno, deepened as everyone awaited the "official" interpretation of what had happened, how, and why.

Within hours of Sandusky's conviction, the news vans had dispersed from Happy Valley, but they would return in a matter of weeks to cover the outcome of yet another investigation.

The Freeh Report Condemns the Process and the Participants

On July 12, 2012, Freeh issued prepared remarks in conjunction with the release of his report. Well aware of the possible attacks on his work, the investigator decided to address, directly, any possible allegations of conflict of interest. He noted that his committee did not release any findings to the task force or board of directors prior to the general release, and stated:

> We have shown no favoritism toward any of the parties, including the Board of Trustees itself, our client. I can tell you that at all times we felt that our demand for total independence—the primary condition of our engagement—was respected.[12]

The findings of his report were far-reaching and devastating. Freeh summarized:

> Our most saddening and sobering finding is the total disregard for the safety and welfare of Sandusky's child victims by the most senior leaders at Penn State. The most powerful men at Penn State failed to take any steps for 14 years to protect the children who Sandusky victimized. Messrs. Spanier, Schultz, Paterno and Curley never demonstrated, through actions or words, any concern for the safety and well-being of Sandusky's victims until after Sandusky's arrest.[13]

Freeh went on to conclude:

> . . . in order to avoid the consequences of bad publicity, the most powerful leaders at Penn State University—Messrs. Spanier, Schultz, Paterno and Curley—repeatedly concealed critical facts relating to Sandusky's child abuse from the authorities, the Board of Trustees, Penn State community,

and the public at large. Although concern to treat the child abuser humanely was expressly stated, no such sentiments were ever expressed by them for Sandusky's victims.[14]

In addition to these scathing summaries, the committee also found that

- University officials exposed one of the victims to additional harm by alerting Sandusky to what McQueary reported that he had seen
- The board of trustees did not perform its oversight duties, did not inquire about important university matters, and did not create an environment where senior university officials felt accountable
- Sandusky's continued access to the PSU football program and facilities provided Sandusky with the currency that enabled him to attract his victims[15]

Freeh's committee also made an extensive series of recommendations to the university, from changes in general governance to a reduction in the importance placed on football in the culture of the institution.

Killing the Messenger: Freeh Is Condemned from All Sides

Reaction to Freeh's report was immediate and vehement, and his detractors had to line up to see who could heap the most scorn on his findings.

Among the strongest was Timothy Lewis, the attorney representing Graham Spanier. In some ways, Spanier had the most to lose from the report. The former president had been fired by the university but not legally charged with any wrongdoing. The report, however, included details that suggested he had broken the law. Lewis accused Freeh of being a "self-appointed accuser who in his zeal to protect victims from a monster . . . recklessly created new victims of his own."[16] Lewis claimed that his client "welcomes the opportunity to respond" to questions while simultaneously stating that Spanier was unavailable to speak with the media. "Penn State University deserved better, the commonwealth of Pennsylvania deserved better, the victims deserved better, and Graham Spanier deserved better,"[17] Lewis insisted. Interested parties would agree with at least part of his summary.

Paterno loyalists clung to a thin line of defense—that the former coach had done what he was legally required to do when he passed along what he allegedly knew to his supervisors. Paterno detractors dismissed such a flimsy argument, insisting that Paterno had a moral obligation to follow up on such a destructive situation; it was hypocritical for a coach who was such a prominent moralizer to rely on a minimalist legal defense and ignore any ethical obligations; Paterno had demonstrated numerous times his nearly universal power over the program—the idea that he would not be a part of the decision-making process about such an important issue contradicted his obvious authority over all things related to football.

Paterno's Statue Removed

Throughout the scandal, Joe Paterno's seven-foot, 900-pound statue outside of Beaver Stadium served as a central symbol of the story. Print and television news teams, unable to obtain interviews with the former coach or university administrators, used the bronze statue as a backdrop in many of their stories. Supporters unable to reach their idol made pilgrimages to his image, delivering all manner of blue-and-white totems: stuffed animals, letters, pictures, and flowers. Pro-Paterno supporters used the statue as a rallying point to begin their protests. When Paterno died, the statue took on even more significance. It also became a flashpoint for any discussion of how the university would address the coach's legacy. Child abuse protection advocates demanded that the statue be removed. Occasionally a plane would circle over the campus trailing an ominous threat: "Take the statue down or we will." Fans took turns "guarding" the statue, in case anyone, including university officials, made any attempt to remove it.

Interim president Rod Erickson faced a conundrum: Leave the statue as it was and it would look like the university continued to support the disgraced coach. Remove it, and it would appear that the university was attempting to wipe clean his memory from the place where he had created his legacy.

Erickson was fully aware of how much the timing of the board's decision to fire Paterno had played in the chaos that followed. He decided to remove the statue, so the remaining questions became how and, particularly, when to implement the decision. The university waited until 10 days after the Freeh report was announced, a long enough time to let the initial emotions of the release subside, but close enough to the release of the report that the report's negative conclusions about Paterno were still fresh.

Shortly after dawn on Sunday morning, July 22, police barricaded the streets in the area, erected a temporary chain-link fence to keep out onlookers, potential protesters, and the press, and covered the statue in a blue tarp. While the statue was being removed and put into storage, a hundred students gathered as close to the scene as possible and chanted "We are Penn State." At the same time that the statue was being removed, the university released a statement from interim president Rod Erickson stating that he had decided to have the statue removed because "it has become a source of division and an obstacle to healing. . . . I believe that, were it to remain, the statue will be a recurring wound to the multitude of individuals across the nation and beyond who have been the victims of child abuse." At the same time, Erickson said that Paterno's name would remain on the campus library that he had provided so much financial support for because it "symbolizes the substantial and lasting contributions to the academic life and educational excellence that the Paterno family has made to Penn State University."[18]

In retrospect, Erickson's decision and explanation appear measured and reasonable, but emotions were running so high at the time that it inevitably was denounced by advocates of various positions. Child protection advocates were incensed that the Paterno name remained anywhere on campus. Paterno supporters were incensed at the removal the coach's image, claiming it was morally wrong, disrespectful, and an attempt to rewrite history.

George Mitchell: The Sports Scandal Authority

The NCAA needed someone to monitor the university's progress, and they turned to a respected figure with the temperament and résumé to get the job done. George Mitchell had vast experience negotiating in the midst of complex, emotional situations—he had served as Senate majority leader, the U.S. special envoy in the Middle East, and the chair of the Northern Ireland peace talks, earning an international reputation for fairness and integrity. He also had experience with sports scandals, having led baseball's 2006 investigation into performance-enhancing drugs.

In announcing Mitchell's appointment as athletic integrity monitor, the NCAA's Emmert said, "Senator Mitchell has impeccable credentials as a fair and experienced arbitrator nationally and globally. He will bring the benefit of his vast experience and knowledge to the execution of the agreement."[19]

The new overseer of PSU's progress approached the role with his customary clarity, gravitas, and consideration for multiple audiences: "I enter this engagement mindful of the fact that this tragedy has deeply affected many lives, starting, of course, with the victims and their families," Mitchell said. "I will do my best to fulfill my independent oversight responsibilities to help ensure that Penn State University moves promptly and decisively to achieve the very high level of trust and integrity needed to fulfill its important mission to those it serves."[20]

A New Round of Charges

On November 1, 2012, the Pennsylvania attorney general's office announced a new set of charges related to the cover-up. In addition to the perjury charges Schultz and Curley already faced, they were now accused of felony obstruction, endangerment, and conspiracy. The biggest announcement, however, was that the state would now charge the university's former president, Graham Spanier, with eight offenses, three of them felonies. The charges included obstruction, endangering the welfare of children, and perjury.

"There has been speculation about charges against Spanier since an internal Penn State investigation unearthed emails that seemed to show Spanier played a role in the decision not to report a 2001 allegation of sex abuse against Sandusky,"[21] noted *Patriot-News* reporter Sara Ganim. Penn State backers who hoped that the story would disappear off the back pages of the paper were once again disappointed: every few weeks, some new development brought the cover-up scandal back into the national spotlight.

The NCAA Weighs In

Internal investigations, individual trials, and policy reviews all took a back seat to the decisions of the National Collegiate Athletic Association that were announced on July 24, 2012. Some PSU administrators feared "the death penalty," the dissolution of the football program, but the Nittany Lions were spared the complete dismantling of their program. Instead, college sports' governing body sanctioned the university with a $60 million penalty, reduced the team's scholarships by 10 for the first year and 20 for each of the next three years, and banned the Nittany Lions from postseason play for four years.

NCAA president Mark Emmert also announced that all of the teams' wins dating back to 1998 were vacated, a stunning blow to the university and the coach's legacy. Not only were 13 teams' records wiped out but the vacation would eliminate Paterno's title as Division I football's winningest coach. In effect, the NCAA's punishment was an enormous blow to the past, present, and future of Penn State football. In announcing the penalties, Emmert stated that "in the Penn State case, the results were perverse and unconscionable. No price the NCAA can levy will repair the grievous damage inflicted by Jerry Sandusky on his victims."[22]

The university had very little room to maneuver in its response to the NCAA decisions: Accept them and bear the heaviest cost of any program in collegiate history; fight them and be accused of being hypocritical about accepting responsibility and failing to comprehend how damaging the Sandusky scandal had been. Penn State president Rodney Erickson described the sanctions as "very heavy," but also stated that he had no choice but to accept them. Appearing on CBS's *Face the Nation*, he said:

> I was faced with a very, very difficult choice. It was made clear to me and to our legal team very early on in the week that we really had a choice, which was multiple years of the death penalty (the loss of the football program) or the sanctions. . . . Given the two alternatives, I felt that it was best to accept the consent decree. This allows us to continue to go on playing football, it allows us to go on helping to support the other intercollegiate athletic teams that we have at the University. The choice that I made really allows us to move forward.[23]

Policy Decisions Remain under Attack

If Penn State's staunchest defenders had been upset at the Freeh report, they were ballistic over the NCAA sanctions. They railed against every aspect of the NCAA decision, from the process used to reach the decision to the moral authority of the organization itself to the severity of the penalties. With Erickson's acceptance, however, it appeared that the school might finally be able to begin to move past the scandal. The court proceedings against Schultz, Curley, and Spanier remained, but the institution itself had begun implementing nearly all of the Freeh recommendations. It was far too early to close the book, but it did appear that it was time to close a chapter.

In the fall of 2012, Penn State players once again ran out from the tunnel in Beaver Stadium to thunderous applause. Now, however, they were led by coach Bill O'Brien, who had been hired to take over a team that faced unprecedented challenges: lost scholarships, players, support, and morale and no hopes for a bowl bid. O'Brien proved to be an exceptional leader who not only energized his team but also struck an appropriate tone to bring perspective to the role of athletics on the campus—he proved to be an ambassador not only for football but for education as well. He was operating in uncharted territory, trying to regain support for his team while simultaneously helping to move the culture of the university toward a more balanced perspective on athletics. By the time the team ended the season with an 8–4 record, a surprisingly large percentage of the discussion about Penn State football was about football. The university still had a long way to go to move past the crisis, but O'Brien's words and his team's actions helped move the organization forward in the first season after the scandal.

Dissension and acrimony remained, however, despite everyone's agreement that the best course for the school and the team was to go forward. Within the university, an ongoing battle over control of the board of trustees began with the 2011 grand jury report, increased with the release of the 2012 Freeh report, and accelerated even further with the NCAA sanctions. In 2012, more than 80 candidates ran for three board positions, many of them adamant that current board members should be removed, Paterno's legacy should be restored, and the university should protect against external institutions' involvement in decisions to alter the university's policies and culture. In 2013, 39 candidates ran for another three positions. Many of those candidates won seats on the board and continued to fight against Freeh, the NCAA, and former board members. Ironically, Penn State's football team, the center of the controversy, may eventually move past the Sandusky scandal faster than the university as a whole.

In January 2013, Pennsylvania governor Tom Corbett, the former attorney general when the original grand jury had been formed and a member of the PSU board of trustees when the university agreed to the NCAA sanctions, filed suit seeking to invalidate portions of the sanctions against PSU based on antitrust regulation. Once again, the timing of Corbett's actions on Penn State gave his critics ammunition. The governor was almost as unpopular across Pennsylvania as the NCAA, and his opponents claimed that the suit was simply an attempt to curry favor with the electorate in the run-up to the election.

A few days after Corbett's announcement, Pennsylvania senator Jake Corman, who represents the state's Centre County, filed suit to ensure that all of the $60 million in fines that were part of the NCAA agreement would be spent in Pennsylvania.

Still to come are the trials of the three administrators who were central to the university's response to the Sandusky charges. Should the former president of one of America's major educational institutions be led off to jail in handcuffs, the Penn State saga will remain in the public eye.

Regardless of how the trials conclude, however, there are still members of the PSU board of trustees, former Nittany Lions, and thousands of other Paterno supporters who will continue to push for the reinstatement of Paterno's record and the statue that once stood outside the stadium. The surviving members of Paterno's family no longer share an agenda with the remaining members of the board and make regular statements that keep the scandal in the news. As long as the pro-JoPa groups continue to push for the restoration of his reputation, they will continue to sabotage efforts by the university to move past the Sandusky scandal.

Conclusion

There is a consistent relationship between how organizations strive to avoid crises and how they deal with them when they occur. The best-run organizations have comprehensive and well-tested crisis plans, but the fact that they practice ethical, effective communication means that they often identify potential problems and confront them before they reach the crisis phase. In other words, ethical organizations with value-driven cultures do such a good job in crisis planning they often avoid major crises before they arise. Conversely, organizations that fail to adhere to their own moral code or see how inaction only creates larger problems often bring these same problems to their approach to handling a crisis when it occurs. The organizations that need the most help are least equipped to find it when things go wrong.

Penn State's child molestation cover-up is an outgrowth of a dysfunctional institution, in which sports, particularly football, had grown so powerful within the organization that athletic administrators no longer honored the chain of command. It was a tragic example of an organization responding to a problem by suppressing information to make it go away. When this failed, administrators were stunningly unprepared to deal with it and continued to act unethically with inevitable results. Had the crisis been sprung on them with no prior knowledge, their response still would have been unprofessional and unethical, but the fact that top administrators had time to prepare a communications strategy and ended up so reactive and disorganized is particularly hard to grasp. Key administrators at the top of the organization knew about the problem for years prior to it going public, and they still appeared to have no well-considered plan in place when it did.

The foundations of effective crisis communication, including careful planning, methodical fact-finding, appeals to existing policy, strategic media relations, etc. were, for the most part, ignored or poorly implemented.

The resultant chaos—misinformation, a dysfunctional chain of command, inadequately informed decisions and announcements, poor relationships with key audiences, etc.—demonstrated that their poor crisis communication plan was a reflection of a flawed policy and unworkable relations among key players.

Penn State's football-centric culture was by no means responsible for Jerry Sandusky's years of abusing young boys—it is probable that he would have found ways to prey on them regardless of his affiliation with the team. Once his crimes were known, however, the Penn State community's obsession with the team, insularity from external checks, and dysfunctional chain of command all factored into the cover-up of his atrocities.

The Freeh report recommended a wide variety of changes that could begin to change the culture of the institution, but cultural change is an extremely challenging goal. When problems run this deeply, organizations often attempt to clean house, removing whoever and whatever was associated with the problem and then starting fresh. To some degree, Penn State has done this, cutting ties the president, coach, and athletic director.

With the introduction of a new president, athletic director, and head football coach, Penn State University moved quickly to address the institutional shortcomings that had led to the crisis. O'Brien, who would spend only two years in Happy Valley, returned the football team to its winning ways and restored integrity to the program, but, more important, constantly reinforced the message that Pennsylvania State University stood for more than a football team. In September 2013, athletic integrity monitor George Mitchell released his report evaluating the university's progress one year into the sanctions. He lauded Penn State's efforts at reform, suggesting that the school had done such an effective job that the penalty on football scholarships should be reduced. The leader most responsible for evaluating the institution's progress signaled that the university was, indeed, changing its ways.

The NCAA acknowledged Mitchell's findings, noting that "Penn State leaders have made continued progress toward ensuring a culture of athletics integrity, and we look forward to full implementation of these efforts."[24]

The recovery from the scandal remains a work in progress. The board of trustees still contains many long-term members who were part of the prior culture, who should have known more about the situation than they have admitted to, and who were decision makers in Paterno's dismissal. These board members will attempt the delicate task of retaining all of the best qualities of the institution while changing how it functions at a very fundamental level. New board members are already acting as change agents, but they differ widely on what they are trying to do and how they are trying to do it. Some are looking forward and, while maintaining respect for Paterno, focusing on moving the institution past the crisis. Others have a different agenda, their highest priority the restoration of Paterno's reputation. The latter group may think they have Penn State's best interests in mind, but the more they focus on Paterno, the longer it will take to resolve the crisis. Differences among the agendas and perspectives of the board members ensure that the next decade will remain a challenging one for the institution.

Penn State University boasts one of the largest and most passionate alumni groups in America, a portion of whom, rightly or wrongly, developed and maintain that loyalty because of their passion for Nittany Lion football and the team's venerable coach, Joe Paterno. Every university in the country has its rituals and sayings, but the most common phrase heard at PSU provides an insight into how Nittany Lion supporters feel about their institution. It is rare to go an hour on the school's massive campus without hearing someone shout out, "We are" and someone else, usually multiple students, respond, "Penn State!" The call-and-response suggests not only school spirit but an unusually intense commingling of identities between the students and the school. That bond will continue to serve as both a hindrance and a help as the institution tries to move forward and find a way past the most painful scandal in its history.

Chapter 9

Individual Gambling Scandals

The Black Sox scandal, professional baseball's racist reaction to Jackie Robinson, the cheating epidemic in college basketball, the NBA's drug and race issues, amphetamine and steroid issues in baseball, the NFL concussion crisis and the collective failure of Penn State University in the Sandusky case emerged from either deep-rooted dysfunction within an organization, a failure on the part of leadership to identify and resolve institutional problems, or both.

The next two chapters address a fundamentally different kind of sports scandal, in which individuals are involved with some improper on-field or off-field behavior that brings their organizations into disrepute. Some of their offenses defy specific rules of the sports organization, and some of their offenses break larger societal rules.

This chapter examines the individual gambling scandals of five men: Paul Hornung, Alex Karras, Denny McLain, Pete Rose, and Tim Donaghy. Some of these men were extremely well known prior to their scandals, and some gained a kind of infamy because of their betting problems. The better known the gamblers were, the more complicated the task for the league administrators, who addressed the scandals while maintaining a delicate balance among the rights of the individual, the rights and responsibilities of the organization, and the social contract among the player, team, organization, and society as a whole.

NFL Gambling: The Golden Boy and the Mad Duck

Paul Hornung played halfback for the Green Bay Packers, and Alex Karras starred as a defense tackle for the Detroit Lions. Both were high-profile NFL players in the 1960s who were the most publicized players on their teams. They are permanently linked, however, not by their on-field performance but by their off-field association with gamblers. When the NFL suspended them for the 1963 season in response to their gambling, it appeared that they were given similar penalties for similar infractions. The players reacted to the suspensions in very different ways, however, and the league's next steps illustrate how sports organizations view employees in the midst of a scandal. Contrition by the offender goes a long way toward helping to move both the player and the organization past the problem, but the opposite is also true—an athlete who refuses to acknowledge the error of his ways makes it difficult for the player and the league to put the scandal to rest. As Hornung and Karras found out, players who create scandals but cooperate in resolving them are rewarded, while players who fail to learn their lessons and help the organization resolve the problems they have created are likely to regret that decision. The first priority of the organization is self-preservation—if the agendas of the league and the player coincide, administrators will work with the athlete, and if they don't, the league will act in its own best interest, regardless of the consequences for the employee.

The Golden Boy

Paul Hornung's nickname, "the Golden Boy," reflects the charmed life he led at almost every stage of his career. In high school, he pitched for the baseball team, starred on the basketball team, and quarterbacked the football team. At Notre Dame University, he lettered in football all four years, the first three at fullback and the final year at quarterback. With his blond hair and winning smile, Hornung looked like the model of an athlete. When he won the Heisman Trophy in 1956, he beat out such notables as Jim Brown, Tommy McDonald, and Johnny Majors.

His fairytale story continued when the Green Bay Packers selected Hornung as the top pick of the 1957 draft. Unfortunately, his professional career did not bring the immediate success that he had enjoyed at every step in his life, and he struggled in his first two seasons at the NFL level. Hornung wasn't alone—the Packers underperformed as well.

The fortunes of the player and the team improved dramatically in 1959, when Vince Lombardi was brought in to run the team. The new coach revamped the offense and built it around the running game, featuring Hornung and Jim Taylor. In the 1960 season, the Golden Boy and the Packers won their first conference title. Horning had the highest-production season in the history of the game: he ran for 13 touchdowns, caught 2 more and threw for 2 others, kicked 15 field goals and 41 extra points for a total of 176 points. In 1961, he was named the league's most valuable player. The combination of his handsome profile and athletic achievements made Hornung a natural for lucrative endorsements: he was so well known and well liked that both major political parties wooed him to run for Wisconsin public office. At the height of his career, it appeared, the Golden Boy could do no wrong.

The Mad Duck

If Hornung represented the glamor of the league, Karras represented the guts. Karras was "the Mad Duck," toiling in the trenches at a position that required a tough, grind-it-out mentality. "For me, Alex Karras will always be a pink giant with a towel wrapped around his waist. He will always have a scowl on his face, a cigar in one paw and a cold beer in the other,"[1] *New York Times* writer Bill Morris recalled years later. In his senior year at the University of Iowa in 1957, Karras won the Outland Trophy as college football's best interior lineman and finished second in the balloting for the Heisman Trophy, despite the fact that he and his coach, Forest Evashevski, barely spoke to each other. Evashevski was no "players' coach," but Karras's relationship with him was no anomaly—it was one of many that demonstrated the player's lifelong antiauthoritarian streak. He was drafted in the first round by the Lions and played his entire professional career in Detroit. The team's consistent mediocrity did not stop Karras from earning Pro Bowl honors four times.

Regardless of the Amount, It's Still Gambling

Polar opposites in style, Hornung and Karras shared individual success on the field, the adoration of hometown fans, and a penchant for doing things their own way. They also shared a fondness for wagering on sports, and in 1962, league officials began hearing rumors that both men were gambling.

Hornung's connection with the betting world began in 1956, when he met Barney Shapiro, a businessman who made his fortune around the gambling industry, particularly Las Vegas hotels and coin-operated amusement games. The football player was drawn to his new friend's business acumen; the businessman enjoyed the company of one of America's most famous athletes. Shapiro also enjoyed hearing Hornung's opinions on upcoming games, information that helped improve his winning percentage of football bets. With his close connection to the gambling industry and regular discussions with Shapiro about sports wagers, it was only a matter of time before Hornung began putting down wagers of his own, despite the league's clear and well-communicated policy against it. In late summer 1959, Hornung began betting through Shapiro on college and NFL games. He continued betting with him for three years, with most of his wagers between $100 and $200, but occasionally placing as much as $500 on a game.

When Hornung's gambling habits went public, Lombardi confronted him about the allegations. Hornung denied them, an enormous offense to a coach who demanded candor and responsibility from his players. It was a misjudgment that would eventually cost him. He learned from his mistakes at the next level, however: when he was interviewed by investigators from the NFL offices, he admitted to gambling and apologized immediately for the infraction.

Publicly, the Packer halfback framed his actions in the most innocuous language possible: "There's nothing mysterious or secret about it," he said. "Barney (Shapiro) and I have talked together during the season and during the off season. I considered betting on some games solely because of his interest in the games, and I bet only through him as a personal friend."[2] His naïveté is a little difficult to comprehend—league rules against gambling were clear-cut, and while it is true that Shapiro was a genuinely close friend, he also made no secret of his connection to the gambling-centric environs of Las Vegas. The explanation was disingenuous, but Hornung accepted full responsibility and publicly stated the words that help any individual and organization move past a scandal: "I made a terrible mistake," Hornung said. "I am truly sorry."[3]

Commissioner Pete Rozelle apparently bought Hornung's story: in his report on the Hornung gambling inquiry, Rozelle noted that the "investigation indicates that Hornung's friend is a personal bettor, not a bookmaker.[4] Rozelle also listed the size of the bets, which implied that the gambling could be interpreted as a set of friendly wagers between buddies, and even noted that the player was close to even in the returns on his wagers.

The commissioner's interpretation may have been accurate but also appears to have put the best possible spin on the star player's situation. Sports organizations reserve their strictest penalties for gambling, because of the potential leverage gambling interests can gain over a player who falls behind on his bets, increasing susceptibility to bribes. Not only did Hornung place bets with a friend who had been partial owner of a Las Vegas hotel that included a casino, he also admitted to providing Shapiro with his "opinion" of games—insider information that would clearly be used for gambling purposes. However Rozelle chose to describe it, the game's biggest star had made far too close a connection with the gambling world.

While the Hornung investigation was going on, the commissioner's office was also looking into allegations against Karras. Rozelle found that the

Lions' lineman had made fewer bets than Hornung, each between $50 or $100, but he decided on a similar punishment: suspension. During the Karras investigation, Rozelle found that five additional Detroit Lions were also gambling. All of them had placed bets on a playoff game, which, coincidentally, involved the Packers. Players from one team were betting on games involving players on another team who were betting on other games. The situation was a public relations nightmare.

Like Hornung, Karras admitted to his transgressions, although his anti-authoritarian ways would not allow him to accept his punishment with the same resignation. "Even when Karras ran afoul of the NFL's rules, he did it in a big way,"[5] Detroit columnist Mike O'Hara noted. Daniel Flynn of the *American Spectator* explained that "part of Karras's bitterness over his suspension stemmed from the league's more lenient policy on gambling when it came to bosses."[6] Flynn noted that a number of NFL owners, including the Giants' Tim Mara, the Colts' Carol Rosenbloom, and the Steelers' Art Rooney were all associated with gambling at one time or another, but none ever faced fines or suspensions. Karras understandably saw a double standard when it came to the men with the authority to hire or fire the commissioner.

In April of 1963, Rozelle announced the suspension of both players. In Rozelle's announcement, the commissioner spoke not only about their transgressions but about the limitations of their mistakes as well:

> There is absolutely no evidence of any criminality. No bribes, no game-fixing or point-shaving. The only evidence uncovered in this investigation . . . was the bets by the players penalized. All of these bets were on their own teams to win or on other NFL games.[7]

The commissioner also fined the additional five Detroit Lions $2,000 each, and, in an unusual move, levied a $4,000 fine on the Lions' team management for laxity of supervision. The amounts of the fines and lengths of suspensions allowed Rozelle to punish all parties without triggering an automatic review from team owners. Anything more needed the approval of the men who were really in charge of the league. Only three years into his tenure, the commissioner wanted to establish himself as an independent arbiter of league punishments and do so without needing permission from the men who really ruled the league.

Reactions to Rozelle's decisions ran the gamut, from complaints that the players had received a slap on the wrist to accusations that the commissioner was too heavy-handed because he was trying to make examples of the highest-profile players. The commissioner described his decisions as "the hardest in his life" and went to great lengths to explain them:

> I thought about it at length. The maximum penalty for a player would be suspension for life. That would be for failure to report a bribe attempt or for trying to shave points. This sport has grown so quickly and gained so much of the approval of the American public that the only way it can be hurt is through gambling. I considered this in reaching my decision. I also took into account that the violations of Hornung and Karras were continuing, not casual. They were continuing, flagrant and increasing. Both players had been informed over and over of the league rule on gambling; the rule is posted in every clubhouse in the league, as well. Yet they continued to gamble. I could only exact from them the most severe penalty short of banishment for life.[8]

Contrasting Approaches to Serving a Suspension

Hornung and Karras served out their suspensions in ways that reflected their personalities. Unblemished to some, Hornung maintained his veneer of respectability, kept as low a profile as the best player in the country's most popular sport could, and counted the days until his return from exile. Karras took a job as a bartender in the Lindell Bar, a raucous sports bar in downtown Detroit, and revitalized a career he had started prior to the NFL as a professional wrestler. During his suspension his wife gave birth to a son, and Karras announced that they would name him Alvin, Pete Rozelle's given first name. His antics kept him on the sports pages and, to some degree, gave him a platform to mock the NFL. He would later claim that he made $4,000 more for one of his wrestling matches than the annual NFL salary he lost in the suspension. Hornung was the model citizen serving his penance; Karras remained the rebel even while in exile. The league would forget neither.

As the suspension drew to a close, Hornung still had to deal with Lombardi, the coach he had lied to and had forced to depend on a lesser running back for an entire season. Rumors swirled that the Green Bay coach would trade him, but Lombardi valued victory over everything. Hornung had been the centerpiece of the Packers' offense, and the coach was willing to forgive a lot, including his star player lying directly to his face, to regain the edge on the field. A less-talented player would have been gone in an instant: Lombardi instructed his wayward star to report to training camp two months before the rest of the team to get in shape, then started him in his first game back.

Karras returned from his suspension with his irreverence intact. Asked to call the opening coin toss in a 1964 game, he declined, telling the referee, "I'm sorry sir, I'm not permitted to gamble."[9]

The Long Memory of NFL Management

Karras retired from football in 1970 and immediately launched a second, equally successful career in the entertainment industry. A series of small parts in television movies in the early 1970s led to a role in the Mel Brooks comedy *Blazing Saddles*. Television executives liked what they saw. In 1974, despite the league's misgivings, Karras was introduced as an analyst for *Monday Night Football*, ABC's premier football telecast, a position he held for three seasons. He would go on to appear in a variety of comic and dramatic roles in film and television, including a starring role in the six-year run of the sitcom *Webster*. Many of the roles cast the lifelong renegade against type, as a benign father figure. The irony was not lost on the coaches and administrators who had worked with him during his football career.

Despite his successful career in television, Karras refused to soften his feelings toward the gambling punishment or the commissioner. In a 1977 interview, Karras told a reporter for the *Des Moines Register*, "I don't like Pete Rozelle, I don't talk to him. I don't know if he likes that or not. I don't think he cares. He suspended me for one season for betting on games, and that was a bull [bleep] rap."[10] Rozelle's antagonist was diagnosed with dementia at age 70, an ailment he partially blamed on his football career. Six years after the diagnosis, he and his wife joined the head trauma lawsuit against the NFL.

League officials appeared to hold on to their grudges as well. "Despite four Pro Bowl appearances, despite being voted to the All-Decade Team of the 1960s, despite a consensus that he was one of the best defensive linemen ever to play the game, Karras was shunned by the Hall of Fame,"[11] noted writer Bill Morris. He was never even named as a finalist for consideration.

Hornung, on the other hand, was inducted into the league's Hall in 1986.

A half century after his suspension, Hornung remained contrite and willing to support the NFL commissioner. In 2012, when NFL Commissioner Roger Goodell handed down sweeping suspensions in the New Orleans Saints' "bounty" scandal, the Golden Boy was one of the first former players to voice his support. "They (the league) have been able to take care of their own in terms of suspensions in the past, and I was one of them, of course,"[12] he told a reporter.

Two gamblers, two suspensions, and two very different responses, by the players and the league, in moving beyond a scandal.

MLB Gambling: Denny McLain and Pete Rose

Football's gambling scandals involved high-profile players who were respected around the league and beloved by their hometown fans. Baseball's gambling scandals, however, involved even higher-profile players, which made their rise and fall all the more dramatic and potentially damaging to their sport.

Denny McLain—Baseball's Last 30-Game Winner

Few players in any sport have experienced the highs and lows of Dennis Dale "Denny" McLain, the Detroit Tiger pitcher as notorious for his self-destructive behavior as his athletic prowess.

As a pitcher, McLain was equal parts talent and audacity. "When you can do it out there between the white lines," he said, "then you can live any way you want."[13] Early in McLain's pro career, a *Sports Illustrated* writer described him as "a hot-tempered, eccentric kid with a million-dollar arm, million-dollar tastes, million-dollar dreams and a ten-cent attitude."[14] His cockiness intimidated batters but alienated opponents, coaches, and even teammates. Because of his exceptional skills, he was extremely critical of those who did not play to his standards and had no problems voicing his opinion about the performance of his teammates to the press. His condemnation occasionally extended to the fan base, as when he complained to an out-of-town writer, "The Detroit fans are the worst I've ever seen anyplace." Understandably, it was a comment he would never live down no matter how many wins he delivered.

McLain's arrogance was one of a number of red flags that indicated his potential for scandal. He was also extremely disorganized with money: despite a star pitcher's salary, he was unable to keep up with, or even keep track of, his bills. "I always had this great urge to go spend money—on anything. I'd get an itch, and the money would be gone,"[15] he explained. McLain's catcher, Bill Freehan, once noted that "the rules for Denny just don't seem to be the same as for the rest of us."[16] This is a common delusion among gamblers, a mixture of entitlement and indestructability that allows them to act as if the odds are always in their favor, despite evidence to the contrary.

Gambling Connections

McLain's relationship with gambling began almost as early as his baseball career: in his mid-teens he was already collecting bets for a local bookie. In his autobiography, McLain displayed an amazing naïveté about the cause of his downfall: "It was illegal, of course, but I really think he [the bookmaker] was just being nice. I was grateful. Running numbers didn't make a gambler out of me. I don't know what did, but it wasn't numbers."[17]

McLain's insatiable thirst for money and complete inability to hold on to it meant that he was constantly searching for the next angle, the next "business opportunity" that would help him catch up on his bills or fund his next extravagance. Conmen know that there's no easier mark than a guy who thinks he's smarter than everyone else, and McLain went through life as if he could always see the angles. He was a great target for a rip-off: loose with money, overly optimistic, and gullible despite a track record of investment mistakes. As long as he was dominant on the mound, however, his poor decision making when off the mound would always be tolerated. Coaches would chastise him, fine him, and threaten to cut him from the team: Denny was too good for them to let go, and he knew it.

McLain arrived at the Tigers in 1963, a raw talent who won a mere two games in his rookie season. In his second year he doubled that total, then exploded for 16 wins in 1965. With increased success came an increased interest in gambling. The Tigers' new ace began placing bets on hockey and basketball with a group of Syrian bookmakers affiliated with organized crime in the Detroit area. He was as bad at gambling as he was good at pitching, so it didn't take him long to fall behind to the bookies, exactly the kind of situation that sports leagues are desperate to avoid.

In February 1967, the Syrian bookmakers convinced McLain and a business partner, Edwin Shober, to bankroll their own bookmaking operation. Desperate for cash, McLain convinced a local bank to lend him additional money, failing to mention that it was liquidity for his new gambling operations. The pitcher was no longer simply consorting with bookmakers—he was one of them.

McLain proved to be no better at taking bets than he was at making them. In August 1967, gambler Eddie Vashon won big, $46,000 on a horserace, and when he visited his bookie to collect, the bookie explained that he had nowhere near that amount of money to pay out, so he directed Vashon to his backers, Edwin Shober and Denny McLain, to collect his winnings. Shober also declined to pay, forcing Vashon to shuttle among minor bookmakers and big-time mobsters in an attempt to collect his winnings.

The frustrated gambler eventually took his case to Tony Giacalone, the enforcer for the Detroit Cosa Nostra. Giacalone failed to resolve the issue for Vashon, but the situation put the mobster in touch with McLain.

As August turned to September, Denny McLain's pitching efficiency tanked during the season's crucial stretch run. Not only didn't he collect a win in September or October, the normally dependable ace didn't finish the fifth inning in any of the five games he started and was pulled before the third in three of them. In mid-September McLain announced that he had hurt his foot, but he offered four different explanations for the injury, ranging from chasing raccoons from his garbage cans to kicking a water cooler in frustration. *Sports Illustrated* reporter Morton Sharnik suggested a more nefarious explanation for McLain's end-of-season swoon. According to Sharnik:

> There is also a fifth version. McLain was ordered to report to Giacalone's boatwell. . . . Once McLain was there, Tony Giacalone and his brother Billy, another Mafioso, went into their "angry act." He gave McLain the full act, including his famous stare. Then he brought his heel down on McLain's toes and told him to get the money up.[18]

McLain was called on to start the final game of the season against the Red Sox with the pennant on the line. He gave up three runs before being pulled a mere two and two-thirds innings into the team's final defeat of the season. Sharnik reported that "according to a gangland source, just prior to McLain's toe injury Billy Giacalone [Tony Giacalone's brother] had made big bets on both the Red Sox and the Twins to win the pennant and later had bet heavily against the Tigers in McLain's final start."[19] Denny McLain was losing money in gambling, behind in payments to dangerous mobsters, and performing poorly in his day job. He needed to turn things around.

Record-Breaking Seasons

Whatever was bothering McLain at the end of the 1967 season, he resolved it by the start of the 1968 season. That year, the 24-year-old Tiger ace had one of the most memorable seasons in baseball history. He completed 28 games, earned an ERA of 1.96, won the American League MVP and Cy Young awards, and helped his team win the World Series. Along the way, he won 31 games, the first pitcher in 34 years to win 30 or more in a season, and the last pitcher to achieve that mark. Based on changes in the way modern pitchers are used, it is possible that McLain will become the final pitcher in the major leagues to earn that many wins in a season.

Win number 31 came against the New York Yankees, and when an aging Mickey Mantle came to the plate in the eighth inning, McLain called catcher Bill Freehan to the mound for a conference. The Tigers had a comfortable lead, and McLain was a huge fan of Mantle's, so he told Freehan to tell Mantle that he was going to groove a pitch straight down the middle, giving the Yankee great a free shot at a home run. Mantle hit McLain's lazy fastball into the outfield seats, and tipped his cap to the pitcher after rounding third. McLain recalled:

> I got the message—"Thanks Denny"—and so did most everyone in Tiger Stadium. But I didn't give a damn. I thought it was hilarious. Still, I could just see the stories in the papers and the questions from the Tigers and the commissioner about "the integrity of the game." The way some baseball people talk, you'd think "the integrity of the Game" ranks right up there with "We the people" and "liberty and justice for all." Sure enough the criticism and inquiries came, everything that I expected. But it was worth it to me to see Mickey reach that milestone.[20]

McLain's regular season performance, in which he posted a 1.96 ERA and pitching nine or more innings 28 times, did not hold up in the World Series. He lost the first and fourth games of the series before winning decisively in the sixth. The Tigers prevailed in Game Seven. When they won, McLain recalls, he was showered with awards, given a big raise, and headed out to the Riviera Hotel ("one of my all-time favorite places to visit"),[21] where he gave some of that raise back at the craps tables. "Everywhere I went," he recalled, "people seemed dedicated to the task of spoiling Denny McLain, and Denny McLain was dedicated to letting them do it."[22]

The 1968 season was no fluke: a year later, McLain won the Cy Young and 24 games—an astounding two-year combination of 55 wins.

1970—A Year of Suspensions

In February of the off-season, however, *Sports Illustrated* broke the story of McLain's gambling involvement, both placing and accepting wagers, and he was called in for questioning before the league commissioner, Bowie Kuhn. McLain admitted to the bookmaking business but denied other details of the magazine story, including ever having met Giacolone. He denied any involvement with the Vashon bet while admitting to lending one of his partners $10,000 to pay the bet off, a curious combination. Kuhn found enough problems with his explanation that he suspended McLain to allow the head of the commissioner's new security office, Henry Fitzgibbon, time to conduct a more detailed investigation.

Kuhn's decision was prudent. Even if McLain was only guilty of the mistakes he admitted to, they were sufficient to warrant suspension. But his explanations were vague and convoluted, and the suspension gave the commissioner an opportunity to get to the facts without having to rely too heavily on the word of a man who demonstrated recklessness in nearly every area of his life. On April 1, Kuhn announced the results of the investigation, a relatively charitable interpretation that suggested that McLain was the victim of a confidence scheme and not a true partner in the bookmaking operation. It was an explanation that McLain would use to cling to in a number of financial fiascos during his career: McLain as the victim, guilty of consorting with the wrong type of people who eventually took advantage of him. Kuhn also announced that the suspension would be lifted on July 1, or nearly halfway through the season.

Before McLain returned to the mound, however, the baseball world received further indication of his recklessness, when the star pitcher declared bankruptcy: the suspension had eliminated his only steady source of income but hadn't stopped him from continuing to burn through money as if it were still flowing. In his filing, he claimed no assets and debts of $400,000.

When he finally returned to the Detroit lineup, he managed to win only three games, losing five, over the rest of the 1970 season. In August, he was suspended a second time, this time for a week by his team, for dumping ice water on two reporters. His return from his second suspension was brief: in September, Kuhn announced McLain's third suspension of the season, telling reporters "certain new allegations have been brought to my attention, including allegations regarding McLain's conduct with respect to the Detroit management and information that on occasions McLain has carried a gun."[23] Only 26 years old, McLain appeared to have peaked on and off the baseball diamond.

The Decline Continues

Detroit management had seen enough. Shortly after the season ended, the Tigers traded McLain to the Washington Senators. A mere three years removed from one of the greatest seasons in pitching history, the former ace unceremoniously left town and for many fans, reporters, and teammates, the move could not come soon enough.

For years, McLain's fastball and look-the-other-way Detroit management had allowed the staff ace to ignore team rules. The unstated agreement worked as long as McLain kept winning, but by the time he showed up in the Senators training camp, years of extended-inning performances and hard living had taken their toll, and he could no longer count on his fast ball to overwhelm batters. Equally important, his new boss in Washington was Ted Williams, a manager who was easily as headstrong as McLain. The combination was toxic, and when McLain lost 22 games, his metamorphosis from staff ace to journeyman was complete. In two seasons, he had gone from the league leader in wins to the league leader in losses. He was shipped off to the Braves, who released him in 1973 after he posted a 6.56 ERA, bringing his colorful career in the majors to a close.

Post-Baseball: From Bad to Worse

Given his personality and track record, it is not surprising that life after baseball did not go well for Denny McLain. He filed for bankruptcy twice more and resurfaced in the press numerous times for a variety of legal offenses.

In nearly all of his business ventures, McLain would show up and trouble would follow. The retired pitcher was hired as the promotions director for a minor league hockey team, but fired for financial irregularities. His plans to purchase a South Carolina radio station ended when he was sued by his partners in the venture.

Despite the fact that gambling had derailed his baseball career, he continued to dabble with the industry. In his autobiography, he noted that "ten years after I'd been suspended from baseball for my unsuccessful attempt to become a bookie, I was doing it for real. And making a bundle."[24] Gambling income was apparently insufficient for his lifestyle, because in 1980, McLain moved to Lakeland, Florida, to become a partner in First Fidelity Financial Services, yet another of his ventures rumored to be connected to the Mafia. The business collapsed in 1982, the subject of a state investigation. McLain professed to be stunned that his partners were involved in illegal activity, particularly since the money was coming in so quickly without having to break the law.

In 1985, he was convicted of racketeering, extortion, and narcotics charges, and sentenced to 23 years in prison. The case was overturned on procedural grounds 2 years later, and when the government reindicted him, McLain pleaded guilty and was given time served and probation. Released from prison, McLain and some associates purchased Peet Packing, a meat company in Chesaning, Michigan. Within two years, the company was bankrupt and McLain was in court facing charges of looting the company's pension fund. He was convicted and sentenced to 8 years in prison.

How does baseball address the legacy of a player as talented and destructive, to himself and others, as Denny McLain? Despite his accomplishments, the former Tiger ace remains a pariah to Major League Baseball, as league officials stay as far away from him as possible and simply hope that he stays out of the sports pages. He remains in "good standing" in the league, but has no real chance of ever being considered for the Hall of Fame, despite some of the most dominant seasons in the history of major league pitching. His biggest fans, who watched him pitch his team into the World Series in the late 1960s, still occasionally argue for his redemption, but McLain continues to undermine their case with his ongoing record of greed and self-indulgence.

The league has washed its hands of McLain, but the Tigers appear to have achieved a more ambivalent relationship with their former star. In June 2008, the team celebrated the 40th anniversary of their 1968 championship, and they invited McLain to take part in the festivities. When the twice-convicted felon and last pitcher to win 30 games stepped onto the field at Detroit's Comerica Park, he was met by a raucous mixture of cheers and boos—one more example of the highs and lows in the life of Denny McLain.

The Hit King: Pete Rose

The image-makers responsible for packaging modern sports are constantly on the lookout for players who embody their games' best qualities, such as toughness, competiveness, and a willingness to work as hard as they possibly can to give their team the best chance to win. In 1963, a 21-year-old rookie burst onto the field for the Cincinnati Reds, and Major League Baseball quickly recognized a new representative of the game.

His name was Pete Rose, and his nickname was Charlie Hustle. He debuted as a second baseman, but was happy to play anywhere between the lines, including first and third base and all three outfield positions. He batted from either side of the plate and demonstrated an insatiable will to win. He had two signature moves: when he walked, he broke into a full-out sprint to first, and when he stole, he dove headfirst into second, third, or home.

Baseball fans, particularly in southwestern Ohio, adored Rose, and, despite the fact that he hit a pedestrian .273 for the season, the new Reds sensation was a lock for the Rookie of the Year Award. He struggled at the plate in his second year in the pros and was even temporarily benched but followed his sophomore slump with a .312 average in his third season, the first of nine consecutive years in which he batted over .300.

Reds management knew a star when they saw one and treated Rose accordingly. "He is Cincinnati. He is the Reds,"[25] said his coach, Sparky Anderson. "Rose played as so many fans imagine they would," wrote Michael Sokolove, "if only they had been blessed with an opportunity: joyously, full-bore every day, never one moment of cheating the paying public."[26] Rose loved baseball, and the game loved him back. In 1968, he was presented with the Hutch Award, given to the player who best exemplified fighting spirit and competitive desire. Over his career, Rose was selected for 17 All-Star teams at a record five different positions and was named the most valuable player in the 1975 World Series. The national sports media echoed the sentiments of the fans and the league, naming Rose the *Sporting News* Player of the Year (1968), *Baseball Digest* Player of the Year (1973), and *Sports Illustrated* Sportsman of the Year (1975). He was an extremely productive player who also benefitted from starring on the dominant team in his era: the Reds played in four World Series between 1970 and 1976, winning twice.

Rose's Run-Ins with the Competition

With his square jaw and combative stance, Rose looked as competitive as he acted. "I'd walk through hell in a gasoline suit to play baseball,"[27] he told reporters. There were times, however, when many fans thought that his competiveness went too far, the biggest example coming in the 1970 All-Star Game. With the game tied in the 12th, Rose scored the winning run by bowling over Ray Fosse and dislocating the catcher's shoulder in the process. For the remainder of his career, the play was used to define him by both his supporters and detractors.

In the days that followed, most fans and members of the press focused on the excitement of a play at the plate that ended an extra-inning game. Over time, however, some critics began to argue that the collision not only was unnecessary but threatened an athlete's career in what was, essentially, an exhibition game. In the years that followed, Fosse's injuries were compounded by the fact that they were misdiagnosed. He went on to a 12-year career in the majors, but his performance was never quite the same after the injury.

Rose was, characteristically, unapologetic. He shrugged off any criticism of the decision to run into Fosse—you play every game to win, he reasoned, regular season, postseason, All-Star Game. In his many retellings of the story, Rose always included a description of how he and Fosse had actually been out together socially on the night before the game, as if even the best of friends had to put aside their relationship once the game began. In a 1974 interview, he told a reporter that "[i]f I didn't hit him the way I did, I couldn't have talked to my father afterwards." In other versions of the story, Rose explained that he had originally intended to slide until he saw Fosse moving up the line and then realized that he had to run into him to score.[28] The incident and Rose's subsequent explanations left many fans ambivalent about the Reds' star, impressed by his tenacity but suspicious that there was nothing Charlie Hustle wouldn't do to win a game.

Three summers later, Rose critics had their suspicions confirmed in a game between the Reds and Cardinals. Breaking up a double play, Rose came in high and late to take out second baseman Bud Harrelson, and the two players began brawling. Players from both sides jumped in, and as historian James Reston wrote, "[N]ear second base, the riot was total; it remains one of the most spectacular melees in baseball history."[29] Rose, it appeared, would do anything to win.

After the game, Rose told the press: "I play hard, but I don't play dirty. If I was a dirty player, I could've leveled him. It's like the 1970 All-Star game. I played that game to win. I've been criticized ever since for that. But that's the way I play."[30]

A Growing Sense of Scandal

In 1978, Rose, already one of the most popular players in the game, became the focus of the sports world as he earned a hit in 44 consecutive games, the longest streak in National League history. The run was not only the biggest story in Cincinnati, it captured the attention of the national sports media. Within the organization, the attention exacerbated a growing problem. "His streak had been wonderful for baseball, glorious for Rose himself, and bad for the Cincinnati ballclub,"[31] wrote James Reston. It was all Rose, all the time, despite the fact that he was playing with exceptional talent, most of whom were now relegated to second-class status. Rose was used to the limelight and unlikely to spread around the attention, so the problem festered in the clubhouse.

Narcissism was only one of Rose's locker room problems: he was also a frequent user, and a big proponent, of "greenies," the diet pills that players used to stay sharp on the field. He was not alone: the pills were widely accepted in the baseball community (and in society at large), but baseball managers were aware of the growing antidrug sentiment in America and were already working on ways to, if not eliminate them from the game, minimize their public connection with it. Like many players of the era, Rose did not seem to think the drug posed any significant problems, to himself or the league.

Beyond the locker room, it was apparent to management that Rose was headed for scandal from other directions as well. For many years, it was common knowledge around the relatively conservative city of Cincinnati that Rose cheated on his wife. Infidelity is commonplace among professional athletes, but Rose was anything but discreet about it. As Rose's marriage dissolved, however, he impregnated one of his mistresses and invited others to sit in the players' family section during games. The fawning press generated by the hit streak would only go so far: at some point, the streak would end and the serial infidelity would remain, and the club would be forced to deal with the repercussions.

Adultery was one problem, gambling was another, and Rose appeared to be as reckless with his wagers as he was with his women. By the time Rose launched his record-breaking hit streak, he was betting heavily with bookmakers just across the river from the Reds' stadium, in northern Kentucky. He felt so untouchable that he stiffed bookmakers and bragged about it, assuming his position as the Reds' star would make him immune from retribution from the bookies, the team, or anyone else who might question his ways. Baseball commissioner Bowie Kuhn directed the league's director of security to interview Rose about the gambling rumors, and Rose denied them. The potential for scandal was increasing on a number of fronts, and hitting streaks could only cover for so many of them.

Home and Away

Publicly, the Reds supported their main attraction, but privately they had seen enough. After 16 years in Cincinnati, Rose and the club could not agree to terms of a new contract, and the local hero jumped to Philadelphia. He brought his winning ways with him: over the next five years, his Phillies team won two pennants and a world championship. He brought his gambling ways as well: amazingly, Rose and Phillies chief executive Bill Giles frequented Philadelphia area racetracks together, with Giles watching his new star bet as much as $500 on a horse race.

Giles, a lifelong baseball man, was particularly blind to Rose's potential for scandal. He was well aware of his star player's frequent use of diet pills but chose to publicly downplay the issue. "Bill Giles knew that Rose's use of greenies was chronic," explained James Reston, "and that he taught younger players how to use the uppers, sometimes in concert with coffee. In the age of cocaine, a much more damaging and socially unacceptable drug, many baseball administrators had adopted a tolerant attitude toward 'diet pills.'"[32] Management's failure to address the issue allowed it to become standard practice in the Philadelphia clubhouse until mid-season in 1980, when a local reporter published a story saying that the physician for the club's Reading farm team, Dr. Patrick Mazza, was under investigation for amphetamine distribution. At the time, the misuse of "diet pills" was a gray area in sports and society—it was difficult to tell who was taking them to shed weight and who was taking them for other reasons. It didn't take long for reporters to make a connection between the doctor and players on the Phillies, however, and the team was quickly engulfed in a scandal over possession and distribution of controlled substances.

The team's reaction was part defense and part offense. All of the players denied the story, and Giles released carefully worded defenses of his ball club. Mazza's trial stretched out past the end of the season and the charges were eventually dismissed. Stung by the criticism and what they perceived to be an invasion of their privacy, many of the players took out their frustrations on the press, furious that reporters who frequented the locker room would break the clubhouse code of silence. Rose was in a particularly difficult position: once again betraying his disregard for the law, he had already given interviews, on the record, in which he had admitted to using diet pills. The charges had the potential to erupt into a major scandal, but the team kept winning. When the Phillies marched through the playoffs and brought Philadelphia the first World Series championship in the city's history, any talk about amphetamines in the clubhouse was buried in an avalanche of feel-good stories. Once again, Rose found, there wasn't a problem that wouldn't go away as long as you continued to win baseball games.

After a brief stint with the Montreal Expos, Rose returned to Cincinnati, where he took over as one of the rare player-managers in modern-day baseball. In the twilight of his career, he began to close in on one of the most important records in baseball: most hits in the history of the game. As he inched closer to the record, Rose was once again at the center of national sports coverage and he was happy to bask in the attention: he began holding press conferences twice a day to deal with the crush of reporters. Baseball historians were quick to note the similarities between Rose and the man whose record he was chasing: Ty Cobb had been known as the most competitive, combative player of his era, respected for his abilities but disliked for his single-minded obsession with winning. Both men had a strained relationship with the game: baseball loved their talents but held them at a distance because of their personality quirks and potential for scandal.

Rose tied Cobb's record on the road, then the Reds returned to Cincinnati, where he broke the record in front of his hometown crowd. As the Reds took the field on the historic night, a plane flew over Riverfront Stadium with a sign reading "Latonia is betting on Pete." Latonia was Rose's favorite racetrack.

Rose's record-breaking performance was all the more remarkable because he achieved it while his private life grew increasingly chaotic. "By the agreement of virtually everyone later . . . Pete Rose's gambling had become pathological by 1985," Reston recounts. "People stopped his lawyers on the street to tell horrifying stories of the huge and crazy bets Rose was placing and to say how the man's life was out of control."[33] Management did little to stop him, and league officials were loath to do anything that would alter the biggest story in sports. To fuel his habit, Rose turned to the sports memorabilia industry, where his signature was in great demand and he insisted that he be paid in cash. But his salary and the extra money from signing sessions couldn't keep up with his gambling losses, and by the end of the season, Rose owed multiple bookies hundreds of thousands of dollars. Major League Baseball now had a disaster in the making: mobsters close to a gambler who not only was the most famous player in the game but a man who made out a lineup card every day of the week. He could influence the outcome of a game with his bat and his glove, but he could also affect the game through his management decisions, changing his defense, starting one pitcher over another, selecting which relief pitcher to insert in a particular situation.

The cash transactions from the memorabilia shows created two problems. First, they kept Rose from confronting his financial situation: as long as he had piles of money sitting around, he failed to recognize the extent of his debt. Second, the cash was loose and barely accountable: Rose quickly lost track of how much was where, and, inevitably, failed to account for the revenue when it came time to pay his taxes.

An Inglorious Departure for the Hit King

A year after becoming the all-time hit king, Rose retired as a player, secure in his position as one of the most successful players in the game's history. He had more at bats and had played in more games than any other player in the game. He held the longest hitting streak in National League history. But most important, he left the game with more hits—4,256—than any other player who had ever played in the majors.

Rose continued as the Reds' manager, but, when he was unable to duplicate the success he had achieved earlier in his career, his frustration mounted and he began to tarnish his reputation. Early in his final season, he got into a furious argument with umpire Dave Pallone about a close play at first base, and, as the dispute escalated, Rose shoved the ump with his forearm, then, after Pallone ejected him, shoved him a second time. The home crowd erupted as Rose left the field, throwing everything from golfballs and marbles to toilet paper and whiskey bottles onto the field.

National League president A. Bartlett Giamatti fined Rose $10,000 and suspended him for 30 days, the longest suspension for a manager in 41 years. The incident was the first in a series of showdowns between the two men, and it gave each a glimpse into the makeup of the other and the struggle that would play out over the next five years. Rose, unaccustomed to accountability, was stunned at the speed and severity of the president's decision and assumed that he would have the decision overturned on appeal. Giamatti, the former president of Yale University, was a moralist with extremely high standards of conduct for himself and for the members of organizations he led. Where some administrators might have perceived Rose's contributions to the game as a reason to give him a pass, Giamatti tended to think in the opposite direction—he held the game's biggest star to higher standards.

The two also differed, dramatically, on their understanding of the appeals process. At a minimum, Rose felt, the court of public opinion would be on his side and would factor into the final outcome. He argued that he had not been given due process and, since the punishment was unprecedented, that he was entitled to equal protection under the law. Rose failed to grasp the difference between traditional law and the rules of baseball. He was given the benefit of the doubt by forcing a review by an executive council of the league, but that proved inconsequential when the three-man council supported Giamatti's original decision.

Rose came away from the experience wary of a baseball executive he found heavy-handed and close-minded. Giamatti may have been the former but was certainly not the latter: his approach was to thoughtfully consider the opinions of all sides in a dispute before rendering a decision. On the other hand, he was a great admirer of Kennesaw Mountain Landis, appreciating the man's love for the game and desire to protect it at all costs, including the careers of players he found to have endangered it. Giamatti also appreciated Landis's supreme authority over the game, granted by the owners and upheld in the courts. He came away from his showdown with Rose wary of a star player who demonstrated arrogance, antiauthoritarianism, and an inability to change his ways. Giamatti would ascend to the role of baseball commissioner in 1989, and the two men would cross paths again.

The Wrong Crowd

There are a number of parallels between Denny McLain and Pete Rose. Both were enormously confident athletes who showed an early affinity for gambling. Both spent their lives refusing to change their self-destructive ways and being eager to blame their problems on misinterpretations, bad luck, and, most frequently, mistakes by the people around them. And both gravitated toward associates whose illegal activities would eventually bring them under the scrutiny of law enforcement.

McLain had gone as far as actually serving as a bookmaker; for Rose, it was hanging around with friends who were dealing drugs. In 1985, Rose began frequenting Gold's Gym on the north side of Cincinnati, a comfortable scene for a macho figure like Rose since it was populated with bodybuilders and gamblers, fast-talking characters with mysterious piles of cash. Workout facilities are often hotbeds of steroid abuse, and it was often a short jump to other forms of drugs, including cocaine. Donald Stenger, a former body-building champion, used the gym that Rose frequented as a front for a highly profitable cocaine business, and Michael Fry, the owner of the Gold's franchise, partnered with him in both businesses.

In 1988, the FBI began looking into the gym based on suspicions of drug activity. To understand how the operation worked, they leaned on a lower-level steroid distributor, Paul Janszen, who also served as one of Rose's flunkies. Janszen did odd jobs for Rose, driving him to events and occasionally placing his bets with local bookies. When the FBI interviewed Janszen in the drug investigation, he kept bringing up tales of Rose's astounding gambling habits. The bets were a tantalizing story, especially for such a high-profile athlete, but the FBI's principal interest was in the drug trade, and unless Janszen tied Rose directly to buying or fronting money for cocaine, he was not central to their investigation. Without the slam-dunk evidence they needed to tie Rose to the drug trade, the FBI continued to concentrate on the supply chain and turned over what they had on the Reds' star to the Internal Revenue Service: Rose had avoided any connection with drug activity but was still going to have to answer the government about untaxed cash.

Called Out

Rose's bookie-stiffing gambling spree, which he made no effort to hide, finally brought him before baseball administrators in February 1989, in a meeting with baseball commissioner Peter Ueberroth, deputy commissioner Fay Vincent, and Rose's old foe and baseball commissioner-designate Bart Giamatti. The leaders of baseball focused on a single question: whether Rose had ever bet on baseball. Rose vehemently, repeatedly denied it. Giamatti then took over the questioning and listed a number of other accusations the commissioner's office had heard about Rose's gambling.

Rose denied each of them, including that he had been part owner of a winning Pik Six horse racing ticket only days earlier. In fact, he had been involved in the horse racing bet, and his denial was a direct lie to the commissioner-designate.

It is impossible to know what potentially scandalous information was available to the administrators at the time of the meeting, whether they had heard rumors of or had substantiated information about drug connections, infidelity, cheating bookmakers, enormous bets made and lost, or unreported income, but it is clear that their primary, possibly solitary, interest was on whether Rose had bet on the game he played and managed—the rest appears to have been unknown or irrelevant.

Rose's appearance in the league's New York offices was guaranteed to generate press speculation and follow-up. Rose bluffed his way through local media, and Ueberroth downplayed the meeting in a discussion with a *New York Times* reporter. The hit leader who had barreled his way through all of the great difficulties in his life may have thought that his meeting with the commissioner had ended the debate, but his answers had simply aroused further suspicions, and the stewards of the game saw no reason to take him at his word: a day after the meeting, Bart Giamatti began organizing an investigation. He chose as his chief investigator John Dowd, who quickly recognized the particular challenges inherent to the position. He could compel testimony from fellow baseball players because they were employed by the league. But the vast majority of important information would not only be held by people outside of baseball, it would be coming from characters associated with Rose's vices—fellow gamblers, bookies, baseball hangers-on, each of whom had an angle and few of whom could be trusted to tell the truth.

Dowd didn't have to wait long for a star witness: he flew to Cincinnati and spent two full days interviewing Paul Janszen. Dowd recognized Janszen's credibility problems: he was a felon who thought that Rose owed him money. Just because Janszen might prove a liability on the witness stand didn't mean that he had no value in the investigation, however—he was a trove of details who could say when and where Rose had bet with whom and how much he had lost. Most important, he confirmed the central allegation in the investigation: Rose had bet on baseball. Janszen also told Dowd that Rose had told him that if he had enough money bet on a game, he would consider throwing it.

"Therein lay the ultimate rationale behind gambling as the game's most serious offense," noted Reston. "It was a mortal danger pointed directly at the integrity of baseball as a fair, honest test of skill. The knife of gambling pointed far more lethally at the heart of the contest than did drug use or child molestation or a host of other tawdry sins."[34]

Janszen provided Dowd with copies of betting slips allegedly written by Rose, and Dowd forced Rose to provide additional writing samples. The investigator submitted both to a handwriting expert, who confirmed that they were written by the same person. Since Janszen's credibility was questionable, Dowd also tracked down a second Rose associate, Ron Peters, who confirmed most of Janszen's allegations. Peters had credibility issues of his own, but the growing pile of evidence all pointed in the same direction: Rose had been betting, betting on baseball, and betting on the Reds while managing the team.

In April, Dowd deposed Rose, reminding him that failure to participate in the investigation would be reported to Giamatti. Rose understood the leverage: fail to cooperate and he would be suspended. Dowd interviewed Rose for two days, presenting him with evidence ranging from the betting slips to audiotapes in which Rose discussed betting on baseball. Rose's testimony was critical in setting in motion the events that followed. To no one's surprise, he went on the offensive, disparaging his accusers, dismissing the physical evidence, and lying about the crucial question of whether he had bet on baseball: The Hit King was all in.

The entire investigation played out on the front of the sports page, the last thing any of the participants preferred. Rose and Giamatti wanted the issue resolved behind closed doors, but a major investigation of one of the most important players in the history of the game was not going to unfold under wraps. Rose and his advisers attempted to shift the focus of the story to procedural problems and prejudicial decisions, putting Giamatti on the defensive as he attempted to simultaneously keep the focus on Rose and justify the investigation. The process wore heavily on the two principals: Giamatti, who was not only exposed to the seamiest side of a major representative of the sport he loved but also forced to defend what he felt was a fair and respectful investigation, and Rose, the blustery, hyperaggressive combatant whose lies finally appeared to be catching up with him.

On May 11, Giamatti informed Rose that he had received the report on the investigation and that he would hold a hearing in two weeks. Rose and his legal team responded with a letter of their own, demanding that Giamatti recuse himself from the case. The commissioner refused, and a week before the scheduled hearing, Rose sued the commissioner in an attempt to stop the hearing. On June 19, the case of *Peter Edward Rose v. A. Bartlett Giamatti* transformed the focus of the case from the investigation's results to the investigatory process and the jurisdiction from the office of the commissioner to an Ohio courtroom under an entirely different set of rules. The roles were now switched, as Rose's lawyers hammered away at the commissioner's conduct.

In the weeks that followed, the showdown between Rose and Giamatti grew increasingly bitter and expensive. Rose hemorrhaged money on his legal defense; the commissioner was physically and emotionally drained by the attacks on his integrity. Both sides recognized the need to resolve the issue out of court, and their representatives met privately to hammer out a deal.

Banished from the Game

On August 23, six months after the investigation began, Giamatti announced that Rose was banished from the game. To avoid any possibility of misinterpretation, the commissioner defined the breadth of the decision: Rose was not and could not be employed by any phase of organized baseball, at any level, nor could he hold a position with any broadcast organization approved by the team. He was barred from any Major League Baseball team clubhouse or front office and wasn't even permitted to play in an Old Timers game sanctioned by the league.

In negotiating the announcement, the two sides had agreed to avoid a formal finding on whether Rose had bet on baseball. At the conclusion of the commissioner's announcement, the first question he fielded from the press was whether he personally believed Rose had bet on baseball. Giamatti deflected the question, but the reporter pushed further, asking for his personal opinion. Giamatti responded: "In the absence of a hearing and therefore in the absence of evidence to the contrary, I am confronted with the factual record of Mr. Dowd. On the basis of that, yes, I have concluded he bet on baseball."[35]

The agreement left open the possibility of Rose returning from his banishment, assuming the player would show sufficient contrition and change his ways. But Giamatti's comments following the announcement stunned Rose and his lawyers. They not only felt that the commissioner had failed to honor the agreement not to cite a finding on the betting allegations but they also assumed that Giamatti's public conclusion might make reinstatement even more complicated than they had assumed, if it were to come at all.

Rose's press conference was even less comfortable than Giamatti's. The now-banished player assumed that he would not be banished for a long time, questioned Giamatti's responses to reporters' questions, denied he had a gambling problem and, therefore, ruled out counseling to help him with it, and appeared to have no plan for what he would do during his separation from baseball. Rose was back on his heels but, as usual, didn't seem to see why he should change anything he was doing.

Eight days after banishing Rose, only 154 days into his tenure as the commissioner of baseball, Giamatti died of a heart attack. Obituaries noted that he had been a longtime smoker, and his lifestyle clearly contributed to his demise, but it was impossible not to consider the toll that the Rose investigation had taken on his life.

Evading Taxes and Responsibility

Rose's ban from baseball may have been the most painful judgment he faced, but it wasn't the only one. His long-standing insistence on cash payments for appearances and signings led the federal government to investigate his tax returns for most of the 1980s, and by the end of the decade, he and his lawyers were working on yet another agreement to limit the damage. In August 1990, he was convicted of tax evasion. He appeared repentant before the judge but still refused to admit that he had bet on baseball.

With his banishment from the sport that defined him, Rose seemed to need the game more than ever. Giamatti had left the door open a crack, promising that his office would consider reinstatement, but only if Rose changed his ways. Even as he told anyone who would listen how important the game was to him, he continued to frequent horse races and accept appearances at casinos. He appeared oblivious to the causes of his demise.

Rose applied for reinstatement to baseball with two of Giamatti's successors—Fay Vincent in 1992 and Bud Selig in 1997. Neither commissioner would receive his application.

In the 15 years that followed the Dowd investigation, Rose continued to deny betting on baseball and the Reds in countless interviews, articles, and personal discussions. All of that changed in 2004 when he released an autobiography in which he admitted to gambling, gambling on baseball, and betting on the Reds. If Rose thought the admission would make him the prodigal son, he greatly miscalculated the public response. Many of his long-term supporters were crushed that they had defended him for years but had been wrong about the central issue in the case, and many of his detractors reveled in the opportunity to drag his name through the mud again. Still others felt that, at that point, his word had no credibility, so it was irrelevant what he said. One final group had simply tired of the sordid story.

Besides, what initially appeared to be the great mea culpa turned out to be less so on close reading. Rose still insisted that he never bet against the Reds, a huge distinction in his mind that was lost on most of his readers. He also made it clear that the reason for the admission was to gain access back into baseball. The book included redundant recitations of his baseball credentials, a barely disguised argument for his admission to the Hall of Fame. His narcissism still did not allow him to understand how much his actions and denials had hurt the game and his supporters. The commissioner's office was unmoved, and the banishment remained in place.

Baseball's Conundrum

Major League Baseball's commissioner has no jurisdiction over the game's Hall of Fame. In 1991, the hall's directors amended their organization's eligibility rules to make anyone on baseball's permanently ineligible list also ineligible to appear on the ballot for the hall. Rose's name never appeared in the amended language, but to date, he is the only person impacted by it. The decision made the balloting process irrelevant: it no longer mattered how voters for Hall of Fame selection—the Baseball Writers Association of America—felt about Rose's inclusion in the hall, because as long as he is banned from Major League Baseball, his name will never appear on a ballot.

In his waning years, baseball's Hit King continues to squander the remnants of his case for reinstatement in the game and acceptance in the hall. He remains convinced that his enormous contributions to the game should stand on their own. The men who ultimately make that decision, in the Major League Baseball executive offices in New York City and the committee rooms of the National Baseball Hall of Fame committee rooms in Cooperstown, New York, disagree.

The NBA Official: Tim Donaghy

Hornung, Karras, McLain, and Rose are the most famous examples of modern professional athletes who brought scandal to their leagues through gambling. In 2007, however, the National Basketball League was forced to respond to a betting scandal from an unexpected source: a referee. By the time it was over, league officials throughout the country were forced to review their policies, not only for the men who played their games, but for the men who officiated them as well.

A Pattern of Deception

Tim Donaghy grew up in an environment steeped in officiating tradition. He is the son of Gerald Donaghy, a veteran NCAA referee, and was raised in Delaware County, Pennsylvania, an area that produced an extraordinary number of professional basketball players, coaches, and officials. During his formative years at Cardinal O'Hara High School, Donaghy developed a reputation as a hard-working basketball and baseball player. In the classroom, however, he was also known for taking academic shortcuts. "I taught him for a year, and I think every homework assignment he turned in to me was copied,"[36] a former teacher later told the New York *Daily News* when his scandal went public. It was at Cardinal O'Hara that Donaghy met James Battista, a fellow student who would also be implicated in the gambling scandal.

Donaghy was suspected of having another student take part of his SAT. The allegations were never proven, but the disputed test scores were high enough to get him into Villanova University, where he was also suspected of cheating, according to one of his high school teachers. As the son of a well-respected college official, however, Donaghy was also given an opportunity to prove himself as a referee, and he worked hard to secure a full-time position officiating basketball games. By 1994, he had established himself as a professional and was hired to work for the NBA. Unfortunately, the ethical cloud that had swirled around his academic career followed him into his professional work as well.

Public and Private Warning Signs

The NBA's first indication that Donaghy might have behavior problems came in January 2005, when a long-running dispute between the referee and a neighbor in West Chester, Pennsylvania, escalated to harassment allegations. Donaghy denied the allegations, claiming that he was the victim, and league officials accepted his explanation but hired a private investigator to look into the possibility of anger management issues as well as rumors that the ref had been gambling in Atlantic City. Donaghy denied those rumors as well, and while Commissioner David Stern once again took him at his word, he also removed Donaghy from the second-round playoff rotation, a high-profile position he had held the prior season. Donaghy moved from Pennsylvania to Florida, presumably leaving his problems behind.

Later that year, however, the FBI, which had been looking into the Gambino crime syndicate in New York City, heard Donaghy's name on a wiretap involving his high school friend, Battista. In November, the FBI opened an investigation of Donaghy that continued for the next two years.

In December 2006, the FBI found, Donaghy began providing insider information via phone to professional gamblers on referee assignments, player health, relationships between players and refs—information that could provide just enough of an edge for a gambler to improve his odds. Donaghy's actions were the sports equivalent of insider trading.

Initially the ref was paid $2,000 per win for his information, an amount eventually increased to $5,000. The FBI wiretaps revealed that on December 13, 2006, Donaghy spoke on the phone with either Thomas Martino or James Battista, the same night that he officiated a Sixers–Celtics game in Philadelphia. The next day, the FBI alleged, Donaghy met with Martino to collect his payment for the information he had provided. Two weeks later, Donaghy spoke with the gambler prior to refereeing a Wizards–Grizzlies game and was then paid a few weeks later in Toronto.

Donaghy's descent into gambling addiction was similar to Hornung's pattern in the NFL. It began with a seemingly innocent, long-term relationship with a friend who operated on the fringes of organized crime and accelerated when the friend began asking for inside tips that would help in betting decisions. It wasn't long before the player himself wanted a taste of the action and began betting on games himself. Once again, the pattern that sports leagues fear the most and fight hardest against was unfolding— small steps that can result in a player (or, in Donaghy's rare case, an official) being connected to organized crime and the temptation to fix a game.

The FBI and the NBA

By June 2007, the FBI had amassed enough evidence to take its case to the NBA. FBI officials met league representatives, laying out their case and requesting cooperation in an attempt to gain the league's support in the investigation. League officials promised full and immediate cooperation, then agreed to keep the investigation quiet and avoid the temptation to question the ref for their own purposes or fire him to avoid additional damage. With both sides agreeing to avoid publicity, the league had time to develop a communications plan.

A scandal this big wouldn't stay out of the press for long, and by early July, reporters began posting stories about rumors of an investigation. The *New York Post* broke the story, an unnamed law enforcement official confirmed the investigation to the Associated Press, and Donaghy's attorney admitted that the ref was under investigation. The media now had a name to go with the rumors, and, of course, immediately began poring over tapes of the games that Donaghy had officiated to attempt to identify any suspicious patterns. They were looking for games that featured significant differences in the number of foul shots per team, game scores in relation to point spreads, or anything else that indicated that the ref was making calls to throw a game one way or the other.

Donaghy realized that the game was up, and on the ninth of July, he resigned from the league.

In the NBA offices, officials were in damage control mode, attempting to at least appear ahead of the fast-moving story. Commissioner David Stern released a statement on July 20 saying:

> We would like to assure our fans that no amount of effort, time or personnel is being spared to assist in this investigation, to bring to justice an individual who has betrayed the most sacred trust in professional sports, and to take the necessary steps to protect against this ever happening again.[37]

On the same day, Dallas Mavericks owner Mark Cuban, a consistent critic of the officiating in the league, attempted to accent the positive in a blog post:

> As bad as the allegations facing the NBA today are, it's also an opportunity to face every allegation that has ever been directed towards the NBA and its officials and preempt them from ever occurring in the future. Calamity can be a catalyst for significant change.
>
> The NBA took a hit today. Behind that hit is a catalyst and opportunity for significant change that could make the NBA stronger than it ever has been. I have complete confidence that David Stern and [NBA Deputy Commissioner/COO] Adam Silver will do just that and the NBA and our officiating will be all the stronger for it.[38]

Four days later, Stern held a press conference to address the case. "This is the most serious situation and the worst situation that I have ever experienced either as a fan of the NBA, a lawyer of the NBA or the commissioner of the NBA,"[39] Stern said. Reporters peppered him with a series of "what did you know and when did you know it?" questions, and Stern stressed the league's cooperation with the FBI and the fact that no other referee was involved in the investigation. Reporting on the news conference, *New York Times* reporter Selena Roberts blasted the commissioner and the league's culture of coddling refs, citing the league's decision to reinstate referees caught in an airline ticket exchange scandal in the 1990s, and citing ethical compromises that "provided a petri dish perfect to develop a rogue official."[40] She concluded: "Protectionism isn't what referees need. Protectionism is how the league got into this fix."[41]

On August 15, 2007, Donaghy appeared in Brooklyn's U.S. District Court to plead guilty to two felonies: conspiracy to commit wire fraud and conspiracy to transmit wagering information over state lines. The maximum penalty for the two counts was 25 years in jail and $500,000 in fines. The charges did not include accusations of point-shaving or game fixing. During court proceedings, Donaghy noted that he suffered from depression and was taking antianxiety drugs and was also being treated for a gambling disorder. While Donaghy appeared in court, his coconspirators, Thomas Martino and James Battista, were also being arraigned.

Meanwhile, on the day of the plea, the NBA released a statement attempting to address the concerns of a growing number of basketball fans:

> As expected, former N.B.A. referee Tim Donaghy pleaded guilty today to betting on N.B.A. games, including games in which he officiated, and providing confidential information to others who bet on N.B.A. games. We will continue with our ongoing and thorough review of the league's officiating program to ensure that the best possible policies and procedures are in place to protect the integrity of our game.[42]

In the firestorm that followed, fans and reporters watched closely to see what changes Stern would make to address the scandal. Interestingly, prior to the 2007–2008 season, he had made two changes that, on the surface, appear counterintuitive. First, he relaxed rules that forbade game officials from gambling at casinos. While critics argued that this could increase gambling losses and bring referees closer to organized crime, Stern reasoned that the rule was unenforceable. In announcing the casino decision, Stern also stated that he would not punish referees who were found to have violated the policy. Stern also announced that referee assignments, which had been announced at game time, would now be announced the morning of the game. Presumably, this would mitigate any advantage that knowledge of referee assignments would have, since anyone who was gambling would have the entire day to react to the information.

The League Attempts to Move Forward

If there is any doubt about the damage a gambling scandal can do to a league, the Donaghy story removes it. Once the news that he had gambled on games he officiated went public, fans and members of the media were far more wary not only of questionable shots or passes by players but also of debatable calls by referees. The integrity of the game suffered considerable damage, and restoring league credibility became a long-term project.

In July 2008, the league moved to improve the league's officiating by hiring two new administrators: retired Army major general Ronald L. Johnson, who was charged with overseeing the referee operations, and retired referee Bernie Fryer, who was appointed as vice president and director of officials. Both proved to be effective in their positions, and Fryer in particular was an excellent choice—he was well respected in the officiating community not only for his refereeing skills but also for his ethical standards, was one of only three league officials who had also played in the NBA, and had retired from the league during the Donaghy scandal, apparently upset at the league's approach to working with officials. Fryer's appointment was embraced by many players, officials, and reporters who covered the game, who felt that he combined an insider's knowledge of the situation with an outsider's passion to improve it. The two appointments came at a particularly challenging time: some referees were being accused of having cozy relationships with star players and others were considered too combative. With the increasing use of video technology, each call the refs made was now analyzed in super–slow motion from multiple angles, increasing the amount of second-guessing over close calls.

Donaghy began serving his sentence on September 23, and while league administrators hoped that his incarceration would create some closure, they continued to work on innovations that would improve the league's image. In October, Stern announced the results of its 14-month investigation into the gambling scandal: Former prosecutor and lead investigator Lawrence B. Pedowitz found that no other officials had bet on games, provided insider information to gamblers, or attempted to alter the outcome of a game. He also concluded that, in the 17 games in which Donaghy had refereed and also provided gamblers with information, there was no evidence that he had manipulated the outcomes. Pedowitz also found that Donaghy's most explosive accusation, that other NBA refs and officials had manipulated the outcome of games, was unfounded.

Critics were unhappy that the league had, essentially, investigated itself and that the findings appeared to conveniently quarantine Donaghy from the rest of the league. But Stern argued that the NBA was working to be as transparent as possible and would take additional steps to increase accountability in the future. He noted that the idea that "criminal activity will exist every place else in the world except in sports is just something that we can't guarantee, but we're going to have the most effective possible system that's ever been devised."[43] The commissioner concluded:

> This is just something that we—I mean, we've always known, but as gambling continues to grow in this country and around the world, this is something that we're going to have to keep addressing to decide when the edge that gamblers try to get should be blunted by public release of information and other rules that we will try to implement.[44]

Lessons Never Learned

If Donaghy was contrite, he didn't show it. While serving his sentence, the disgraced referee wrote *Personal Foul: A First-Person Account of the Scandal that Rocked the NBA,* an attempt to rehabilitate his image while tarnishing that of the league. He admitted to gambling but insisted that he had never fixed a game, arguing that a traditional fix was unnecessary because insider knowledge about which officials disliked which players and coaches would be sufficient to make a winning bet. Donaghy's line of reasoning was frustrating, but his next line of work was appalling. Released from prison in November 2009 after serving 11 months, he founded a Web site, Refpicks .com, that provides gambling tips on a variety of sports, including the NBA. The self-described gambling addict apparently thought it was reasonable to make his next career move an even closer connection to the gambling industry. Donaghy's book would also keep him in the news, as he eventually sued the publisher for breach of contract and civil theft and was awarded $1.6 million. With the convicted felon happy to spout online about point spreads and ref biases for various NBA games, the public relations nightmare that was Tim Donaghy refused to go away.

In 2014, as this book was being written, Refpicks.com was still an active site and Tim Donaghy was featured prominently on the home page. Donaghy's biography on the site boasts his "winning percentage" and claims that he has an advantage over other handicappers because of his insider experience as an official and his knowledge of what affects the scores of games. The league's response is to ignore him as much as possible, but his multimedia presence serves as a reminder of the ongoing danger that gambling poses to the integrity of sports.

Conclusion

Football, baseball, basketball. Players and referees. Gambling scandals transcend specific sports or the roles of the participants. Leagues vary in their policies, but they have all been tarnished by hardcore gamblers unwilling or unable to control their addictions. These gamblers are often coddled individuals who have broken social and organizational rules throughout their lives but have not suffered the consequences because of their athletic talents, connections, or positions. Some of them, such as Hornung, renounce their decisions and change their ways. Others, such as Rose, McLain, and Donaghy, never grasp the destructiveness of their behavior, despite the damage it has done to their careers, personal relationships, and reputations. Instead, they rail against their persecution, blame their mistakes on naïveté or poor selections of friends, and continue to act as though they are misunderstood or are victims of circumstance. In the end, they refuse to acknowledge or curtail the conduct that has led to their demise.

The leagues are not without blame. League administrators often promote the hero worship culture that reinforces the message that their members are different and that rules do not apply to them. When league interests are threatened, administrators are often insular and self-protective, traits that can hinder the changes necessary for the health of the organization.

NBA commissioner David Stern's warning that gambling is big and getting bigger in America is prescient. Betting is increasingly acceptable to Americans, technological advances continue to make gambling more accessible, and the media, particularly cable and network television, offer ever-expanding revenue and coverage for major league sports.

League administrators must continue to address the growing gambling problem by developing policies on multiple fronts, including early and ongoing education programs, closer monitoring of employees, penalties big enough to alter behavior, support for members who seek assistance, and even more transparent approaches to sharing information with fans and the media. The stakes are high and getting higher, as the continued growth of gambling threatens the integrity of the games.

Chapter 10

The Social Contract: Scandals That Transcend Sports

Sports and society occasionally differ on how seriously they judge particular forms of misconduct. For example, deliberately losing a game is the most egregious sin in sports but a relatively minor violation in general society, while a DUI conviction is a serious offense to the general public but a trifling infraction to some professional athletes.

If the misbehavior is sufficiently inexcusable, however, sports and society reinforce each other's values in their response. As Shakespeare wrote in *Hamlet,* murder is "most foul, dangerous, and unnatural." It is irrelevant whether the murderer is a professional athlete.

Or is it?

This chapter examines murder scandals involving a trio of sports figures: O. J. Simpson, Rae Carruth, and Ray Lewis. All three are African American males who emerged from difficult economic circumstances to excel in college and professional football. Many Americans are convinced that they each committed murder, but only one (Carruth) was convicted. Simpson was found not guilty and Lewis not only wasn't convicted but clearly didn't kill anyone.

Media coverage of the scandals differed significantly, based on the player's popularity, his status in the league (active vs. retired) at the time of the crime, and, to some degree, the sensational qualities of the murder. At the time of the crimes, Carruth was a competent starter in his third season, Lewis was a Pro Bowl standout in his fourth year in the league, and Simpson was a retired Hall of Famer. All three of the cases had sensational elements, none more than Simpson's, which was a particularly brutal stabbing involving a beautiful woman and occurring in a media-rich environment. The murders associated with Lewis also involved a knife, but the victims (two African American males) were relatively unknown and the environment (the late-night club scene in Atlanta) was less likely to attract significant media coverage. Carruth's crime, the only one of the three to be premeditated, involved the contract shooting of his pregnant girlfriend, two elements that clearly added to the sensational nature of his crime.

The Lewis and Carruth stories received some degree of national coverage but, as they progressed, became more local stories, frequently relegated to the sports page. Neither is remotely comparable to the coverage of the murders Simpson was charged with: his story dominated the American news media as much as any story in modern American history. There were significant differences among the scandals, the players' complicity, and the trial results, but each seriously damaged the image of the NFL.

O. J. Simpson

For most of his life, Orenthal James "O. J." Simpson, nicknamed "Juice," succeeded in whatever he tried to do and looked good doing it. Raised in a San Francisco housing project, Simpson was a football phenomenon from an early age. He was the star athlete at his high school, a nationally acclaimed running back in junior college, and the leading rusher in the nation for consecutive seasons at one of the nation's premier programs, the University of Southern California. In 1968, he was awarded the Heisman Trophy, and a year later the Buffalo Bills made him the first pick in the NFL draft.

A powerhouse on the field, Simpson was equally charismatic off of it. He was admired by men, attractive to women, and, a rare marketing commodity, a crossover athlete who appealed to both black and white audiences. Before his NFL career even began, he was already a multimedia phenomenon, with movie and television roles and an impressive list of endorsement contracts. "Simpson's potential is nearly limitless," veteran sportswriter Frank Deford reported when the Bills drafted their new star. "He is not only charming and good-looking, but still unaffected. His appeal is established, almost as if his career had been programmed by a market research agency. He grew up in Northern California, grew famous in Southern California and will (if he goes to Buffalo) establish still another metropolitan popularity base in the East."[1]

The Bills were a small-market team with a sporadic record, however, and Simpson was unsure of whether he could thrive in northwestern New York state. His negotiations with the team were contentious, including a public request to be traded, but he eventually agreed to a contract. Once he put on the uniform, he quickly established himself as one of the premier players in the league, and the accolades quickly followed. The Juice won the league's rushing title four times, including 1973, when he became the first player in NFL history to run for more than 2,000 yards in a season. He played in six pro bowls and was named the NFL player of the year three times. After nine years in small-market Buffalo, he played his final two years for the San Francisco 49ers before retiring in 1979 as the second-leading rusher in league history. O. J. was elected to the pro football Hall of Fame in 1985, the same year that he married his second wife, the blond and beautiful Nicole Brown.

During his career, Simpson's list of endorsements was as long as it was varied: Honeybaked Ham, Dingo Boots, Calistoga Water, the pX Corporation, and, most famously, Hertz Rental Cars, which included a series of television commercials featuring the former running back dashing through an airport, dodging obstacles the same way he ran past opponents on the football field.

When his football career was over, Simpson returned to Southern California to pursue an acting career. Between 1988 and 1994, Simpson costarred in a trio of *Naked Gun* films, a series of low comedies in which he played a bumbling detective. By this phase of his career, Simpson was almost as well known as a media personality as he was as a football player, and his public image reflected his character in the films—a happy-go-lucky guy laughing his way through life. His private world, however, was a different story: as his media career progressed, his marriage to Nicole Brown disintegrated. In 1989, Simpson's wife filed charges of domestic abuse, he pleaded guilty, and the couple separated, divorcing in 1992. The same year, Hertz, the source of his biggest endorsement contract, quietly began to deemphasize Simpson in its advertising campaign.

The Double Murder That Shocked the Nation

Just after midnight on June 12, 1994, police found the bodies of Nicole Brown Simpson and her friend, Ronald Goldman, outside of her home in Brentwood, California. The scene was a bloodbath: O. J.'s ex-wife had been slashed across the upper torso and throat, and Goldman had been stabbed 22 times. Since his relationship with his wife had been contentious in the years after their divorce, Simpson was an immediate suspect. He was also wealthy, famous, and well connected, however, so police proceeded cautiously with the case, bringing him in for questioning but not immediately arresting him.

It took five days, but the police eventually charged Simpson with double homicide. When he did not turn himself in, he was declared a fugitive. Simpson was spotted in the back of a Ford Bronco driven by a friend, and police began to follow the vehicle. National television broke into traditional programming to report breathlessly on what became an infamous low-speed "chase," as Simpson traversed 60 miles of Los Angeles freeways until the episode ended anticlimactically, with Simpson returning to his home in Brentwood, followed by a string of police cars. The media coverage of the "chase" was excessive, but a harbinger of the sensationalism to come.

The Trial of the Century

Simpson's trial began on January 25, 1995, and the suspect's notoriety and the murders' sensational details combined to produce a perfect media storm: over the next eight months, American newspapers published daily reports of the most minute details of the case, network news covered the story on a nightly basis, and 24-hour cable, still relatively new, made the Simpson case the centerpiece of its programming. The trial was a national obsession, with Americans debating courtroom strategies, the veracity of the witnesses, and the relevance of the evidence. In the process, the trial exposed and exacerbated the nation's racial divide, with the vast majority of the white population convinced of Simpson's guilt and a large portion of the African American population convinced that he had been unfairly targeted by a racist system.

On October 3, 1995, Simpson was acquitted of both counts of murder. America's response was intense but divided, mostly along racial lines. Many African Americans cheered the verdict, while the vast majority of white Americans were outraged, convinced that the football star had walked away from the crime because his expensive legal "dream team" had obfuscated the facts and confused the jury.

The Juice was loose, but only briefly: 20 days after his acquittal, he was back in court on civil charges in a wrongful death suit brought by the victims' families. The second trial dragged on far longer than the first, and in February of 1997, a jury found him liable for the deaths of both victims and awarded their estates a $33.5 million judgment. The decision was anticlimactic and largely symbolic, however, since Simpson would serve no jail time and claimed that he did not have the money to pay the judgment. He was ordered to turn over his golf clubs and his Heisman trophy, but was a free man, his every public appearance a symbol of injustice to the majority of Americans who thought he had gotten away with murder.

The NFL Holds Fast

Most of the companies that had signed Simpson as a spokesperson began to distance themselves from him as soon as the homicides were announced, not waiting for the conclusion of the trial. From a marketing perspective, the legal outcome was irrelevant: it was essential for organizations to disassociate their brands as quickly as possible from any person even remotely connected with such a gruesome crime. How to handle Simpson was far more complicated for the pitchman's former employer, however. Simpson was not only the most famous player in the history of the Buffalo Bills, he was also a prominent member of the NFL's Hall of Fame. What should a sports league do when one of its most well-known players is accused of a horrible crime but is no longer participating in the games?

In some ways, the acquittal was even worse for the league than a conviction might have been. Had Simpson been locked away, he would have been out of sight and, to some degree, out of mind. But he was free and unapologetic, and his public appearances were an ongoing reminder that a man appeared to have gotten away with a grisly double murder and that part of the reason he got off may have been the fame and fortune that he had gained through the NFL.

Baltimore Sun columnist John Steadman preempted discussion about the league's options with an unequivocal defense: "As a sportswriter who voted for Simpson's election to both the college and pro football halls of fame, let it be said with strong conviction that what he was able to do on the field should be the only yardstick of evaluation," Steadman wrote, "The Pro Football Hall of Fame doesn't have to act. It can keep Simpson in place among its deified heroes because good citizenship has nothing to do with getting elected."[2] Steadman didn't simply advocate inaction, he guaranteed it: "The Pro Football Hall of Fame won't make a move, unless advised to depart from its rules by the urging of commissioner Paul Tagliabue or the hall's board of directors, which has a federal judge among its membership."[3]

Steadman proved correct: Hall of Fame officials refused to consider Simpson's removal. The administrators could have rationalized their decision based on the jury's decision: despite the public's verdict, he had been found not guilty. Such a defense would have been problematic if Simpson eventually was convicted, however, so they defended their decision by relying on existing policy: not only was the election process based entirely on the players' productivity on the field but there was no review process to reevaluate a player who had been accepted. Despite passionate protests from many football fans and sportswriters, the league held fast: Simpson would remain in the hall.

Legal Troubles Continue

When the trial ended, Simpson vowed to continue the search for his ex-wife's killer, an additional affront to the sensibilities of the majority of

Americans. He was free but a pariah in his own world. His entertainment career was over, although over the next few years he agreed to be involved in two extremely offensive media projects: a video game in which his image was used for a team called "Assassins" that featured a knife-wielding mascot and a coauthored book called *If I Did It,* in which he denied having killed his wife but explained how he would have done it had he committed the crime. Both projects simply added to the disgust people felt toward him. His lawyers managed to shield his pensions, nearly $400,000, from the civil judgment, and he was able to generate income by selling memorabilia and signing autographs. And, in some bizarre way, he continued to capitalize on his notoriety. "The provenance of fame is pointless," noted sportswriter Richard Hoffer. "Being known—whether it's for double murders or rushing records—is all that matters. O. J. Simpson cadged free drinks and scored sweet babes ("curb girls," his handlers called them) in his exile exactly as he did in his glory years. His fame insulated him from prison, poverty, and a life without golf. . . ."[4]

Simpson's pattern of violent behavior and avoiding incarceration also continued. Four years after his civil conviction, he was arrested on battery and auto burglary charges related to a road rage incident in Florida but was found not guilty in the case.

Justice for O. J. Simpson was delayed, but, ultimately, not denied. In September 2007, Simpson and five associates broke into a cheap Las Vegas hotel room to recover a collection of sports collectables from two memorabilia dealers. Two of Simpson's accomplices were carrying guns, which significantly increased the gravity of the crime. Simpson's defense was that the items in question belonged to him, but the local district attorney concluded otherwise. Prosecutors zeroed in on the former NFL star and offered plea deals to four of his associates, all of whom testified for the prosecution and eventually received probation for their parts in the crime.

In October 2008, Simpson's string of court victories came to an end. Thirteen years to the day after he was acquitted in the double homicide, the NFL Hall of Famer was convicted on 12 counts, including conspiracy, burglary, armed robbery, and kidnapping, in the Las Vegas case. Simpson was sentenced to 9 to 33 years in prison. The legal decision was somewhat anticlimactic: "By the time O. J. Simpson stood up in court late Friday to hear the spray of guilty verdicts on robbery and kidnapping charges that may send him to prison for the rest of his life, he was already so far removed from the heights of his fame and popularity that an entire generation of young Americans was barely aware that he had ever been a football star,"[5] noted a reporter for the *New York Times.*

In the years that followed, O. J.'s name occasionally resurfaced in the press when he attempted an appeal or a current running back threatened one of his records, but in general, his conviction closed the book, and he was left to languish behind bars.

Clinging to a Policy, Regardless of Public Perception

Simpson's felony convictions eliminated the defense that he could not be banned from a Hall of Fame because he had never been convicted of a serious crime, but football administrators remained adamant that his status remain unchanged: there was simply no process for dismissing a member of the college or professional halls of fame.

The College Football Hall of Fame, which had inducted the former USC star in 1983, considered how a candidate had lived his or her life as part of its selection process, but had no written policy on morality or ethics for accepted candidates. Following Simpson's 2008 conviction, Steve Hatchell, president of the National Football Foundation, stated that Simpson's status would be reviewed, but there were no plans to remove him; and he remains a member of the hall today.

In Canton, Ohio, the eligibility and retention policies for members of professional football's Hall of Fame were clear and consistent: criteria for selection are limited to a player's on-field accomplishments, and there are no procedures for reviewing the status of an inductee once he has been selected. Simpson had been accepted and would not be removed. In Buffalo, the Bills relied on the hall's policy to reinforce their own and refused to remove Simpson from the team's Hall of Fame.

In the years since Simpson began his sentence, media members still raise the occasional question about the star-turned-prisoner's status. When a *USA Today* columnist challenged the NFL Hall of Fame's refusal to review Simpson's case in 2007, Joe Horrigan, the Hall of Fame's vice president of communications/exhibits, responded:

> Did he play for the Buffalo Bills? Yes. We can't say he did not. Did he have a great career as a Buffalo Bill? Yes. We can't say he did not. . . . He was elected based on his playing career, and he remains there based on his playing career. There are no provisions in the bylaws to ever remove someone from the Hall of Fame. . . . He's one of 241. For the moment, we feel comfortable with our criteria for election to the Hall of Fame, which are based solely on a player's on-the-field performance.[6]

In a 2010 opinion piece, NBC Sports reporter Gregg Rosenthal revisited the question, asking whether a retired player should be considered any different from an active one, since he collects a pension from, and continues to represent, the organization. What about other players, such as Lawrence Taylor, a legendary linebacker who was also tried (but not convicted) on a rape charge? "The NFL should be proud of every man enshrined in Canton, and every parent who takes a child to the Hall of Fame shouldn't have to quickly nudge him or her along when they linger before the image of a man who has posed both for a bronze bust and for a mug shot,"[7] Rosenthal argued.

Rosenthal suggested that the NFL follow recent decisions from Major League Baseball. When MLB banned Pete Rose from the game, the Hall of Fame in Cooperstown used the decision as a cover for its own refusal to allow a vote on his candidacy. "There should be a procedure in place for cutting ties with men who commit heinous acts after their careers end," Rosenthal suggested. "Whether it's done via hard-and-fast rules or on a case-by-case basis, former players should be subject to the same type of banishment that sports like baseball aren't bashful about using, when justified."[8]

Regardless of the consensus of football fans or the indignation of the occasional sports columnist, Orenthal James Simpson remains a member in good standing in the halls reserved for the most revered players in football. In Canton, the busts of members are arranged in the order in which they are inducted, so Simpson is almost directly in the center. The plate that accompanies his bust lists his on-field accomplishments, nothing more and nothing less.

Rae Carruth

Rae Carruth was born Rae Lamar Wiggins, a name he abandoned after his biological father left the family. His mother, Theodry, raised him in a crime-ridden section of Sacramento, California, and when she married his stepfather, Rae accepted his mother's new husband's name as well.

From an early age, Carruth dominated in sports but displayed a quiet, almost shy persona once the games had ended. The combination made him popular with women, and he quickly learned to juggle multiple romances, a pattern that he would follow throughout his athletic career.

Carruth earned a scholarship to the University of Colorado in 1992, where he had over a thousand yards' receiving in back-to-back seasons. During his sophomore year, he fathered a son with a girlfriend back in Sacramento. He did not return to Sacramento but stayed on in Boulder, and in 1997 was drafted in the first round by the Carolina Panthers, who offered him a four-year $3.7 million contract.

Carolina coaches were convinced that they had made the right choice when the team's new star led all rookies in number of catches and receiving yards in his first year in the league. In his second year, however, he was forced to the sideline with a broken foot after only two games, the start of a long and frustrating year of rehabilitation to get back on the field.

Carruth's third season as a Panther started out with promise: He made 14 catches in the first 5 games, and his private life appeared to be stabilizing as well: he was happy to learn that his new girlfriend, Cherica Adams, was pregnant with his second child. In October 1999, however, Carruth's life changed abruptly when he suffered an ankle sprain in a game against the 49ers, an injury that would keep him out of the lineup for a month. Rae's physical problems were compounded by financial ones, as writer Peter Richmond noted:

> Frequently injured, no longer a starter, Rae had by now become that singularly sorry football phenomenon: a first-round draft pick gone bust. Taxes and agents had taken half the bonus. He'd invested in a car-title-loan scam that had promised the trappings of easy money—and lost his money. He'd hired former wide receiver Tank Black, later indicted on fraud charges, to manage his money. He'd signed a contract on a new house, but he'd had to pull out when he couldn't get the financing, and the owners had sued him.[9]

The change in Carruth's football status affected his role as a father-to-be, according to Adams' mother, Saundra: "He seemed to be more pressured after his injury—more pressured about money and how much the baby was going to cost him."[10] Initially supportive of Adams's pregnancy, Carruth now urged Adams to abort the baby, but she refused. The struggling wide receiver began considering increasingly desperate alternatives to escape his constraints. He reached out to an accomplice, Michael Kennedy, and began planning ways to eliminate his pregnant girlfriend, their child, or both. Some of the ideas were as bizarre as they were horrific: Kennedy later testified that Carruth suggested that he could accompany Adams to a childbirth course, then have Kennedy beat her up after the class so that she would miscarry. The scenarios were fanciful but cold-blooded: it was apparent that Carruth planned on finding a way to end his financial burdens.

The Adams Ambush

On the evening of November 15, 1999, Carruth and Adams attended a movie in Charlotte, then stopped back at his house so that she could get her BMW. From his home, Carruth called Kennedy to alert him that the two were leaving the house in separate cars. Shortly after midnight, Carruth led Adams to a deserted, windy stretch called Rea Road on the outskirts of Charlotte. He slowed his vehicle to a crawl, forcing Adams to reduce her speed. A car carrying three men, Kennedy, Van Brett Watkins, and Stanley Abraham Jr., pulled alongside Adams's car, and Watkins shot Adams four times, in the chest, neck, and abdomen. One of the bullets came within an inch of her unborn child.

The four men sped off in different directions, leaving Adams alone in the dark. Despite her wounds, the pregnant woman managed to call 911, describe the shooting, and provide Carruth's license plate number. When the paramedics arrived, Adams, unable to speak, used a notepad to write a description of the attack.

At the hospital, doctors performed an emergency caesarean section to save Adams's child, a baby boy born 10 weeks premature. Shortly after the operation, Adams slipped into a coma. The mother and child were listed in critical condition.

Carruth Is Arrested, the NFL Responds

With Adams's description to work from, police quickly identified the suspects. Nine days after the shooting, they arrested Carruth and charged him with conspiracy to commit murder. Within two more days, the police had arrested his coconspirators.

The Carolina Panthers excused their star receiver from team activities as soon as the word of the shooting went public. On the day of the arrest, team officials released a statement saying that, in accordance with NFL rules, Carruth would most likely be placed on a paid leave of absence.

Quarterback Steve Beuerlein told the press: "I'd be lying if I said we weren't all surprised that this whole thing could ever develop. In my heart I wanted to and still want to believe that he's not involved. But that's because he's a teammate. He's a part of our family."[11]

Panthers coach George Seifert told reporters: "I'm certainly disappointed. I think all of us all along were concerned about the young lady and the baby and certainly Rae being involved in this. We were hoping that it wouldn't come down to this."[12]

On December 2, the team placed their troubled wide receiver on leave of absence without pay.

Since Adams was still alive when the prosecutor announced the charges, Carruth could be freed on bail, which was set at $3 million. He posted a bond and was released. Adams died on December 14, however, and prosecutors immediately announced that the charges against the four men were upgraded to first-degree murder and issued an arrest warrant for Carruth. When he didn't turn himself in, the FBI began searching for him. The Carolina Panthers announced that they had cut him.

Carruth's plan to flee was as ill conceived as the murder plot. His mother, fearing for his safety, provided his bail bondsman with a description of the woman she thought he was with and the car that they would be driving. Within 24 hours of Carruth's disappearance, FBI agents found their target in the trunk of a Toyota Camry in a motel parking lot more than 400 miles from his home in Charlotte.

Trials for the Player and the League

At Carruth's trial, prosecutors presented an overwhelming case. The player's parade of ex-girlfriends testified that he expressed resentment about paying child support and hoped that Adams would have a miscarriage. Kennedy, the driver in the shooting, testified that Carruth had provided him with $100 to buy the murder weapon and had set up the ambush and slowed his car to force Adams to stop. And finally, prosecutors played their most emotional card, the audiotape of Adams's phone call from the scene of the crime.

Carruth's defense team presented a forensic psychologist who testified as to Carruth's ability to resolve conflicts in a nonviolent manner and argued that Watkins had made a statement in jail that he had shot Adams in retribution against Carruth for a drug deal gone bad, a statement Watkins denied. Carolina Panther fans were horrified that their star player might have been involved in such a crime. North Carolina citizens had an additional reason to be upset: the defendant had been declared indigent, so the costs of his trial lawyers, jury consultant, and investigative team were paid for by the state's taxpayers.

On January 22, 2001, the jury acquitted Carruth of first-degree murder, the charge that was punishable by death, but found him guilty of conspiracy to commit murder, discharging a firearm into occupied territory, and using an instrument with intent to destroy an unborn child. Judge Charles Lamm sentenced the former star to 24 years and 4 months in jail, with no eligibility for parole.

The Carolina Panthers released a statement saying, "This has been a most difficult ordeal for everyone involved. We respect the legal process that has run its course."[13] The NFL did not release a statement.

Appeals Denied

Throughout the scandal, the Carolina Panthers and the NFL provided minimal communication with fans or the general public. The team released terse statements to announce the organizations' rapid movements to distance themselves as thoroughly and quickly as possible from the player and the crime; league representatives said next to nothing.

Unfortunately for them, Carruth would not disappear entirely from the sports pages. During the trial, Adams's mother gained emergency custody of the newborn child, and Carruth countered by filing for permanent custody of the son who had almost died from his mother's bullet wounds. It was a claim that *Sports Illustrated* writer Thomas Lake called "one of the more brazen counterclaims in the annals of U.S. jurisprudence."[14] It was one more demonstration of the world according to Rae Carruth.

In the decade following his conviction, the former wide receiver gave a series of interviews denying any involvement in Adams's murder and continued to press to overturn his sentence. From 2001 to 2011, in legal venues from Mecklenburg, North Carolina, to the Supreme Court in Washington, D.C., his lawyers appealed the conviction on the grounds that Adams's 911 phone call and the note she scribbled at the hospital were inadmissible evidence and should never have been introduced in his trial. In the end, the appeals court denied their requests—not because some of the evidence should not have been admitted, but because there was sufficient evidence from other sources to show Carruth's guilt.

In September 2012, the Carruth story surfaced again in a *Sports Illustrated* article that detailed the status of the former wide receiver; his son, who was born with cerebral palsy because of the trauma on the day of his birth; and the boy's grandmother, who remains his primary caregiver.

Carruth's projected release date from the North Carolina Department of Corrections is October 22, 2018. Long after his release, his crime, a conspiracy to shoot dead the mother of his unborn child, will remain one of the most significant scandals in the history of professional football.

Ray Lewis

One way for an organization to counter bad publicity is by diverting attention to positive stories. If the NFL couldn't stop the media from covering Rae Carruth, it could at least offer up the narrative of other well-known athletes, and the NFL worked hard to promote its biggest names. Among them was the tenacious, highly quotable middle linebacker for the Baltimore Ravens, Ray Lewis.

As the 1999 football season came to an end, Lewis was emerging as the league's most recognizable defensive star. In his fourth year as a pro, he led the NFL in tackles, sacked quarterbacks eight times, forced a fumble, and intercepted three passes, earning him his third consecutive trip to the Pro Bowl. He was talented, passionate, and charismatic, and league officials were happy to promote him as one of the biggest personalities in professional football. Unfortunately, by the time the postseason was over, he would be more notorious than famous, yet another NFL player involved in a murder case. Even worse for the league, the scene of the crime would be the Super Bowl.

A Portrait of Tenacity

Like Simpson, Lewis was born into challenging circumstances and used his athleticism to play his way out. Like Carruth, variations in his name demonstrated the turmoil of his home life.

Lewis's mother, Sunseria, was 16 when he was born, and his father, Elbert Ray Jackson, was absent for most of his formative years. When he entered high school, Sunseria's son took the last name of his mother's boyfriend, Ray Lewis.

Lewis was a tenacious force on the high school football field in Bartow, Florida, attracting recruiters from a variety of top-tier universities. He selected the University of Miami Hurricanes, a team that reflected his talent and personality. The 'Canes featured some of the most coveted athletes in the country but had earned a reputation for wreaking havoc on and off the field. When Lewis joined the team in 1993, he quickly made the defensive unit his own, as a fierce tackler who demanded maximum effort from himself and his teammates. In his three seasons with Miami, he became as famous for his passionate sideline speeches as he was for his dominant play. In his junior year, the anchor of the Hurricanes defense finished second in the nation in voting for the Butkus Award, which is awarded to the nation's top linebacker, and by the time he finished his college career, he had the fifth most tackles in Hurricanes history.

In 1996, Lewis was snatched up as the 26th pick in the first round of the NFL draft by the Baltimore Ravens, a team that was already defined by its dominating defense. He immediately moved into the middle linebacker position and led the Ravens in tackles in the first of his 17 years with the team. In 13 of those years, he would be selected to the Pro Bowl.

Super Bowl Celebration Ends in Tragedy

The Ravens failed to make the playoffs after the 1999 season, but Lewis still decided to attend the Super Bowl in Atlanta, Georgia. Following the game,

Lewis and his entourage went out to enjoy the city's nightlife, partying at a series of clubs.

At about 4:00 a.m. the next morning, the Ravens' star and his acquaintances were leaving the Cobalt Lounge nightclub to return to the 40-foot-long Lincoln Navigator limousine that Lewis had hired for the weekend. Among his associates were Joseph Sweeting and Reginald Oakley. An argument broke out between Lewis's group and members of a second group that was leaving the club at the same time. There are conflicting reports about what happened next, but all of the witnesses agreed that the argument escalated, and when it was over, two men from the second group, Richard Lollar and Jacinth Baker, had been stabbed to death.

"Keep Your Mouth Shut"

Immediately after the stabbings, Lewis and his associates fled the scene in his limousine. Members of Lewis's entourage later provided conflicting testimony about what happened in the hours that followed, but everyone agreed that Lewis instructed everyone in the car to "keep your mouth shut." Evelyn Sparks, a friend of Lewis's who was in the limo at the time, later testified that she saw one of Lewis's associates dispose of a bag of clothes, presumably the blood-splattered suit that Lewis was wearing, in a dumpster behind a fast-food restaurant. The suit that Lewis was wearing on the night of the murders was never recovered.

Police questioned Lewis on the day of the killings, and he provided incomplete and misleading statements about what he had seen. The following day he was arrested. In Georgia, it is possible to convict an individual on a murder charge if that person aids in the commission of a murder or participates in another crime during the incident. Lewis was charged with six felony counts, two of them murder. Scheduled to play in the league's Pro Bowl the following week, Lewis missed the game because he was in jail.

Most of the witnesses in the case agreed that Lewis did not throw any punches in the fight, and Lewis contended that he was in the limo at the time of the physical confrontation. No one involved in the case ever testified that Lewis committed the murders. He was, however, at the scene when the killings occurred and immediately afterward, and in the weeks that followed, attempted to cover up the crime.

In the days following the murders, the details of the killings became increasingly muddled in a set of claims and counterclaims by participants and bystanders. It became difficult to get a clear picture of who did what, but if reporters couldn't include in their stories the specifics of the double murder, they could at least recap what they knew about Lewis's past brushes with the law. It was not a pretty story. Reporters noted that over the six years prior to the murders Lewis had been involved in four other altercations involving brawls, batteries, and assaults, none of which had resulted in a conviction or even found their way into a courtroom. Many of the stories about the Lewis scandal referenced the Carruth case. NFL fans were growing increasingly suspicious that, while the details of the Atlanta slayings were unclear, it appeared that another professional football player was involved in, and might be getting away with, murder.

Unlike the Panthers, the Ravens were not so willing to part ways with their player as quickly as possible. Part of the reason may have been confusion over the facts of the case: it was a confusing story involving multiple contradictory claims. But part of the reason may have also been Lewis's contributions to the team: he was the Ravens' biggest star. Lewis had signed a four-year $26 million extension in November 1998, and his arrest was a massive blow to the Ravens' rabid supporters. "The city is heartbroken," a Baltimore-area radio sports personality said, "the fans loved him. Ray Lewis was building a legend here."[15]

The Case Falls Apart

The trial of Lewis, Oakley, and Sweeting began on May 15, 2000, and it quickly became apparent that the prosecution had a shaky case. Witnesses contradicted each other or provided inconclusive testimony, and no one came forward to say that Lewis had a hand in the actual murders. The defense exploited the gaps and contradictions, and it appeared that there was enough confusion to make an argument for reasonable doubt.

The cover-up, however, was another story. Lewis's lawyers conceded that their client had failed to cooperate with the investigation and encouraged other witnesses to do the same, facts corroborated by a variety of witnesses. Lewis's murder charge looked like a reach, but it was apparent that he had obstructed justice. Both sides began to scramble for a way out.

On June 5, Lewis reached a deal with prosecutors in which the murder charges were dropped in exchange for his testimony against his codefendants and a guilty plea to a misdemeanor charge of obstruction of justice. He was sentenced to 12 months' probation, the maximum sentence for a full-time offender, but no longer faced jail time.

Public perceptions of Lewis were in a state of flux. No one doubted that he had been present when the murders occurred, but his defense team was unequivocal in stating that he had no hand in the killings. Why, then, would he plead guilty to impeding the investigation and agree to turn on his codefendants?

NFL officials, still reeling from the ongoing Carruth murder case, were anxious for any good news, and they found enough of it in the plea bargain to try to move past the scandal. On the same day the judge agreed to the deal, Baltimore Ravens owner Art Modell and NFL commissioner Paul Tagliabue both released statements about Lewis's status.

Modell's statement read:

> From the beginning of this tough situation for all involved, we believed in and supported Ray Lewis. We also believe in the court system and the due process that found Ray to be innocent of the very serious charges. He can now get on with his life, including his work with the Ravens. As I said at Ray's bond hearing in February, Ray is a good young man. Even during these difficult past four months, he has made the effort to help his family, his teammates, and others who rely on his good will and generosity. It will be great to see Ray back in our facilities and on the field soon.[16]

The wording was disingenuous. Lewis had not been found innocent of the charges, the charges had been dropped because the prosecutor was attempting to salvage something from a confusing case with multiple witnesses providing contradictory testimony. The best the prosecutor could do was leverage Lewis's mistakes in the cover-up into testimony against the men they thought wielded the knives.

Tagliabue's statement was less enthusiastic and more cautionary:

> Today's developments will help put this tragic incident behind us. Ray Lewis has been entirely cleared of the charge that he was responsible for the loss of life that occurred in Atlanta in late January. There are many lessons to be learned as we review this case. If anyone in the NFL needed a reminder that high-profile professional athletes need to be extraordinarily careful in their associations and activities, Ray Lewis' experience provides that reminder. We will continue to work as hard as we can to ensure that our players do not become involved in these types of situations.[17]

Modell's top priority was getting his best player back on the field to start the season. He might achieve his goal if Lewis could escape a league suspension. Tagliabue's more measured response reflected a different set of priorities. The Carruth case was still in the headlines, and there were still unanswered questions about Lewis's conduct during and after the murders. The commissioner also knew that Lewis's plea meant that he was about to spend even more time in the public eye, testifying against his former friends. Like the Black Sox eight decades earlier, Lewis had slipped through the courts but still had to face the league's commissioner.

The day after the plea agreement was announced, Lewis took the stand for the prosecution. He testified that his codefendants had purchased knives at a Sports Authority store while he was attending an autograph-signing session. He went on to testify that he had not wanted to get involved in the fight and had actually tried to stop it because he knew that it could jeopardize his football career. In addition, he stated in court that codefendant Joseph Sweeting had showed him how he had repeatedly stabbed one of the victims on the night of the fight and that he had seen the other codefendant, Reginald Oakley, fighting with one of the victims.

If the prosecutors thought cutting a deal with Lewis would produce testimony that would at least allow them to salvage something from their case, they were wrong. Six days after Lewis testified, the jury needed less than six hours of deliberation to find Sweeting and Oakley not guilty. When the verdict was read, Lewis was already hundreds of miles away, at the Baltimore Ravens' practice facility. Once again, football fans were suspicious: two men were dead, an NFL player was somehow in the middle of it, and nobody was going to jail.

The Commissioner's Decision

Paul Tagliabue met with Lewis and his lawyers on July 10, and nine days later the commissioner announced that Lewis would not be suspended. "It's the courts who have the primary responsibility in this case," Tagliabue said. "We're not a substitute for the courts."[18] The announcement settled a big issue for Ravens fans, who had been concerned about the ramifications for the team's approaching season.

Tagliabue still held out the possibility of financial punishment, however, and on August 17, he delivered: a $250,000 fine, the largest ever imposed on an NFL player that did not involve substance abuse. In announcing his decision, Tagliabue also threatened Lewis with an additional $250,000 fine if he violated the terms of his probation. In his ruling, the commissioner stated that Lewis's failure to tell the police the entire story "fueled perception that he had something to hide," and said that he believed that the episode "had caused great harm to other players and to the league."[19] The commissioner concluded:

> When an NFL player engages in and admits to misconduct of the type to which Mr. Lewis has plead here, the biggest losers are thousands of other

NFL players, present, past and future. Such admitted misconduct clearly contributes to the negative stereotyping of NFL players.[20]

Tagliabue's focus on the league's reputation resulted in a rare public relations miscalculation by the savvy commissioner. By suggesting that the real losers in the case were the thousands of NFL players, past, present, and future, he gave NFL critics the opportunity to point out that the league still didn't have its priorities straight—the real losers were the two dead men and their families.

Lewis, who was no longer threatened by jail time or a suspension, felt that he had moved past the matter and was caught off guard by the fine. If Tagliabue had assumed that the Ravens' linebacker would be contrite, he misjudged Ray Lewis, who immediately appealed the decision. The team simultaneously announced support for his decision. The appeal went nowhere—a year later, Tagliabue denied it—but over the probation period, Lewis honored the conditions of the agreement and received no additional fines.

All's Well That Ends Well

By the start of the 2000 regular season, Ray Lewis had returned to his role as middle linebacker and undisputed leader of the Ravens. At the conclusion of the season, Lewis's team played in the Super Bowl. In the enormous media spotlight that accompanies the run-up to the championship game, reporters continuously peppered the now-infamous defensive captain with questions about the murder and the trial. Lewis ignored almost everything scandal-related and responded almost exclusively to questions about football.

The Ravens won the championship and Lewis was named the game's most valuable player. Shortly after their victory parade, relatives of the two stabbing victims sued him in civil court. Publicly, Lewis's lawyers claimed that the suit was totally without merit. Privately, they negotiated. Both cases were settled out of court.

In 8 of the 10 years that followed, Lewis earned trips to the Pro Bowl. As the accolades continued to pile up, the details of the murder trail began to fade. Within a few years, Lewis began to pick up endorsements from national organizations again. Nowhere was his redemption more obvious or more complete than in the way he was treated by the top officials in the NFL: a decade after the murders, Lewis was once again one of the most prominent representatives of the league and Commissioner Roger Goodell in particular embraced him as one of the most public faces of the game.

Throughout the rest of his career, Lewis continued to play at an incredibly high level and did an inordinate amount of volunteer work. His Ray Lewis 52 Foundation was among the most active charities in the Baltimore sports community, providing school supplies and food in underprivileged areas around the city. For the most part, he steered clear of additional controversies, with the exception of the end of the 2012 season, when he was one of a number of players accused of ingesting a concoction based on deer antlers, a substance banned by the league. Lewis denied the charge and the stories quickly passed.

On January 2, 2013, Lewis announced that he would retire at the end of the season. In his coverage of the announcement, NPR reporter Mike Pesca criticized the NFL and the media that cover it for their presentation of the news:

> Baltimore Ravens linebacker Ray Lewis' announcement of his retirement Wednesday was cause for reflection, celebration, some sadness—and not a single mention by two of the largest purveyors of NFL information of his role in a murder trial. As of 3 p.m. ET, the NFL's home page had links to 10 different stories or interviews about Lewis. Not one mentioned his role in a murder trial in 2000. ESPN's archives have stories on the trial and reflections on Lewis' character, but neither the current home page nor the NFL front mentions the stabbing deaths outside a nightclub in Atlanta, hours after the city hosted Super Bowl XXXIV.[21]

As Lewis's team progressed through the postseason, his team and the league did their best to downplay stories revisiting the murders. When a *USA Today* reporter broached the subject with Lewis, the Ravens' star was ready with a response: "Really, really. Why would I talk about that? That was 13 years ago."[22]

The Ravens defeated New England in the AFC championship game, 28–13. Following the game, the wife of a player on the losing team tweeted: "Proud of my husband and the Pats. By the way, if anyone is bored, please go to Ray Lewis' Wikipedia page. 6 kids 4 wives. Acquitted for murder. Paid a family off. Yay. What a hall of fame player! A true role model!" She issued an apology a day later, but the seed was planted. The tweet not only was a reminder of Lewis's role in the killings, it was a demonstration of the new media landscape. Sports organizations, already battling traditional media systems to control the agenda, were now forced to deal with social media as well.

The Ravens went on to win their second championship in Super Bowl XLVII, providing a storybook finish to their star's career. Within days of the championship, Lewis was entertaining employment offers for roles including television analyst and motivational speaker. He also got a very public and enthusiastic endorsement from Roger Goodell, who invited him to serve as a special adviser to the commissioner:

> He's a tremendous voice of reason. He's someone that has a unique pulse of the players and that's helpful to me. . . . He means a great deal to this commissioner, and I could tell you that I will always seek out his input. He will stay involved, I'm certain of it, in football and that perspective that he has is something I'll reach out for on a regular basis. . . . He was able to take, obviously, an unfortunate incident, and he grew from a bad situation and he made very positive changes in his life and the lives of many others. That's a great thing.[23]

Reporting on Lewis's retirement announcement, *Orlando Sentinel* columnist Mike Bianchi wrote that the Ravens' linebacker had "pulled off the greatest comeback story in the history of sports. He is considered a role model, a team leader, a man known for his hard work on the field and his charitable work off of it." But, Bianchi noted, "amid this week-long celebration and commemoration of Ray Lewis' brilliant, Hall of Fame career, let us not forget that he was once charged with killing Richard Lollar and Jacinth Baker—two men whose murders were never solved. Two men whose families are, no doubt, still haunted by the fact that brutal, bloody killers are still out there somewhere running free."[24]

The NFL's Mixed Approach to Murders

The three cases in this chapter illustrate the public relations problems that sports leagues face when their players are involved in the most horrible and high-profile crimes.

O. J. Simpson had retired and established an identity beyond football when the murders he was charged with occurred, reducing but not eliminating the damage to the NFL's reputation. But the crime was so sensational and America's fascination so intense that any person or organization even remotely connected with the scandal could not escape the media coverage. The organization was going to take a hit no matter how it responded. It was effective in addressing its most problematic area of exposure, the Hall of Fame question, by repeatedly referring to existing policy as if to say it had no options to consider.

The Rae Carruth case was arguably even more horrific than the Simpson case, since it involved premeditation and a pregnant victim. The player was also an active member of an NFL roster, creating a closer connection between the scandal and the organization. The team and the league distanced themselves from the criminal as quickly and thoroughly as possible while respecting the player's rights as an employee. They also maintained a minimalist approach to communication. Time has worked in the league's favor, as the player is rarely heard from anymore, and when he is covered is described as a pariah.

The most nuanced of the three scandals was the Lewis case, which was complicated by a number of factors. At the time of the scandal, the athlete was not only an active player, but a pro bowler and one of the most prominent members of the league. He did not commit the murders but clearly obstructed their investigation. The crime occurred relatively early in what turned out to be a Hall of Fame career, so unless the NFL decided to banish him, an unlikely decision, it was apparent that the league was going to have to deal with Ray Lewis, one way or the other, for a very long time. Finally, the crime was never solved, adding to the sense of injustice and never really allowing Lewis, or the league, to put the story to rest. Lewis's on-field successes eventually overshadowed his involvement with the case, but reporters would always have a controversy to include in their profiles of the player, regardless of how many tackles he made. For many years after the judicial process was completed, they would continue to seek comment from the families of the murder victims. Since no one was ever held responsible for the murders, the survivors' bitterness only grew deeper.

In the Lewis case, the NFL administrators decided on an extremely long-term, if risky and ethically questionable, approach, embracing the player (over time) and eventually repositioning him as one of the most important faces of the game. Lewis is a charismatic, talented, and natural leader, and some fans have been willing to forgive if not forget. The strategy could only work if the future Hall of Famer kept out of trouble, which he did, but the league was correct in trusting in a basic tenet of human nature: if you win often enough, people are capable of accepting pretty much anything.

It is highly probable that Lewis will be elected to the Professional Football Hall of Fame in 2018, his first year of eligibility. If he is, his induction will take place in Canton, Ohio, about 20 miles south of the burial plots of the two men who were murdered on the night of his Super Bowl party.

Limited Long-Term Solutions

In 1997, the NFL was the first major sports organization in America to introduce a violent-crime policy. The new rule required any employee charged with violent criminal activity to undergo a mandatory psychological evaluation and, if directed, appropriate counseling, and called for a fine or suspension of players convicted of a violent crime and suspension without pay and possible dismissal for repeat offenders, at the discretion of the league commissioner. The crimes covered included the use or threat of physical violence, the use of a deadly weapon, illegal possession of a weapon, hate crimes, the destruction of property, and domestic violence.

During the Carruth murder coverage, *New York Times* reporter Mike Freeman noted:

> While nearly a dozen highly publicized arrests of N.F.L. players in recent months in violent acts against women have created a public relations nightmare for professional football, some league officials say that the image belies a more complicated reality. The number of players charged with violent crimes has actually declined over the last three years, N.F.L. executives say. They attribute the reduction to programs the league created in March 1997 that use counseling, fines and the threat of suspension or banishment to deter players from violent crime. But interviews with dozens of N.F.L. players, coaches and team executives showed a deep consensus within professional football: people think the league is still not doing enough to combat off-field violence.[25]

In his coverage of Rae Carruth's trial for *GQ Magazine*, reporter Peter Richmond echoed Freeman's thoughts but also attempted to explain the troubled relationship between NFL players and women:

> Football is a violent sport, growing far more violent and mean and attitudinal every year, and it has been played by men who have traditionally been violent against their women. This has been the case since Jim Brown, the greatest running back ever to play the game, garnered the first of a half-dozen charges of violence against women, ranging from spousal battery to rape to the sexual molestation of two teenage girls. Brown, who has never been convicted of a single charge, begat O. J., the second-greatest running back, who, at this writing, continues to seek out Nicole's true killers. O. J. begat Michael Irvin of the Dallas Cowboys, who, prior to one of his frequent cocaine–sex bacchanals a few years back, cavity-searched one of his girls a little too hard for the liking of her cop boyfriend, who then took out a hit on Irvin. It wasn't just Irvin who dodged a bullet that time. It was the NFL, which retired Irvin with pomp and circumstance. . . .
>
> . . . The NFL claims it is doing more than ever to educate its recruits. Its preseason three-and-a-half-day symposia are supposed to make its rookies duly aware of their newfound responsibilities to their fans and their leagues and

the kids who put their posters on the wall: To avoid the sleaze joints. Steer clear of the hucksters. Grow up quick. But what is it really doing? When the NFL parades its first-round draft picks to a podium on national television and slathers them in their first frosting of celebrity, its message effectively and immediately neutralizes all the good-behavior seminars. On that day, the commissioner is not only handing each of the players a guarantee of several million dollars; he is also giving them the whispered assurance that the league likes them just the way they are. No need to grow up too fast. Ultimately, the league refused to ban Ray Lewis and his brutal peers because it needed them on the playing field, and that mandate speaks more loudly than a lecture about good citizenship—especially to a remarkably immature kid like Rae.[26]

In the months following the trials of Carruth and Lewis, the players' union met to discuss the problem of off-field violence in the league. "One violent act—you're gone," recommended one player, "that should be the N.F.L.'s new motto."[27] But Tagliabue and successive commissioners are hampered from making the additional changes needed to significantly reduce off-field violence by a number of intractable problems. Their game rewards violent behavior and, as much as society makes a distinction between on-field and off-field activity, players don't easily alter their mindset when the game ends. The most talented players are coddled from an early age, stunting their emotional maturity and reinforcing the idea that regular societal rules do not apply to them. Finally, there is the very practical issue of labor relations: right-to-work laws and union rules significantly restrict the legal options of sports administrators. Despite their rhetoric to the contrary, unions tend to support players in termination cases, regardless of the circumstances: it is not always as simple as firing a player for breaking the law.

Since becoming the NFL commissioner in 2006, Roger Goodell has increased the amount of counseling available to players and the frequency and size of penalties for off-field malfeasance. But dozens of NFL players are still charged every year with violent crimes. In 2013, tight end Aaron Hernandez appeared to be poised for a breakout year with the New England Patriots. In June of that year, however, the team unceremoniously cut him from the roster. His career was over—he had been charged with murder.

Chapter 11

Ethics, Effectiveness, and a Changing Environment

The history of American sports scandals demonstrates that are as many kinds of crises as there are ways for organizations to address them. But which approaches are the most ethical and which are the most effective? Crisis communication professionals have always stressed that the two questions are closely related—that the most successful emergency communications strategies are grounded in ethical standards and practices. This linkage is borne out by the examples presented here: When the leaders of sports organizations respond to scandals with honesty and transparency, address all key audiences, and act based on the long-term ramifications of their decisions, they resolve crises more effectively. When they take shortcuts, fail to address all of their constituents, or worst of all, cover up scandalous behavior, they not only fail to resolve their problems, they usually make them worse.

The principles of crisis communication management transcend a particular sport or type of crisis, but the sports landscape continues to evolve. As a result, there are trends that increase the probability of scandal and others that reduce the likelihood that players will make headlines for the wrong reasons. Changes in technology, economics, and culture all factor into the future of sports scandal.

Trends That Lead to More Scandal

In some cases, external forces such as fundamental changes to America's media system have increased the likelihood of scandal. In others, internal forces, such as sports organizations' failure to develop or implement effective policies, have led to additional problems.

New Media, New Challenges

The evolution of the relationship between media and sports is a story of change, gradual at first, increasingly rapid as the country moved into a new era of communication. In the early 20th century, newspapers helped fuel the nation's interest in professional sports, particularly baseball, but the impact of the medium was limited by the delivery system—papers could only offer readers yesterday's scores. For two decades that was sufficient—newspapers were happy to cover a mostly positive story that was cheap and convenient to cover, and fans were happy with the statistics and text that summarized the previous day's game.

In August 1921, that dynamic began to fundamentally change when, for the first time in American history, a radio station aired a broadcast of a professional baseball game. The station was KDKA, and the game was a win by the hometown Pittsburgh Pirates over the Philadelphia Phillies at Forbes Field. It was a simple affair, a relatively crude broadcast going out a limited distance and heard by a small audience, but, for the first time, a fan could know about a pro game as it was happening without buying a ticket. Eighteen years later, television station W2XBS brought two cameras to Ebbets Field and transmitted a doubleheader between the Cincinnati Reds and the Brooklyn Dodgers to an estimated 400 television sets in the New York area. Thirty-three thousand fans were at the stadium; 3,000 watched it on TV. Two months later, the same company came to the same field and broadcast the first television images of a professional football game. America's sports fans were no longer limited to going to the game or reading about it the next day—fans could now listen to or watch the game, in real time, at a local pub or in their own houses.

The men who controlled America's professional sports were wary, to say the least, of the impact broadcasting could have on their games, particularly their revenues. The fear was that fans who could hear and, eventually see, the games could decide to stay home to enjoy the game. The reality was that the broadcasts were free publicity, a massive, regular advertisement to come see their games. While the games' stewards didn't realize it right away, the new media connections would also quickly become a brand-new source of money—broadcast rights contracts—and this income would grow to the point that broadcasting rights would be on a par with (in some cases, even surpass) the value of ticket sales. Even the most farsighted owners and administrators could not have predicted how much the media would alter the economics of their games.

While media were changing sports, sports were changing media. As the three networks (NBC, ABC, and CBS) grew, they made sports programming a staple in their lineups, paying increasingly larger broadcast rights fees while making sports a much bigger part of the public consciousness. Within a few decades, sports programming spread from a weekend phenomenon to a daily staple in the American media diet.

The explosion of cable television and increase in sports-focused radio programming in the 1970s and 1980s added even more customers who tuned in to even more stations and created an even greater demand for sports programming. But along with their live game coverage, these new media also began to offer entire shows devoted to sports analysis. Reporting on sports' seamier side, including both on- and off-field controversies, began to compete with more traditional coverage. It was no longer enough to show the game or report the scores; fans wanted to know more about the players, and the ever-growing variety of media devoted to sports were happy to provide the stories. Scandal was, of course, part of the package.

In 1979, entrepreneur Bill Rasmussen launched ESPN, the first cable network devoted entirely to sports programming. Critics predicted that his network would fail for various reasons, the biggest of which was that there wasn't enough content to fill every hour of the day. His detractors could not have been more wrong: today, there is so much sports programming available that ESPN has created entirely new outlets devoted to subcategories of sports, with cable stations specializing in topics such as "classic" games and college athletics. The company generates $6.5 billion annually in revenue from subscriptions alone before factoring in advertising revenue; and male consumers have identified ESPN as their favorite network for 14 consecutive years.[1] Success inevitably leads to imitation, and in August 2013, the FOX network launched its own sports-only station under the assumption that there was not only enough programming to fill multiple 24-hour networks devoted to athletics, but enough fan interest to keep them all profitable.

In the last two decades, sports-oriented radio and television programming has continued to grow despite the introduction of an entirely new and powerful medium—the Internet. With unlimited bandwidth, Web entrepreneurs offer an alternative form of sports reporting that is portable, ubiquitous, and extremely popular with younger, more tech-savvy sports fans. Web sites run the gamut in terms of sports programming, from extremely broad sites that cover sports from around the world to extremely focused sites concentrating on subspecialties, such as a single sport's draft prospects, statistical history, etc. Not only do these sites increase the opportunity for sports scandal coverage, but they have changed the standards for the reporting: Web sites don't require the start-up or maintenance capital required by traditional media, so they are less likely to be staffed by trained professionals and less likely to adhere to the reporting standards of journalism organizations. This increases the chance that they will report slanderous and incorrect information, which may then be retransmitted by news consumers regardless of traditional media coverage, increasing the distribution of information about scandals, real or imagined.

Social Media Add a New Twist

The new media also include social media, an entirely different and far more democratic form of information distribution. Facebook, YouTube, Twitter, etc., have hundreds of millions of users and are growing far faster than traditional media, displacing and, to some degree, replacing systems that have been in place for decades. They are also far less filtered than traditional media: nearly anyone can post relatively unfiltered content and generate wide distribution. As a result, rumors about sports scandals now reach millions of fans without passing through the traditional fact-checking that stops insufficiently sourced stories from airing in more professional channels. These new systems also act to notify traditional media of potential scandals and as megaphones for traditional media, retransmitting scandalous stories that appear on television and radio or in print and dramatically increasing their reach.

The new media do not simply transmit information, they also record it. The nearly universal availability of cell phones in America makes everyone a potential reporter: there are now countless opportunities to capture audio and video of an athlete in any public situation, from a postgame autograph signing to a strip club bacchanal. Once captured, the sounds and images can be uploaded and widely distributed from nearly any location in seconds. Prior to camera phones, stories about a player doing something scandalous in public were passed along by word of mouth from those on the scene or occasionally through a gossip column to a larger audience, with only the most sensational stories about the biggest athletes actually making it into the major media. With so many camera phones in so many places, far more of athletes' public mistakes are now captured, transmitted by a social medium, and then almost instantly retransmitted by additional versions of the same medium or effortlessly converted and retransmitted by other social media. This is particularly true of stories with visual elements, which not only are more likely to be picked up by both social and traditional media than those without visual elements but are also more likely to be read, clicked on, and discussed by news consumers.

We Have Met the Enemy, and He Is Us

League administrators worried about camera phones, YouTube videos, and tweets in the hands of fans and wannabe reporters must also worry about these media in the hands of their own athletes. An increasing percentage of sports scandals is generated by players creating, capturing, and distributing scandalous information on their own, about themselves.

In 2000, NBA all-star Allen Iverson released a rap CD that included disparaging references to gays, women, and African Americans and included the line, "Man enough to pull a gun, man enough to squeeze it." The NBA was inundated with complaints, but the Philadelphia 76er refused to disassociate himself from his controversial lyrics and the league's image suffered as one of its most prominent representatives reinforced its worst stereotypes. The rap problem gave way to a larger, even less-controlled phenomenon—Twitter—as demonstrated by three incidents in 2010. In January, Washington Wizard Gilbert Arenas exacerbated his own scandal involving guns in his locker room by tweeting, "i wake up this morning and see i was the new JOHN WAYNE..lmao media is too funny." In September, one day after a gunman opened fire in a library in Texas, University of Oklahoma wide receiver Jaz Reynolds tweeted, "Hey everyone in Austin, tx. . .kill yourself #evillaugh." And a month later, Buffalo Bills receiver Stevie Johnson offended many religious Americans when he dropped a game-winning touchdown and then tweeted, "@StevieJohnson13: 'I PRAISE YOU 24/7!!!!!!' AND THIS HOW YOU DO ME!!!!! YOU EXPECT ME TO LEARN FROM THIS??? HOW???!!! ILL NEVER FORGET THIS!! EVER!!! THX THO. . ." Later in the season, Johnson created even more controversy by tweeting a picture of his penis to his 22,000 Twitter followers. His indiscretions were overshadowed by those of Vikings quarterback Brett Favre, who was accused of forwarding a photo of his penis to a young Jets employee. Apparently Johnson learned little from all of these Twitter disasters: 12 days after the 2013 Boston Marathon bombing, he tweeted a joke about a bomb attack on Foxborough Stadium. The increase in scandalous tweets, texts, YouTube postings, etc., shows no sign of abating, and emerging technologies promise even more ways for players to create public relations disasters in the future.

It may seem hard to believe that multimillionaire adults who receive regular warnings from their organizations about the dangers of social media would intentionally do something so humiliating to themselves and their leagues. Some of them still fail to appreciate how permanent images are and how little control they have over their distribution. Many younger players, raised in a culture of social media, fail to recognize traditional privacy boundaries or simply don't understand how other groups will respond to words and images that may be part of their upbringing but are frowned upon by other segments of society. Furthermore, their occupation lends itself to extremely high highs and extremely low lows—following a particularly important win or devastating loss, these athletes are likely to express something that they might want to take back, given the chance. If they say it in the locker room, it can be contained. If they tweet the same sentiment, the control is lost forever.

Some players naively assume they can retract a message and erase any trace of it, a technological impossibility, while others clumsily attempt to use the same medium that got them into trouble to attempt to get out of it. In the case of the Oklahoma receiver who joked about a shooting at a rival school, the apology he tweeted was as offensive to some Texans as his original statement. Others respond to the reaction to their scandalous tweets by claiming that their Twitter accounts have been hacked, rarely true, generating a new falsehood that they have to address and extending coverage of the original scandal.

Sports leagues recognize the scandal potential of these new media, but they are extremely limited in their ability to control them. Professional athletes, protected by the First Amendment, their agents, and their union, have the right to generate their own media content without supervision from the league. College players, ostensibly representing their universities, have less control and more restrictions than their professional counterparts, and some coaches have had limited success with social media policies. If a star player who is essential to a team's success misuses social media, however, his coach is likely to keep the player and ride out the scandal to win the next game. With each succeeding year, players at all levels of sport are more and more conversant in and dependent on these forms of media, and as a result, self-generated scandals transmitted by social media are the fastest-growing cause of crises in sports today.

Trends That Lead to Fewer Scandals

Not all trends increase the probability of sports scandals—a few actually work to reduce them. These include improvements in league policies and procedures and, to some degree, an increase in the salaries paid to athletes.

Training and Penalties on the Rise

Increasingly aware that scandals harm the bottom line of their organizations, sports leagues have attempted to be more proactive in working to avoid scandals in the first place. The majority of them are employing a carrot-and-stick approach, rewarding positive conduct and increasing the penalties for improper behavior.

At the collegiate level, the historic response to the Penn State child abuse scandal is one example of college sports attempting to keep such a disaster from happening again. The unprecedented penalties—the vacating of 111 wins, a $60 million fine, the reduction in scholarships, and the four-year bowl ban—were not only an unprecedented punishment for the university and its sports program but a deliberate warning to other schools to strengthen their conduct policies. In announcing the decision, NCAA president Mark Emmert did not limit his rebuke to Penn State University or even college football, but took on the entire athletic-centric culture of higher education. PSU introduced an extensive range of policy changes, not only about sexual misconduct but about the way football is regarded on its campus. Other universities have responded to the PSU crisis by reevaluating their own policies and procedures to minimize scandalous activity by their student athletes. Over the following decades, it will become clear whether these changes have any effect.

At the professional level, sports organizations rocked by a seemingly endless parade of scandals have revised their own policies. New players are required to attend seminars that address everything from player codes of conduct (on and off the field) to drugs and alcohol, etc. Teams have extended individual counseling services to players, and some organizations even go so far as to distribute a phone number that players can call at any time to reduce the possibility of drunken driving charges. Recent stories about the startling percentage of professional athletes who end up bankrupt have prompted leagues to offer financial planning guidance to rookies who are suddenly transformed from college students to multimillionaires.

Leagues continue to refine and provide communications about their drug policies. Sports organizations have made progress, but plenty of room for improvement remains. In 2009, the *Wall Street Journal* published an evaluation of the antidoping policies of major sports according to the policy accessibility to the public, severity of sanctions for offenders, and administration of the code. Reporters found that America's big four sports lagged behind other sports organizations such as the U.S. Boxing Federation, NASCAR, and the International Olympic Committee. The report ranked the NFL as the most effective of the four major leagues, with a precipitous drop-off for the NBA, NHL, and MLB, which all had similar rankings. The study ranked the NCAA's antidoping policy slightly below that of professional baseball.[2] "On the whole, the sporting world has come far,"[3] the *Journal* concluded.

Leagues have also beefed up penalties for conduct detrimental to the sport. Administrators are now handing down larger fines and longer suspensions for on-field infractions such as dangerous tackles in football, fights in baseball and basketball, and so forth, as well as off-field infractions, including the use of performance-enhancing or recreational drugs.

Professional and collegiate sports programs have also increased their commitment to community relations programs—creating situations in which organizational representatives interact on a regular basis with key audiences (members of the media, fans, community groups) to improve the perception of athletes and create a reservoir of goodwill to tap into when a crisis does occur. This is a longstanding public relations practice, and like other businesses, sports organizations have come to understand that this proactive approach is not simply a good thing to do, it is a cost-effective one as well. Programs that cost a few tens of thousands of dollars are well worth the investment when they can prevent scandals that can cost institutions millions of dollars in reduced ticket sales, lower viewership and listenership, and damaged relationships with key constituents. There is a limit to the effectiveness of these programs—many athletes, like other people, inevitably make mistakes, and bad behavior by high-profile figures is going to receive an inordinate amount of media coverage no matter how much public relations activity precedes it. But organizations that are proactive in establishing relationships with key audience members will probably be involved in fewer scandals, and when they do occur, they are more likely to resolve their problems faster.

Higher Salaries, Fewer Scandals?

One of fans' biggest complaints about players in professional sports is the enormous amount of money athletes make to play their games. Ironically, escalating player salaries actually reduces the possibility of at least one form of scandal: an athlete accepting a bribe to throw a game.

A player who is offered a bribe must consider the opportunity in terms of risks and rewards: not simply whether he will get away with it but what he jeopardizes if he takes the offer. In the early 20th century, players were paid poorly and infrequently, with very few fortunate enough to receive a contract that would provide any long-term security. A bribe was a chance to make money immediately, a tax-free wad of cash that, in theory, no one but the athlete and the gambler would know about. If the player didn't get caught, he was ahead by the amount of the bribe over his regular earnings. If he did get caught, it still might be the right financial decision if the bribe was big enough relative to his regular pay. Besides, banishment from one league did not apply to another and if an athlete was talented enough, some other team would have no problem adding him to the roster, regardless of earlier infractions.

The money in modern professional sports completely upends that line of reasoning. What would it cost to bribe a player who makes $10 million a year, with a decade of earning potential in front of him? Every dollar that goes into the bribe is one less that can be invested in the crooked wager, quickly approaching a point of diminishing returns. In the modern game, if a player is important enough to influence the outcome of a game, he is often paid enough to inoculate him from the fix. As historian Daniel Ginzburg noted about one sport:

> It is unlikely that gamblers could successfully fix a major league baseball game today. In contrast to the players of 70 years ago, today's players realize that they will be punished severely for engaging in corrupt activity. Even more important, the earning power of players is so high that it is hard to imagine anyone throwing away a career in which he will earn millions of dollars to get involved in a game fixing scandal. The amount of money it would take to fix a game today would be tremendous, and far more than a gambler could earn betting on fixed games.[4]

The massive increase in player salaries does not eliminate fixes: mobsters often simply move on to more economically favorable situations, such as the college ranks or the lower-paid professional sports or turn their attention to officials such as NBA official Tim Donaghy, since salaries for professional referees have not kept pace with the increases seen by athletes. Some athletes are simply inordinate risk takers, or have some enormous enmity about the team and may accept a bribe regardless of their salary. Furthermore, high wages do not ensure that a player won't put himself in a position where he throws a game for other reasons: gambling debts, drug problems, blackmail, etc., can ensnare even the wealthiest player. And finally, the potential for high salaries can also encourage scandalous behavior, such as when marginal players take performance-enhancing drugs to gain big contracts. But there is no question that one very positive and unintended consequence of multimillion-dollar salaries is that gamblers have a more difficult time convincing players to throw games for money.

The Hall of Fame Conundrum

When a sports organization fails to prevent a scandal, it not only is forced to deal with a crisis when it occurs it also creates the potential for scandal down the road, a kind of public relations time bomb that reexplodes when a player retires. At the least, the athlete's mistake is revisited as part of his retirement story. At the most, the scandal becomes central to a player's consideration for the sport's Hall of Fame. In fact, depending on the nature of the crisis, the scandalous behavior may be a primary reason the player is a candidate for the hall—some of baseball's most productive players in the last two decades not only used performance-enhancing drugs, they set records in their sports because they used them. This is the worst possible scenario for a sport, when the enshrinement of its greatest players is entangled in a debate about scandalous behavior.

It is possible, but unlikely, for a sport to use a player's candidacy for its Hall of Fame as the final opportunity to right the wrong, denying him the highest possible recognition as a form of punishment. This rarely works, however. First, consideration for a Hall of Fame is limited to very few players, so it will have no impact on the vast majority of players involved in scandal. Second, a player under consideration for the hall will have many supporters regardless of his shortcomings, and among their defenses of their candidate will be the faults of the league policies or the shortcomings of those already enshrined—two conversations sports administrators prefer to avoid.

Sports leagues vary in terms the selection process, including the criteria for evaluation. Some limit consideration to the player's career and on-field contributions; others consider the athlete's off-field life during and after his career. Some attempt a kind of compromise, withholding consideration for a number of ballots as a form of penance, while others have eligibility windows that can turn protest votes into permanent banishment. Whether or not Dennis Rodman's career statistics make him a legitimate candidate for the Naismith Basketball Hall of Fame, any debate on the topic will always include his eccentric behavior during and after his NBA career. The candidacies of Pete Rose, Roger Clemens, Alex Rodriguez, and Barry Bonds may be Cooperstown's final opportunity to address their shortcomings, but they also ensure that their scandalous behavior is never really out of the limelight. And even when a player connected with problematic behavior is inducted, he does not leave the scandals behind when he passes into the hall. When Michael Irvin was inducted into the National Football Hall of Fame in 2007, he spent almost as much time in his acceptance speech apologizing for his years of misconduct as he did thanking the people who had supported him. Halls of fame are designed to honor a sport's greatest players, but, ironically, the process can also serve a final reminder of those players' biggest shortcomings.

Recommendations for Ethical and Effective Scandal Communications

Sports organizations can never eliminate scandals, but administrators can continue to develop comprehensive, proactive, and ethical programs that reduce the chance that they will happen and minimize the damage when they occur. These programs must be designed to address the problem before, when, and after a scandal occurs.

Prior to Scandals

Planning is far more difficult in the midst of an emergency, so the most effective crisis communication preparation occurs ahead of potential problems. The plan should be developed with input from every relevant department in the organization and should be viewed as an everyday part of organizational activities, following the credo that prevention is better than the cure.

The starting point is the organization's mission statement, which serves as the guiding document for all of the organization's policies. The mission statement should be written in a clear and succinct manner and should encapsulate the core values of the institution. Senior leaders should solicit input from various constituents but ultimately are responsible for the final statement as well as the distribution of the message and reinforcement of the principles.

The values in the organization's mission statement should be integrated into every phase of an employee's experience. Search committees should consider the statement when making a hiring decision, although this is not always realistic when making personnel decisions in sports: many coaches either place ethical issues far below talent evaluation when selecting players or assume that they will be able to change a troubled player or minimize the potential for scandal when he joins the organization.

Once an employee has been hired, the leaders of the organization must use the orientation process to introduce and reinforce the mission statement to the new member, setting conduct expectations, explaining the organization's support systems for avoiding problems, and explaining the ramifications to the player and to the organization if a problem occurs. The organization should be as proactive as legally possible, stressing the employee's responsibility and the negative consequences of poor decisions. Since major professional sports are all unionized, these messages should be coordinated with similar messages from the players' representatives. This introductory program can be done at the league level and on a team-by-team basis. It is essential for the organization to begin as early as possible to convey the importance of avoiding the mistakes that lead to a scandal.

It is also essential for other employees, particularly leaders in an organization, to reflect the mission statement's core values in their day-to-day activities. When players see coaches, administrators, and owners whose actions demonstrate the organization's stated values, they are more likely to mimic those values themselves and accept the policies of the institution. When there is a disconnect between the stated values and the conduct of leaders of the organization, when rules are not applied fairly, employees understand that the mission statement is irrelevant and are more likely to act accordingly. The stated values and the actions of the organization must be consistent for management to have credibility in helping a player avoid controversy.

Senior management must also develop a crisis communications plan that prepares the organization in the event of a scandal. This begins with a threat analysis, a scandal matrix based on the likelihood that each type of problem will occur and the degree of damage each type of problem could cause. This includes the traditional types of scandals (controversial statements, on-field incidents, antisocial activities, illegal activities, addictions, including drugs, alcohol, and gambling, cheating, etc.) as well as problems that are more likely with individual players. Administrators must then develop a plan to deal with each of these types of scandals, including media relations, instructions to the individual player, outreach to important constituents, etc. The plan should be as thorough and detailed as possible and should be tested to determine its strengths and weaknesses.

Finally, the organization must develop an ongoing communications program with all key audiences to achieve the larger goal of establishing and maintaining strong, trust-based relationships with important constituents. These include players and staff, members of the media, team supporters from season ticket holders to casual fans, potential supporters, government officials, league officials, and members of the community around the team's facilities. While these relationships are critical to the success of the organization, they are particularly important during crises. They can only be developed over time, and that time cannot be in the midst of an emergency.

When Scandals Occur

When a scandal does occur, the most critical elements in addressing it are speed and credibility.

The earlier that organizational leaders know about a crisis, the better their chances of dealing with it. A team that becomes aware of a crisis before it goes public has a critical window to plan the steps that are necessary to address the problem. Conversely, if the first time a team president hears about a scandal is when he is asked to comment on it by a member of the press, his organization is at a significant disadvantage in controlling the outcome.

While organizations deal best with crises when they know about them early, it is also important for administrators to understand the responsibilities that come with knowing scandalous information for both legal and public relations purposes. It is probable that, as the scandal unfolds, members of the organization will be asked the classic "what did you know and when did you know it?" question, and members of various audiences, particularly in the press, will likely trace the actions and words of administrators back to the point where they admitted to being aware of the problem to reconstruct their reaction to it.

Players, like everyone else, are loath to admit to mistakes, so it is difficult for their organization to convince them that the first thing they should do after a blunder is to inform their bosses about it. No one likes their worst moments to be known to their employers—but they have to understand that the information is eventually going to come out and that the best chance they have for resolving the issue effectively is by giving the organization the time needed to implement a crisis containment strategy. Since different players acknowledge different mistakes in different ways, organizations must be prepared to respond based on early notice, some notice, no notice at all, or even continued denial after the scandal goes public.

Once the organization's leaders are aware of the scandal, their first task is to collect as much pertinent, verifiable information as possible. The information should include details about the scandal, identification of the participants in and witnesses to the misbehavior, legal liabilities, team and league policies related to the infraction, and any other relevant facts about the case. Normally, one senior-level member of the organization is appointed to perform this task.

While the information is being collected, the organization must develop a communications strategy for addressing various publics, mostly through the media. A second senior-level member of the organization is usually responsible for this function. The message should be limited to addressing verified information using clear, unambiguous language. It should not accept or assign blame at this point in the process.

If the leadership of the organization determines that an apology is necessary, the chief communications official should determine who should make the apology, what it should say, and how and when it should be delivered. Whether the apologist is the athlete involved in the scandal or an administrator representing the organization, that person should receive sufficient assistance in creating and delivering the statement that it is perceived as sincere and thorough. The apologist should reference the mistake, clarify any negative misconceptions about the scandal, accept whatever responsibility is necessary, and announce the steps being taken to rectify the problem. Most important, the message must include a full and unconditional apology to all affected parties. This last component is usually the most difficult to convince the speaker to say. Apology messages are frequently presented conditionally ("To the degree that I offended anyone . . ."), wrapped in an explanation that blames others ("My statements were taken out of context . . ."), or, perversely, blame the offended ("If anyone mistakenly interpreted my words . . ."). When making an apology, it is human nature to want to deflect responsibility or provide an explanation as much as possible. When hearing an apology, however, it is also human nature to be less than satisfied when the apology is incomplete, insincere, or attempts to shift responsibility. The best apologies are simple, direct, and clearly assume responsibility for the error. They help achieve the primary objective—moving past the scandal—in three critical ways: demonstrating that the athlete is aware of and has taken responsibility for the mistake, creating an opportunity for the aggrieved parties to forgive the transgressor, and giving the media less opportunity to continue to cover the story.

The apology should be delivered in the most controlled environment possible and should not include any additional interaction between the apologist and the organization's audiences, particularly the media. There may be a time for additional discussion with various groups, such as members of the press, but that decision should come after the peak of the coverage has passed. If an apology to a person who has been harmed by the scandal is necessary, that apology should be delivered privately. The more sincere and comprehensive the apology, the faster the scandal is likely to pass and the less it is likely to damage the player, the team, and the league.

Postscandal

The media eventually exhaust their coverage of even the largest scandal—public interest wanes, other scandals arise, etc. But scandals are never truly "over"—they become part of the public's perception of the player, team, and league. If the mistake is relatively small, for example if a player makes a stupid tweet, it is a small component of that perception. If it is large, such as the murder charges against O. J. Simpson or Rae Carruth, it defines the athlete. While the scandal never completely goes away, effective organizations recognize that they can use the situation to address the root problems that contributed to it—hopefully minimizing the chance for similar new problems.

In a crisis, organizational leaders must balance multiple factors: the rights of players, the anger of publics, agreements with unions, etc. They must also address a normally disparate group of team owners, and, above all, act "in the best interests of the game." Sometimes their response is underwhelming: MLB commissioner Bud Selig looked the other way on performance-enhancing drugs while players hit a record number of home runs and baseball regained its fan base. Two decades later, he faces the no-win decision of how to address admitted drug abusers with Hall of Fame credentials. Even worse, the underlying problem continues to fester: Selig still has not resolved the steroid issue, and a few players continue to benefit from gaming the system. Sometimes their response is overkill: Kennesaw Mountain Landis, with his imposing name, imperious glare, and adoring press, was considered by many to be the savior of baseball when he banished eight Black Sox from the game. If one or two of those players may have been innocent, many agreed at the time, better that he err in favor of too many rather than too few to remove the cancer from the game. Over time, however, an increasing number of baseball fans have come to disagree with his decision, eulogizing Shoeless Joe Jackson and arguing that his World Series statistics proved that Landis had gone too far. This, despite the fact that cheating scandals continued in baseball after Landis's sweeping decision, which caused other fans to accuse him of not having gone far enough. For administrators, striking a balance is extremely difficult.

The first challenge for authorities is to administer justice, but the second challenge is to develop sufficient deterrents to discourage other athletes from making similar mistakes. Although it is an impossible standard to expect organizational leaders to develop penalties and policies that eliminate scandal from sports, it is important for them to take the long view not only to help resolve the immediate scandal but to help minimize future problems as well.

Crises—and Sports—Are Here to Stay

In some ways, it is amazing that sports have survived their long association with scandal. Multiple members of the 1919 Black Sox conspired to throw the World Series. Racism, the vilest trait of modern society, played out in full view on the baseball diamond as Jackie Robinson struggled for acceptance in the majors. Gamblers turned college basketball players into coconspirators in the 1950s, and multiple cases of pedophilia by an assistant coach went unreported by the president, athletic director, and legendary football coach at one of the country's great universities. Neither the last pitcher to win 30 games in a season nor the man with the most hits of any player in professional baseball are in Cooperstown because of their uncontrollable addiction to gambling, while the bust of a running back who most Americans are convinced stabbed two people to death holds a prominent position in the Professional Football Hall of Fame. Some of the best baseball players of the century got that way by taking drugs and some of the best football players of the century are crippled by injuries the men who ran their league understood better than they did.

There is no indication that sports scandals are on the decline. In the summer of 2013, New England Patriot tight end Aaron Hernandez was charged with murder and MLB suspended a record 13 players, including Alex Rodriguez, the highest-paid athlete in the league, for taking performance-enhancing drugs.

Despite the continued evidence of the dark side of sports, the games are as popular—possibly even more popular—than ever before. Teams and leagues have become more sophisticated at dealing with scandals, hiring personal counselors, crisis managers, and media consultants to contain the damage. Most sports administrators continue to make a good faith effort to eradicate the problems that damage their sports. Some fans have become either more jaded, no longer surprised at offensive conduct, or more forgiving, accepting that athletes, like everyone else in society, make mistakes. A third set chooses to emphasize the positive, recognizing that as disappointing as all of these scandals can be, the miscreants represent a small percentage of the people involved with the games.

Sports administrators must continue to do everything they can to protect the integrity of their games and the health of the athletes who play them. At the same time, the trajectory of sports in American society should give them comfort—they should have faith that the games themselves manage to transcend even the most damaging scandals. Some athletes, like some other members of society, will inevitably misbehave, but the popularity of the games they play demonstrates that no matter what mistakes they make, sports in America will always survive.

Notes

Chapter 1. Anatomy of a Scandal

1. Andy Behrens, "Been Caught Stealing: MLB Warns Phillies About Stealing Signs," *Yahoo! Sports,* last modified May 12, 2010, http://sports.yahoo.com/fantasy/blog/roto_arcade/post/Been-Caught-Stealing-MLB-warns-Phillies-about-s?urn=fantasy,240535.

2. "Belichick Draws $500,000 Fine, but Avoids Suspension," *ESPN.com News Services,* last modified September 14, 2007, http://sports.espn.go.com/nfl/news/story?id=3018338.

3. Pablo S. Torre, "How (and Why) Athletes Go Broke," *Sports Illustrated,* last modified March 23, 2009, http://sportsillustrated.cnn.com/vault/article/magazine/MAG1153364/2.

Chapter 2. The Black Sox Scandal (1919)

1. Gustav W. Axelson, *"Commy": The Life Story of Charles A. Comiskey* (Chicago: Reilly & Lee, 1919).

2. William K. Klingaman, *1919: The Year Our World Began* (New York: St. Martin's Press, 1987), 564.

3. Daniel A. Nathan, *Saying It's So: A Cultural History of the Black Sox Scandal* (Chicago: University of Illinois Press, 2003), 15.

4. Lee Allen, *100 Years of Baseball* (New York: Bartholomew House, 1950).

5. Daniel E. Ginsburg, *The Fix Is In: A History of Baseball Gambling and Game Fixing Scandals* (Jefferson, NC: McFarland, 1995), 18.

6. Roger I. Abrams, *The Dark Side of the Diamond* (Burlington, MA: Rounder Books, 2007), 65.

7. Eliot Asinof, *Eight Men Out* (New York: Holt, Rinehart and Winston, 1963).

8. Gene Carney, *Burying the Black Sox: How Baseball's Cover-Up of the 1919 World Series Fix Almost Succeeded* (Washington, D.C.: Potomac Books, 2006), 21.

9. Hugh Fullerton, "White Sox Dope to Win This One," *Chicago Herald and Examiner,* October 6, 1919, 11.

10. Hugh Fullerton, "Fullerton Says Seven Members of the White Sox Will Be Missing Next Spring," *Chicago Herald and Examiner,* October 10, 1919, 9. http://www.historicbaseball.com/scplayers/jacksonmedia.html#ENote6.

11. Ibid.

12. Nathan, *Saying It's So,* 19.

13. Stanley H. Teitelbaum, *Athletes Who Indulge Their Dark Side: Sex, Drugs, and Cover-Ups* (Santa Barbara, CA: Praeger, 2010), 142.

14. Harold Seymour, *Baseball: The Golden Age* (New York: Oxford University Press, 1971), 355.

15. Ginsburg, *The Fix Is In,* 130.

16. *Chicago Tribune,* September 29, 1920, 2.

17. Ibid., 3.

18. Asinof, *Eight Men Out.*

19. *Cincinnati Enquirer,* September 29, 1920, 2.

20. Ginsburg, *The Fix Is In,* 142.

21. "Baseball Leaders Won't Let White Sox Return to the Game," *New York Times,* August 4, 1921, 1.

22. Abrams, *The Dark Side of the Diamond,* 69.

23. Ginsburg, *The Fix Is In,* 163.

24. Seymour, *Baseball: The Golden Age,* 331.

Chapter 3. Baseball's Reaction to Jackie Robinson (1947–1956)

1. Jules Tygiel, *Baseball's Great Experiment: Jackie Robinson and His Legacy* (New York: Oxford University Press, 1997), 13.

2. Ibid., 26.

3. Ibid., 33.

4. Jonathan Eig, *Opening Day: The Story of Jackie Robinson's First Season* (New York: Simon & Schuster, 2007), 21.

5. Scott Simon, *Jackie Robinson and the Integration of Baseball* (Hoboken: John Wiley & Sons, Inc., 2002), 43.

6. Eig, *Opening Day,* 23.

7. Ibid., 28.

8. David Faulkner, *Great Time Coming: The Life of Jackie Robinson, from Baseball to Birmingham* (New York: Simon & Schuster, 1995), 162.

9. Tygiel, *Baseball's Great Experiment,* 41.

10. Jules Tygiel, ed., *The Jackie Robinson Reader: Perspectives on an American Hero* (New York: Penguin Group, 1997), 130–131.

11. Ibid., 31.

12. Ibid., 133.

13. Ibid., 133.

14. Faulkner, *Great Time Coming,* 164.

15. Simon, *Jackie Robinson,* 121.

16. Kelly E. Rusinack, "Baseball on the Radical Agenda: The *Daily Worker* and *Sunday Worker* Journalistic Campaign to Desegregate Major League Baseball, 1933–1947," in *Jackie Robinson: Race, Sports and the American Dream*, ed. Joseph Dorinson and Joram Warmund (Armonk, NY: M. E. Sharpe, 1998), 76.

Chapter 4. Point-Shaving in College Basketball (1947–1951)

1. "Sport: Lifting the Curtain," *Time*, December 3, 1951, http://content.time .com/time/magazine/article/0,9171,889399,00.html.

2. Albert J. Figone, "Gambling and College Basketball: The Scandal of 1951," *Journal of Sport History* 16, no. 1 (Spring 1989): 47.

3. Charles Rosen, *Scandals of '51: How the Gamblers Almost Killed College Basketball* (Canada: Holt, Rinehart and Winston), 119.

4. "Basketball Fixer, 5 Players Sentenced," *News and Courier* (Charleston, SC), November 20, 1951, http://news.google.com/newspapers?nid=2506&dat=195111 20&id=_hNZAAAAIBAJ&sjid=PUYNAAAAIBAJ&pg=3813,4566545.

5. "Sport: Lifting the Curtain."

6. "Education: Basketball vs. Learning," *Time*, December 17, 1951, http://content .time.com/time/magazine/article/0,9171,859468,00.html.

7. "Kentucky's Dr. Donovan Blasts at Judge Streit," *Milwaukee (WI) Journal*, May 21, 1952, http://news.google.com/newspapers?nid=1499&dat=19520521&id =bvspAAAAIBAJ&sjid=zSMEAAAAIBAJ&pg=4398,2618673.

8. "Kentucky's Dr. Donovan Blasts at Judge Streit."

9. Rosen, *Scandals of '51*, 191.

Chapter 5. Race and Drug Issues in the National Basketball Association (1970s and 1980s)

1. David Halberstam, *The Breaks of the Game* (New York: Alfred A. Knopf, 1981), 11.

2. Gary A. Sailes, "Betting Against the Odds: An Overview of Black Sports Participation," in *African Americans in Sport*, ed. Gary A. Sailes (New Brunswick, NJ: Transaction Publishers, 1998), 24.

3. Halberstam, *The Breaks of the Game*, 148.

4. Ibid., 30.

5. John Papanek, "There's an Ill Wind Blowing for the NBA," *Sports Illus-trated*, February 26, 1979, http://sportsillustrated.cnn.com/vault/article/magazine/ MAG1094653/1/index.htm.

6. Billy Hawkins, "The Dominant Images of Black Men in America: The Rep-resentation of O. J. Simpson," in *African Americans in Sport*, ed. Gary A. Sailes (New Brunswick, NJ: Transaction Publishers, 1998), 40.

7. Papanek, "There's an Ill Wind Blowing for the NBA."

8. Ibid.

9. Jennifer Robison, "Decades of Drug Use: Data From the '60s and '70s," last modified July 2, 2002, http://www.gallup.com/poll/6331/decades-drug-use-data -from-60s-70s.aspx.

10. Ibid.

11. Halberstam, *The Breaks of the Game*, 198.

12. Ibid., 199.

13. Dana E. Mastroa, Erin Blecha, and Anita Atwell Seatec, "Characterizations of Criminal Athletes: A Systematic Examination of Sports News Depictions of Race and Crime," *Journal of Broadcasting & Electronic Media* 55, no. 4 (2011): 526–542, http://www.tandfonline.com/doi/full/10.1080/08838151.2011.620664.

14. Selena Roberts, "Marijuana and Pro Basketball—A Special Report; N.B.A's Uncontrolled Substance," *New York Times*, October 26, 1997.

15. Richard Lapchick, Antoinette Lecky, and Aaron Trigg, *The 2012 Racial and Gender Report Card: National Basketball Association* (Orlando, FL: Institute for Diversity and Ethics in Sport, 2012), http://web.bus.ucf.edu/documents/sport/2012 -NBA-RGRC.pdf.

Chapter 6. Amphetamines and Steroids in Major League Baseball (1940s–Current)

1. Jim Bouton, *Ball Four* (New York: Macmillan General Reference, 1971), 45.

2. "'Greenies' the Drug of Choice: Amphetamines Baseball's Longest-Lasting Addiction," *Vancouver Province* (British Columbia), May 17, 2005.

3. United Press International, "Ueberroth to Start Drug-Testing Program," May 8, 1985, http://articles.sun-sentinel.com/1985-05-08/sports/8501180251_1 _grand-jury-drug-trafficking-testing-program.

4. Associated Press, "Smith's Blast Puts Holes in Baseball's Alleged Anti-Drug Campaign," *Lewiston (ME) Daily Sun*, July 29, 1987.

5. Francis T. Vincent Jr., *Memo: Baseball's Drug Policy and Prevention Program*, June 7, 1991, http://www.bizofbaseball.com/docs/1991Memo_Baseballs _Drug_Policy_And_Prevention_Program.pdf.

6. Tim Marchman, "DUST-UP: The Great Steroids Debate: How Have Drugs Changed Baseball?," *Los Angeles Times*, March 13, 2007.

7. Ibid.

8. Bill Madden, "Aaron: I'm Sad for Baseball," *New York Daily News*, February 29, 2004.

9. Duff Wilson, "Medical Adviser for Baseball Lists Exaggerated Credentials," *New York Times*, March 30, 2005, http://www.nytimes.com/2005/03/30/sports/ baseball/30doctor.html?_r=0.

10. Ibid.

11. Christine Hauser, "Baseball Announces Steroids Investigation," *New York Times*, March 30, 2006, http://www.nytimes.com/2006/03/30/sports/baseball/31cnd -base.html?_r=0

12. Mark Fainaru-Wada and Lance Williams, *Game of Shadows: Barry Bonds, BALCO, and the Steroids Scandal That Rocked Professional Sports* (New York: Gotham Books, 2006), 245.

13. Associated Press, "Amphetamine Testing Changes Behavior," *Augusta (GA) Chronicle,* September 29, 2006.

14. Ibid.

15. Paul White, "Selig: Policy Focused on Amphetamines," *USA Today,* July 12, 2006.

16. Ibid.

17. Tom Verducci, "Believe Him or Not," *Sports Illustrated,* February 25, 2008, http://sportsillustrated.cnn.com/vault/article/magazine/MAG1109688/index.htm.

18. ESPN.com News Services, "Barry Bonds Found Guilty of Obstruction," April 14, 2011, http://sports.espn.go.com/mlb/news/story?id=6347014.

19. Paul Hagen, "A-Rod Gets Ban through 2014; 12 Get 50 Games," MLB.com, August 6, 2013.

20. Bob Ford, "Selig Drops the Ball on A-Rod," *Philadelphia (PA) Inquirer,* August 6, 2013.

Chapter 7. Concussions and the National Football League (1900–Current)

1. Linda Carroll and David Rosner, *The Concussion Crisis: Anatomy of a Silent Epidemic* (New York: Simon & Schuster, 2011), 41.

2. Jere Longman, "N.F.L. Linemen Tip the Scales," *New York Times,* January 28, 2011, http://www.nytimes.com/2011/01/29/sports/football/29weight.html?pagewanted =all&_r=0.

3. Greg Easterbrook, "TMQ Sizes Up Players, Writes Haiku," ESPN online, http://espn.go.com/espn/page2/story/_/id/6933214/tmq-mel-kiper-jr-size-increase -football-players.

4. Jim Avila, Enjoli Francis, and Lauren Pearle, "Former NFL Players File Lawsuit Against League on Concussions," ABC News, June 7, 2012, http://abcnews.go .com/US/nfl-players-file-lawsuit-league-concussions/story?id=16514359.

5. Shaheen Lakhan and Annette Kirchgessner, *Chronic Traumatic Encephalopathy: The Dangers of Getting "Dinged,"* Springer Plus, March 12, 2012.

6. Gary S. Solomon, Karen M. Johnston, and Mark R. Lovell, *The Heads-UP on Sports Concussion* (Champaign, IL: Human Kinetics, 2006), 8.

7. P. McCrory, W. Meeuwiss, K. Johnston, J. Dvorak, M. Aubry, M. Molloy, and R. Cantu, (2009) *Consensus Statement on Concussion in Sport—The 3rd International Conference on Concussion in Sport Held in Zurich, November 2008,* SAJSM, 21:36–46.

8. Solomon, Johnston, and Lovell, *The Heads-UP on Sports Concussion,* 10.

9. Julian Bailes, "Brain Injury: Science Waging War on Concussions," in *When Winning Costs Too Much: Steroids, Supplements and Scandal in Today's Sports,* ed. John McCloskey and Julian Bailes (New York: Taylor Trade Publishing, 2005), 174.

10. Ibid., 157.

11. Carroll and Rosner, *The Concussion Crisis*, 10.

12. Bailes, "Brain Injury," 171.

13. Carroll and Rosner, *The Concussion Crisis*, 10.

14. Gay Culverhouse, *Throwaway Players: The Concussion Crisis from Pee Wee Football to the NFL* (Lake Forest, CA: Behler Publications, LLC, 2012), 39.

15. M. S. Ferrara, M. McCrea, C. L. Peterson et al., "A Survey of Practice Patterns in Concussion Assessment and Management," *Journal of Athletic Training* 36 (2001): 145–149.

16. Solomon, Johnston, and Lovell, *The Heads-UP on Sports Concussion*, 3.

17. Culverhouse, *Throwaway Players*, 33.

18. Peter Keating, "Doctor Yes: Elliot Pellman, the NFL's Top Medical Adviser, Claims It's Okay for Players with Concussions to Get Back in the Game. Time for a Second Opinion," *ESPN The Magazine*, October 28, 2006, http://sports.espn.go.com/espnmag/story?id=3644940.

19. Selena Roberts, "The Many Perils of Unqualified Hypocrisy," *New York Times*, May 6, 2007.

20. Culverhouse, *Throwaway Players*, 59.

21. National Football League Press Release, "NFL Adopts Stricter Statement on Return-To-Play Following Concussions," December 2, 2009.

22. Sam Borden, "N.F.L. Plans Broader Concussion Research," *New York Times*, October 3, 2011.

23. Avila, Francis, and Pearle, "Former NFL Players File Lawsuit."

24. Ibid.

25. Ibid.

26. Judy Battista, "Amid Success and Unrest, Goodell Remains Resolute," *New York Times*, December 23, 2012.

27. Sean Gregory, "How Far Will Roger Goodell Go, to Protect the Game He Loves?" *Time*, December 17, 2012.

28. Ken Belson, "N.F.L. Agrees to Settle Concussion Suit for $765 Million," *New York Times*, August 30, 2013.

29. Peter King, "Concussion Lawsuit a Win for the NFL," SportsIllustrated.com, August 30, 2013.

30. John P. Martin, "NFL, Players Settle Lawsuits," *Philadelphia (PA) Inquirer*, August 30, 2013.

31. Mark Fainaru-Wada and Steve Fainaru, "NFL Reports Remain Inconsistent," ESPN.com, December 13, 2012, http://espn.go.com/espn/otl/story/_/id/8706409/nfl-concussion-program-marked-inconsistencies-making-difficult-assess-whether-league-making-progress-issue.

32. Steve Coll, "Is Chaos a Friend of the N.F.L.," *New Yorker Magazine*, December 26, 2012.

33. Sean Gregory, "Can Roger Goodell Save Football?" *Time*, December 12, 2012, 42.

Chapter 8. The Penn State University Football Child Molestation Scandal (2009–2013)

1. Sally Jenkins, "Joe Paterno's Last Interview," *Washington Post*, January 14, 2012.

2. Jeff Frantz, "Penn State Coach Joe Paterno Returns Home to Crowd of Students, Tells Them 'I'm Proud of You,'" *Patriot-News* (PA), November 8, 2011.

3. "Penn State's Joe Paterno Retires, Says He's 'Devastated' Over Child Sex Scandal," *Patriot-News* (PA), November 9, 2011.

4. Jenkins, "Joe Paterno's Last Interview."

5. Sara Ganim, "Penn State Student Riots Were Another Blow to School's Pride, Sister of Sandusky Victim Says," *Patriot-News* (PA), November 10, 2011.

6. Jessica Hopper, "Jerry Sandusky to Bob Costas in Exclusive 'Rock Center' Interview: 'I Shouldn't Have Showered with Those Kids,'" *Rock Center*, http://rockcenter.nbcnews.com/_news/2011/11/14/8804779-jerry-sandusky-to-bob-costas-in-exclusive-rock-center-interview-i-shouldnt-have-showered-with-those-kids?lite.

7. Jenkins, "Joe Paterno's Last Interview."

8. Ibid.

9. Ibid.

10. Ibid.

11. Ibid.

12. Louis Freeh, "Remarks of Louis Freeh in Conjunction with the Announcement of Publication of Report Regarding the Pennsylvania State University," July 12, 2012, 2.

13. Ibid., 4.

14. Ibid.

15. "Report of the Special Investigative Counsel Regarding the Actions of the Pennsylvania State University Related to the Child Sexual Abuse Committed by Gerald A. Sandusky," July 12, 2012, 15–17.

16. Sara Ganim, "Graham Spanier's Attorneys Refute Freeh Report, but Answer Few Questions," *Patriot-News* (PA), August 22, 2012.

17. Ibid.

18. "Paterno Statue Taken Down," *Politico*, July 22, 2012.

19. "Former Sen. Mitchell Selected as Penn State Athletics Integrity Monitor," National Collegiate Athletic Association press release, August 1, 2012.

20. Ibid.

21. Sara Ganim, "Ex-PSU President Graham Spanier Charged with Obstruction, Endangerment and Perjury; More Charges Filed Against Other Administrators," *Patriot-News* (PA), November 1, 2012.

22. "Penn State Sanctions: $60M, Bowl Ban," *ESPN.com News Services*, July 24, 2012, http://espn.go.com/college-football/story/_/id/8191027/penn-state-nittany-lions-hit-60-million-fine-4-year-bowl-ban-wins-dating-1998.

23. "Penn State Head: 'Heavy' Sanctions Better Than Alternative," *Face the Nation*, July 29, 2012, http://www.cbsnews.com/8301-3460_162-57481917/penn-state-head-heavy-sanctions-better-than-alternative/.

24. Mike Dawson, "Penn State Praised in First Annual Report from NCAA Monitor George Mitchell," *CentreDaily.com*, September 6, 2013, http://www.centredaily.com/2013/09/06/3774049/penn-state-praised-in-first-annual.html.

Chapter 9. Individual Gambling Scandals

1. Bill Morris, "A League Outlaw with an Endearing Scowl," *New York Times*, October 13, 2012, http://www.nytimes.com/2012/10/14/sports/football/alex-karras-played-role-of-league-outlaw-for-lions.html?_r=1&.

2. Tex Maule, "Players Are Not Just People," *Sports Illustrated*, April 29, 1963.

3. "Shocking Moments in NFL History," ESPN.com, http://espn.go.com/page2/s/list/football/shocking/moments.html.

4. Maule, "Players Are Not Just People."

5. Mike O'Hara, "Alex Karras Acted Big, Talked Big and Played Big on the Football Field," http://www.detroitlions.com/news/ohara/article-1/OHara-Alex-Karras-acted-big-talked-big-and-played-big-on-the-football-field/896bf25e-0201-44b7-8fb5-e735fd9bd52d.

6. Daniel J. Flynn, "The Gambler," *American Spectator*, October 12, 2012.

7. Maule, "Players Are Not Just People."

8. Ibid.

9. Bob Glauber, "The Life and Times of Lion King, Alex Karras (1935–2012)," *Newsday*, October 13, 2012.

10. Gary Mihoces, "Longtime Lion, Actor Karras Dies at 77," *USA Today*, October 10, 2012.

11. Morris, "A League Outlaw with an Endearing Scowl."

12. Jimmy Smith, "Paul Hornung Faced a 1-time NFL Year Suspension, He Knows What's in Store for Sean Payton." *Times-Picayune* (LA), March 21, 2012, http://www.nola.com/saints/index.ssf/2012/03/paul_hornung_faced_a_1-time_nf.html.

13. Mark Mulvoy, "Dizzy Dream for Jet-set Denny," *Sports Illustrated*, July 29, 1968.

14. Ibid.

15. Ibid.

16. "The Downfall of Denny McLain: McLain-Kuhn: The Prequel to Rose-Vincent," *Baseball Prospectus*, February 28, 2003, http://www.baseballprospectus.com/article.php?articleid=1666.

17. Denny McLain, *Strikeout: The Story of Denny McLain* (St. Louis: Sporting News Publishing, 1988), 23.

18. Morton Sharnik, "Downfall of a Hero," *Sports Illustrated*, February 23, 1970.

19. Ibid.

20. McLain, *Strikeout*, 44.

21. Ibid., 47.

22. Ibid.

23. Associated Press, "Silent For Once: McLain Hiding Out," *Owosso (MI) Argus-Press,* September 11, 1970, 12.

24. McLain, *Strikeout,* 87.

25. *Baseball Almanac,* http://www.baseball-almanac.com/quotes/quorose.shtml.

26. Michael Y. Sokolove, *Hustle: The Myth, Life and Lies of Pete Rose* (New York: Simon & Schuster, 2005), 1–2.

27. *Baseball Almanac.*

28. "All-Star Memories: The Pete Rose, Ray Fosse Collision," *FOXSportsOhio,* http://www.foxsportsohio.com/foxsohio/topics/m/video/59032454/all-star-memories -the-pete-rose-ray-fosse-collision.htm.

29. James Reston Jr., *Collision at Home Plate: The Lives of Pete Rose and Bart Giamatti* (New York: Edward Burlingame Books, 1991), 69.

30. Ibid., 71.

31. Ibid., 136.

32. Ibid., 170.

33. Ibid., 211.

34. Ibid., 277.

35. Ibid., 307.

36. Mike Jaccarino, "Bad Bounces along His Way," *Daily News (NY),* July 29, 2007.

37. "Donaghy under Investigation for Betting on NBA Games," *ESPN.com,* July 20, 2007, http://sports.espn.go.com/nba/news/story?id=2943095.

38. Ibid.

39. Jennifer Fermino, "Commish Rips 'Traitor' Ref—Calls Whistlegate 'Isolated Incident,'" *New York Post,* July 25, 2007.

40. Selena Roberts, "Sports of the Times; N.B.A. Put Referees Above the Law," *New York Times,* July 25, 2007.

41. Ibid.

42. Howard Beck and Michael S. Schmidt, "Referee Pleads Guilty to Gambling Charges," *New York Times,* August 16, 2007.

43. Michael S. Schmidt, "League Finds Donaghy Was Sole Referee Culprit," *New York Times,* October 2, 2008.

44. Ibid.

Chapter 10. The Social Contract: Scandals That Transcend Sports

1. Frank DeFord, "Ready If You Are, O. J.," *Sports Illustrated,* July 14, 1969.

2. John Steadman, "Halls of Fame Should Keep O. J., Add Cannon, Too," *Baltimore (MD) Sun,* June 20, 1994.

3. Ibid.

4. Richard Hoffer, "Is It Good for the Juice? Trading on His Celebrity, O. J. Simpson Survives in Style," *Sports Illustrated,* October 1, 2007.

5. Steve Friess, "Many Stark Contrasts as Simpson Is Convicted," *New York Times,* October 4, 2008.

6. Christine Brennan, "Pro Football Hall Needs O. J. Exit Strategy," *USA Today*, September 19, 2007.

7. Gregg Rosenthal, "NFL Should Ban Former Players Who Tarnish the Shield," *NBCSports.com*, May 6, 2010.

8. Ibid.

9. Peter Richmond, "Rae Carruth, the Women Who Loved Him, and the One He Wanted Dead," *GQ Magazine*, May 2001.

10. Michael Bamberger, "First Degree Tragedy," *Sports Illustrated*, December 27, 1999.

11. "Pro Football; Carruth Arrested in Shooting of Woman," *New York Times*, November 26, 1999.

12. Ibid.

13. Associated Press, "Guilty on Three of Four: Jury Acquits Carruth on First-degree Murder Charge," January 19, 2001.

14. Thomas Lake, "The Boy They Couldn't Kill," *Sports Illustrated*, September 17, 2012.

15. Peter King, "Ravens Star Ray Lewis Sits in Jail on Murder Charges. Is He a Victim or a Killer?," *Sports Illustrated*, February 14, 2000.

16. "Lewis Murder Charges Dropped," *CNNSI.com*, June 5, 2000.

17. Ibid.

18. "Tagliabue Won't Suspend Ray Lewis," *New York Times*, July 20, 2000.

19. Dave Goldberg, "NFL Fines Ray Lewis $250,000," *ABCNews.com*, August 8, 2000.

20. Ibid.

21. Mike Pesca, "On Ray Lewis' Retirement, Some Media Fail to Mention 2000 Murder Case," *National Public Radio*, January 2, 2013.

22. Carrie Wells, "Years Later, Murder Case Still Echoes for Ray Lewis, Families," *Baltimore (MD) Sun*, January 10, 2013.

23. "Roger Goodell Has a Job for Ray Lewis," *USA Today*, January 13, 2013.

24. Mike Bianchi, "As We Celebrate Ray Lewis, Don't Forget Murder Victims," *Orlando (FL) Sentinel*, January 5, 2013.

25. Mike Freeman, "Pro Football; Stains from the Police Blotter Leave N.F.L. Embarrassed," *New York Times*, January 9, 2000.

26. Richmond, "Rae Carruth."

27. Mike Freeman, "Pro Football; N.F.L. and Union Weigh Players' Violent Acts," *New York Times*, March 26, 2000.

Chapter 11. Ethics, Effectiveness, and a Changing Environment

1. Derek Thompson, "The Global Dominance of ESPN: Why Hasn't Anybody Figured Out How to Beat 'The Worldwide Leader in Sports'?," *Atlantic*, August 13, 2013.

2. "A Sports Fan's Guide to Drug Testing," *Wall Street Journal*, November 12, 2009.

3. Ibid.

4. Daniel E. Ginsburg, *The Fix Is In: A History of Baseball Gambling and Game Fixing Scandals* (Jefferson, NC: McFarland, 1995), 291.

Index

About the Author

EDWARD J. LORDAN, PhD, is a professor of communication studies at West Chester University outside of Philadelphia, Pennsylvania. He has published more than 20 academic papers related to media studies, including 3 books: *Essentials of Public Relations Management*; *Politics, Ink: How Cartoonists Skewer America's Politicians, from King George III to George Dubya*; and *The Case for Combat: How Presidents Persuade Americans to Go to War*. Lordan has served on the faculties of Temple University, Villanova University, and Saint Louis University. He earned his doctorate from the Newhouse School at Syracuse University.